Boost your PC's performance

Other Computer Titles

by

Robert Penfold

Boost your PC's performance

Robert Penfold

Bernard Babani (publishing) Ltd
The Grampians
Shepherds Bush Road
London W6 7NF
England
www.babanibooks.com

PLEASE NOTE

Although every care has been taken with the production of this book to ensure that any projects, designs, modifications and/or programs, etc., contained herewith, operate in a correct and safe manner and also that any components specified are normally available in Great Britain, the Publishers and Author do not accept responsibility in any way for the failure (including fault in design) of any projects, design, modification or program to work correctly or to cause damage to any equipment that it may be connected to or used in conjunction with, or in respect of any other damage or injury that may be so caused, nor do the Publishers accept responsibility in any way for the failure to obtain specified components.

Notice is also given that if equipment that is still under warranty is modified in any way or used or connected with home-built equipment then that warranty may be void.

© 2004 BERNARD BABANI (publishing) LTD

First Published - August 2004

Reprinted - February 2005

British Library Cataloguing in Publication Data
A catalogue record for this book is available from the British Library

ISBN 0 85934 541 6

Cover Design by Gregor Arthur
Printed and bound in Great Britain by Cox & Wyman

Preface

Ever since the earliest home computers and PCs were produced there has been a quest for greater speed. The early computers were relatively crude and could not even perform basic text processing very quickly. Whatever type of software you were using, a faster computer would run it that much better. The PCs of today run more than a thousand times faster than the original PC, and speed is slightly less of an issue than was once the case. The average PC can now run some applications, including the basic business types, at more than adequate speeds. Using a faster PC is unlikely to bring any benefits with software such as this.

The speed issue has by no means gone away though, and most computer applications have become far more demanding over the years. Games in particular seem to get more complex to take advantage of advances in the hardware. This year's games run really well if you happen to have next year's fastest PC! Digital video and other applications that were not a practical proposition with the early PCs are now a reality, but place high demands on the hardware. With these programs it is still a case of the faster the PC, the better the results.

For many PC users the speed issue is more one of keeping the original speed of the PC rather than trying to boost it. On the face of it a PC should still work at the same speed after a few months of use because it has exactly the same hardware as when it was new. In practice there is often a noticeable slowdown, but this is nothing to do with the hardware. It is due to the fragmentation of the hard disc, excessive background tasks, a build-up of "rubbish" files on the hard disc, and other issues that are primarily software related. This type of thing often gives a greatly extended boot time plus a general reduction in speed.

If you need to boost the speed of your PC, this book shows how it can be achieved using hardware upgrades such as a faster processor or more memory. If your PC is slowing down, this book demonstrates how to use the built-in facilities of Windows to make it run like new again. It also shows how to use third-party software to tune a PC for optimum results and to effectively speed-up an Internet connection. If your PC suddenly slows down, it might have been infected by a computer pest. Spotting and dealing with the increasing problem of these pests, such as dialers and spyware, is also covered.

It is not necessary to be a computer expert in order to use the methods featured here. Obviously, due care needs to be taken when dealing with the operating system, but the built-in Windows tools are safe provided a bit of common sense is exercised when using them. The same is true of most third-party tuning utilities. It is advisable not to attempt hardware upgrades unless you have a reasonable amount of experience with using PCs and you are a practical person. These upgrades do not require a great deal of skill though, and in most cases the only tool needed is a screwdriver.

Robert Penfold

Trademarks

Microsoft, Windows, Windows XP, Windows Me, Windows 98 and Windows 95 are either registered trademarks or trademarks of Microsoft Corporation.

All other brand and product names used in this book are recognised trademarks, or registered trademarks of their respective companies. There is no intent to use any trademarks generically and readers should investigate ownership of a trademark before using it for any purpose.

Contents

2

Third-party programs 69

3

Viruses and other pests 95

4

Backup and Restore 153

The built-in
facilities

Efficient files

There are two aspects to tuning a PC's software for the best performance. Clearly, one of these is to get the PC operating efficiently in the first place. Less obviously, having set up the PC to work efficiently, there is the problem of keeping everything working well. On the face of it, once set up correctly there should be nothing more to do. In practice the situation is more difficult than this, and it is quite normal for a PC to run noticeably slower after it has been in use for a few months. In fact it can noticeably slow down in the space of a few weeks.

So why does a PC tend to slow down over a period of time? The fall-off in performance is usually due to the hard disc drive taking longer to load files into memory, but the problem is not really caused by the hardware. A PC's hardware normally works at full tilt or not at all. The problem has more to do with the number of files on the hard disc drive. Most people add more programs and data to their PCs over a period of time. Each program that is added places its own entries in the Windows Registry and makes it grow ever bigger. The newly added files for each program tend to be spread all over the hard disc rather than being grouped neatly together. Getting a PC to run efficiently therefore consists largely of removing unnecessary files and keeping the remaining files organised properly on the hard disc drive.

Hidden tools

There are numerous utility programs available that help to get a PC working efficiently and keep it that way, but it would be a mistake to overlook the built-in tools of Windows itself. It would be a mistake, but it would also be quite easy because they are buried quite deep in the

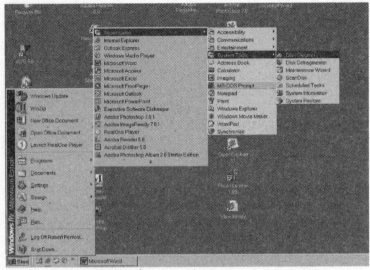

Fig.1.1 The System Tools are buried deep in the menu system

menu structure (Figure 1.1). From the Start menu select Programs, Accessories, System Tools, and then the required program. A good one to start with is Disk Cleanup. The Disk Cleanup program used in this example is the one in Windows ME, but essentially the same facility is available in Windows XP.

As its name suggests, Disk Cleanup looks for unnecessary files on the selected disc drive. The initial window of Figure 1.2 appears, and the drop-down menu is used to select the appropriate drive, which will usually be the default option of drive C. The program then scans the disc for files that it thinks are no longer required, and a summary of its findings is then displayed (Figure 1.3). It is not possible to select files for deletion on an individual basis, and there will usually be too many of

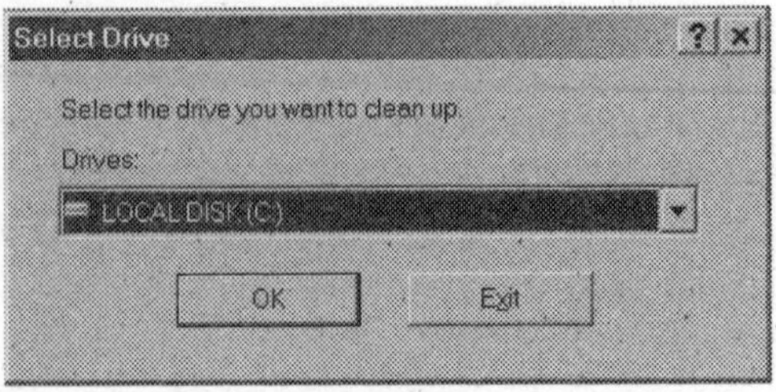

Fig.1.2 Select the appropriate drive from the drop-down menu

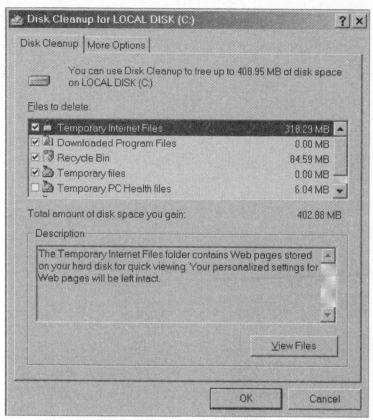

Fig.1.3 Files in various categories can be selected

them for this to be a practical proposition. Instead, you are presented
with various file categories, and all the files in a category can be erased
by first ticking the corresponding checkbox. The OK button is operated
once all the categories for deletion have been selected.

The categories are slightly different between Windows ME and XP, but
the main ones are the same for both operating systems. The Temporary
Internet Files are copies of the files downloaded when viewing Internet
pages. These are stored on the hard disc in order to speed up access if
you go back to the same page. Rather than downloading the page
again, the copy stored on the disc is used. Of course, this only works if
the page has not changed since your last visit, or if most of the files used

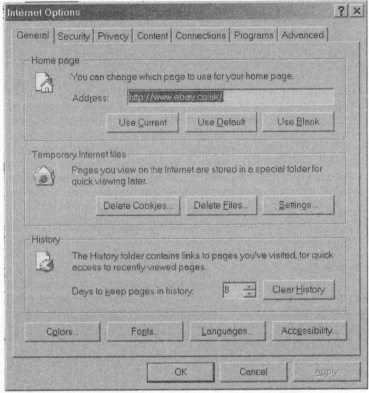

Fig.1.4 The General section of the Internet Options window

in the page are still the same. It is otherwise necessary for the page to be downloaded again, and a copy of the new page stored in the cache on the hard disc. This leads to a gradual build-up of files on the hard disc, especially if you do research on the Internet and visit dozens of sites.

Maximum size

The files are not stored indefinitely on the disc, and Windows automatically deletes the oldest files once a certain a certain amount of disc space has been used. It is easy to alter the maximum amount of disc space that is used for this temporary storage. Start by going into Internet Explorer

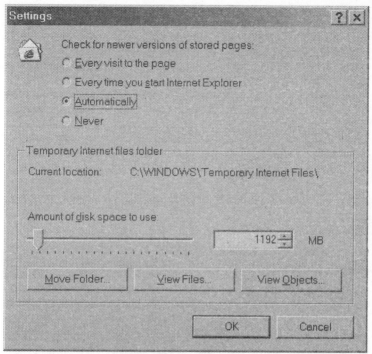

Fig.1.5 The Settings window enables the cache size to be altered

and then selecting Internet Options from the Tools menu. This produces a window like the one in Figure 1.4. The General tab will probably be selected by default, but if necessary select it manually.

The temporary Internet files can be erased by operating the Delete Files button near the middle of the window. To alter the maximum amount of space used for these temporary files, operate the Settings button just to the right of the Delete Files button, which will produce the window of Figure 1.5. Use the slider control to set the required cache size and then operate the OK button. This makes the change take effect and moves things back to the Internet Properties window. Operate the OK button in this window to close it.

Is it worth reducing the size of the cache for temporary Internet files and deleting its contents from time to time? This really depends on the setup you are using and the way in which it is used. With a broadband Internet connection the caching system does not necessarily bring great benefits, since most pages will probably download quite quickly. It will only be of real help when downloading pages that contain large files or when accessing sites that are stored on slow or very busy servers. When using an ordinary dialup connection the benefits of caching are likely to be much greater. Of course, caching is ineffective with any system if you do not keep going back to the same old web pages, or you do but there are substantial changes each time you visit them.

In practice, and regardless of the theory, the caching system does seem to be ineffective when you have a cache that occupies hundreds of megabytes or more of hard disc space, with what is likely to be tens of thousands of files. If you use Windows Explorer to go into the Temporary Internet folder it could well take the program half a minute to produce a list of all the files, and the number of files could well be in excess of 50,000. This gives a hint as to why the caching system can become inefficient.

A large cache of temporary Internet files can be particularly inefficient if there is a lack of vacant hard disc space. Allocating a large amount of space for temporary Internet storage could greatly reduce the amount of disc space left for other forms of temporary storage, causing a significant reduction in the overall performance of the PC. If spare hard disc space is strictly limited, it is definitely a good idea to reduce the amount of space allocated to storing temporary Internet files.

Having erased the temporary Internet cache, it is likely that Internet access will be a bit slower initially when using your favourite sites. This will be especially noticeable with slow sites or when using a dialup connection. However, the cached files will be reinstated after visiting each of these sites for the first time, so any slowdown will be only temporary.

Temporary files

Returning to the categories of files listed by the Disk Cleanup program, the Temporary Files category contains files that that have been placed in a "TEMP" folder by applications programs. Many applications generate temporary files, which are normally erased when the program is closed. However, some of these files get left behind, possibly due to a program shutting down abnormally. Some programs are not designed quite as well as they might be and habitually leave temporary files on the hard disc drive. The files included in this category are temporary types that

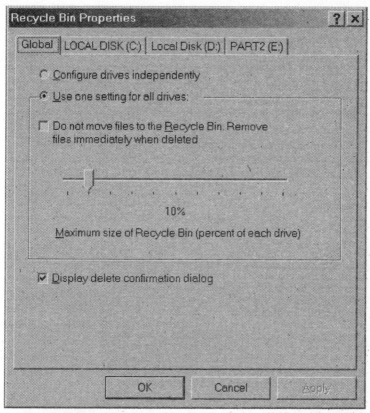

Fig.1.6 The maximum size of the Recycle Bin can be changed using the slider control

are more than one week old, and it should be safe to delete them. Doing so is unlikely to free much hard disc space though.

Recycle Bin

As most Windows users are no doubt aware, when you delete files they are not deleted immediately but are instead placed in the Recycle Bin. The Recycle Bin is just a folder on drive C:, but it is one that is normally handled by Windows or by the user via the special facilities. Of course,

Windows does not continue storing deleted files indefinitely. There is an upper limit to the size of the Recycle Bin, and eventually old deleted files will be completely removed in order to make space for newer ones.

The default size for the Recycle Bin is quite large, so a substantial number of files can be amassed over a period of time. It can be altered by right-clicking on the Recycle Bin icon and selecting Properties from the pop-up menu. This produces the window of Figure 1.6, and the maximum size of the Recycle Bin can then be set via the slider control. Note that the percentage set here is the percentage of each drive's full capacity that will be used for storing deleted files. It does not represent the percentage of free disc space that will be used for this purpose. Accordingly, it is best to settle for a small figure here if a disc's capacity has been largely used up.

By default, the same percentage is used for all the discs. If preferred though, the "Configure drives independently" radio button can be selected. The size of the Recycle Bin can then be set individually for each drive. Simply operate the tab for the drive you wish to alter and then use the slider control to set the required maximum size.

It is not necessary to utilise the Recycle Bin at all. It can be switched off by ticking the checkbox just above the slider control, and deleted files will then be fully erased at once. It is not really necessary to use this option, since the Recycle Bin can be circumvented by holding down the shift key when deleting files. The usual warning message will still appear so that you have a chance to change your mind before the files are deleted. This message can be suppressed by ticking the checkbox near the bottom of the Recycle Bin Properties window.

When fully deleting files, whether via the Disk Cleanup program or by other means, bear in mind that Windows offers no way of retrieving files once they have been fully deleted. It is often possible to retrieve deleted files using an undelete utility, but there is no guarantee that this will be possible. It will certainly not be possible to retrieve a file once the disc space it occupied has been overwritten by another file. Even with a partially overwritten file there is little prospect of retrieving anything worthwhile.

The rest

The other categories in the Disk Cleanup program tend to be those concerned with things such as diagnostics. These files are not necessarily of any use, but there will probably be little point in deleting them. The number of files and the disc space that they occupy will both be quite small, if there are actually any files at all.

Defragmenters

Many users tend to assume that files are automatically stored on the hard disc on the basis of one continuous section of disc per file. Unfortunately, it does not necessarily operate in this fashion. When Windows is first installed on a PC it is likely that files will be added in this way. The application programs are then installed, and things will probably continue in an organised fashion with files stored on the disc as single clumps of data. Even if things have progressed well thus far, matters soon take a turn for the worse when the user starts deleting files, adding new files or programs, deleting more files, and so on.

Gaps are produced in the continuous block of data when files are deleted. Windows utilises the gaps when new data is added, but it will use them even if each one is not large enough to take a complete file. If necessary, it will use dozens of these small vacant areas to accommodate a large file. This can result in a large file being spread across the disc in numerous tiny packets of data, which makes reading the file a relatively slow and inefficient business.

The computer can seriously slow down when a substantial number of files get fragmented in this way.

There are programs called defragmenters that reorganise the files on a disc drive so that, as far as reasonably possible, large files are not fragmented.   A program of this type is available   in   the

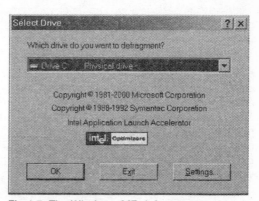

Fig.1.7 The Windows ME defragmenter

System Tools submenu as the Disk Defragmenter. This utility has something of a checkered past, and in older versions of Windows it gave odd results with some disc drives. At some point in the proceedings the

1   The built-in facilities

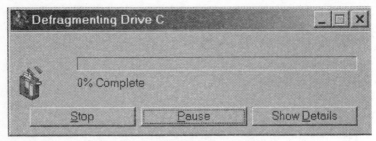

Fig.1.8 A bargraph shows how things are progressing

estimated time to completion would start to rise and usually kept rising with the process never finishing. Provided you are using a reasonably modern version of Windows there should be no problem of this type and the Disk Defragmenter program should work well.

On launching the Windows ME version of the program a window like the one shown in Figure 1.7 is displayed. The drop-down menu is used to select the disc drive that will be processed and then the OK button is

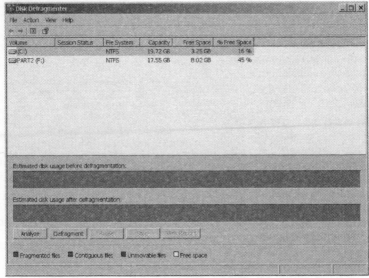

Fig.1.9 The Windows XP defragmenter program

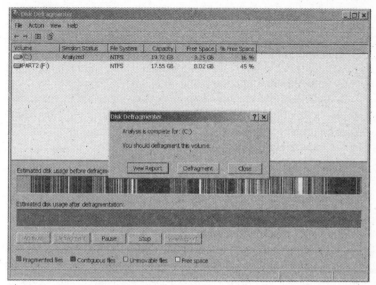

Fig.1.10 The result of analysing drive C

operated. This produces a small window like the one shown in Figure 1.8 which indicates how far the disc processing has progressed, and will eventually report that the process has been completed. With a large disc that is badly fragmented this can take several hours.

XP defragmenter

The defragmenter program supplied as part of Windows XP is more sophisticated than the Windows ME version. Launching the program produces a large window like the one shown in Figure 1.9. The drives that can be defragmented are listed in the main section of the window, and in this case there are two drives that are actually partitions on the same physical drive. These are treated as two separate entities by the operating system, and they are therefore processed in that way by defragmenter programs.

While it is possible to jump straight in and start processing the selected drive, this version of Disk Defragmenter offers the alternative of first analysing the drive to determine how badly (or otherwise) it is fragmented. There is little point in defragmenting a disc that is performing well. To

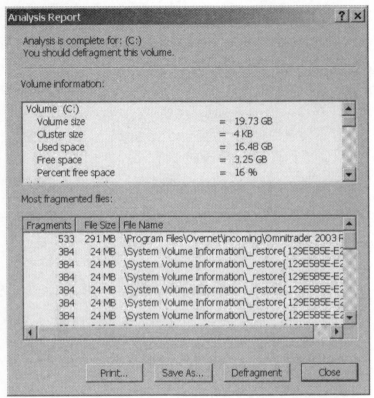

Fig.1.11 Some general information about the disc can be provided

analyse the disc either operate the Analyze button near the bottom left-hand corner of the window or select Analyze from the Actions menu. In this example the analysis produced the result shown in Figure 1.10.

A small window pops up and indicates whether it is worthwhile defragmenting the disc. In this example it indicates that the disc is severely fragmented and that the defragmenter program should be set to work. There is a bar across the window that shows fragmented files in red and the contiguous files in blue (mid and dark grey respectively in Figure 1.10). Although a lot of contiguous files are in evidence, together with unused disc space and unmovable system files, there is a significant amount of red scattered along the bar. More information about the state

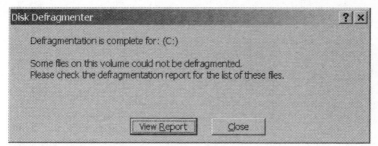

Fig.1.12 Complete defragmentation is not always possible

of the disc can be obtained by operating the View Report button in the pop-up window. This produces some general information about the hard disc, in addition to more specific information about individual files (Figure 1.11).

In order to go ahead with the processing operate the Defragment button in the pop-up window. You can jump straight to this stage, without analysing the disc first, by operating the Defragment button in the main

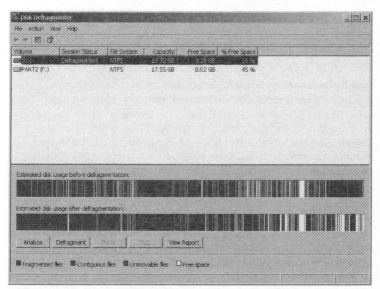

Fig.1.13 "Before" and "after" diagrams are provided

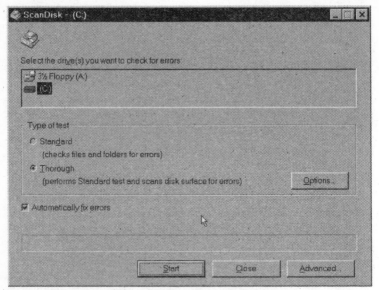

Fig.1.14 Standard and Thorough modes are available

window. Either way, the lower part of the window will show two bars, with the upper one showing the initial state of the disc, and the lower bar shows how the process is progressing.

Eventually the process will be completed and a window like the one in Figure 1.12 will appear. This will often report that, as in this case, it was not possible to fully defragment the disc. However, there should be a substantial improvement in speed. Regular use of Disk Defragmenter should gradually get the disc to the point where it is fully defragmented, or nearly so. The two bars in the lower section of the main window show the "before" and "after" states of the disc (Figure 1.13).

Scandisk

Scandisk is another of the Windows System Tools, and it is familiar to most Windows users. If Windows is improperly shut down Scandisk will normally be run automatically when the PC is next started. Although it is mainly run by Windows itself, it is possible for the user to run it at any time. Due to its tendency to pop up unannounced during booting,

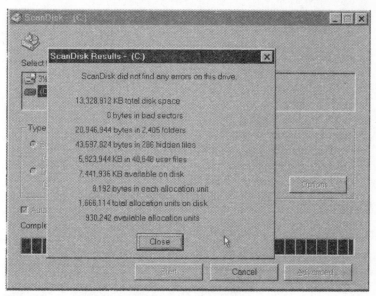

Fig.1.15 A summary of the results is provided

Scandisk tends to be regarded as a nuisance by many users, but it is a very useful piece of software.

The purpose of Scandisk is to examine the file and folder structure of a disc in a search for errors. It is worthwhile using this program when a PC seems to take a long time to complete disc accesses, has a tendency to crash, takes much longer than normal to boot into Windows, or shows a reluctance to start up or close down properly. Note that Scandisk is not available under Windows XP, but it is available in Windows ME and its predecessors. Windows XP has Check Disk, see page 18.

The Scandisk utility offers two modes of operation. These are Standard and Thorough modes, and you operate the radio buttons to select the one you require (Figure 1.14). The Standard check looks for irregularities in the file and folder structure. This includes simple things like filenames that do not adhere to the rules, as well as more serious problems such as one sector of the disc being assigned to more than one file. Program crashes can leave problems of these types, so it is not a bad idea to run Scandisk if a program comes to an unscheduled finish. If you tick the appropriate checkbox Scandisk will try to repair any errors that it finds.

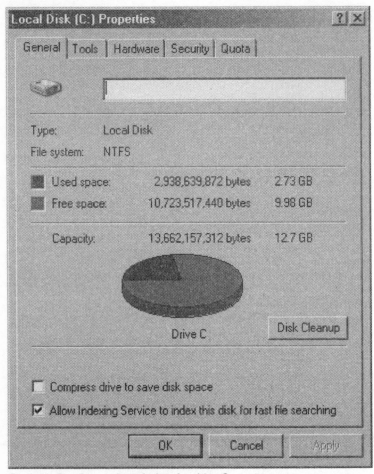

Fig.1.16 The Properties window for drive C

Initially I recommend using the Standard mode with the checkbox ticked. This test should be relatively fast, taking no more than a few minutes. If the program discovers any problems it will report them via onscreen messages, and at the end it also gives a brief summary of its findings (Figure 1.15). Unfortunately, if Scandisk does find some errors and fixes them, this does not necessarily mean that Windows will then work perfectly.

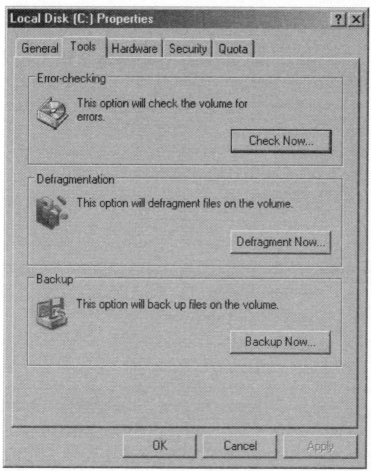

Fig.1.17 The Tools section of the Properties window

The problems will be fixed in the sense that filenames will adhere to the
rules, linked files will be unlinked so that each sector of the disc is
assigned to only one file, and so on. Any damaged files may not be fully
restored using Scandisk. If one file partly overwrites another file there is
no way that a utility program such as Scandisk can restore the overwritten
part of the file. Unless you have a backup copy the damaged file will be
lost permanently. However, Scandisk should at least restore order to the

disc if things have gone wrong, improving the chances of getting things running smoothly again.

The Thorough mode performs the same tests as the Standard mode, but it additionally carries out a surface scan of the disc. In other words, it checks that there are no weak spots on the disc that are causing data to become corrupted. It is certainly worth using the Thorough mode if you suspect that the disc itself may be causing problems. Note though, that a thorough check of this type on a large hard disc drive will take quite a long time. It will probably take several hours rather than a few minutes for the test to be completed.

Check Disk

The Windows XP equivalent of Scandisk is the Check Disk program. This is supplied in two versions, which are a graphical user interface program and a command line utility (Chkdsk.exe). For most purposes the graphical user interface program will suffice, and this is easily accessed. In My Computer or Windows Explorer, right-click the entry for the drive you wish to check and then choose Properties from the popup menu. This produces a window like the one of Figure 1.16, which gives some basic information about the drive.

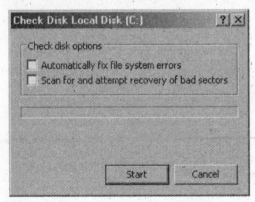

Fig.1.18 Leave both checkboxes blank

Operate the Tools tab to switch to a Window like the one in Figure 1.17, which includes an error checking facility. Left-clicking the Check Now button produces the small window of Figure 1.18, where two options are available via the checkboxes. Initially it is probably best to leave both checkboxes blank, and to go ahead with the checking process by operating the Start button. The program will then check the disc for errors, showing its progress in the lower section of the Window (Figure

1.19). Once the process has completed, the program will either report that there were no errors or give a list of the problems that were detected.

If faults were detected, it is advisable to run the program again, but using one or both of the options provided by the checkboxes. One option sets the

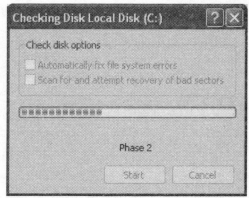

Fig.1.19 A bargraph shows how things are progressing

program to automatically fix any errors that are detected. This is the quicker of the two options. The second option results in the program going through a very thorough checking process. It will try to recover data from any bad sectors on the disc. Using this option helps to minimise the damage caused by disc errors, but with large drives it can many hours for the task to be completed. Once underway there is no way out of the program other than switching off the computer, which has the potential to increase the number of disc errors and is definitely not a good idea.

The program is unable to fix errors in a disc that is currently in use, which means that it can not check the boot drive while Windows is

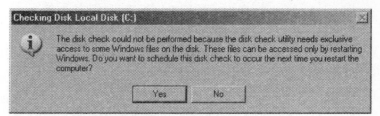

Fig.1.20 It is not possible to check a disc that is in use

running. Trying to check a disc that is currently in use produces the error message of Figure 1.20. To go ahead with the checking and fixing

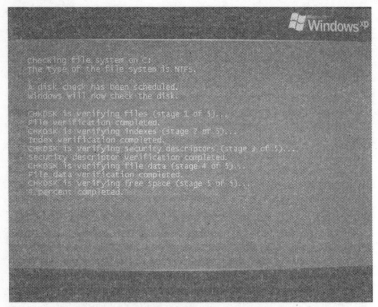

Fig.1.21 Checking takes place during the boot sequence

process, operate the Yes button and restart the computer. The checking program will be launched during the boot process, before the boot drive is left with any open files. The screen will show how things are progressing (Figure 1.21), and the boot process will continue once the disc checker has completed its task.

Users of Windows 9x operating systems soon become used to Scandisk running automatically during the boot routine if the computer has not been shout down properly. Check Disk is likely to run automatically at boot-up if a system having a FAT32 boot disc is shut down abnormally, but it is unlikely to run automatically in systems that have a NTFS boot disc. This is because the NTFS system is better able to recover from abnormal disc activity, making it unnecessary to run Check Disk at the slightest excuse. There is probably no point in running Check Disk manually if the computer was not shut down properly, because it is unlikely that any disc writing errors would have been produced.

Deletion

A program such as Disk Cleanup can remove certain types of file that are no longer required, but it can not manage your data files for you. Only you know which data files are likely to be needed in the future and should be retained on the hard disc drive. The rest can be copied onto some form of removable media before they are deleted from the disc. Of course, it is not essential to make archive copies if you are sure that the files will never be needed again, but it is advisable to take copies "just in case".

You could try erasing programs and other files that are no longer needed, but this type of thing has to be undertaken with great care. In the days of MS/DOS it was perfectly acceptable to delete a program and any files associated with it if you no longer wished to use the program. Matters are very different with Windows, where most software is installed into the operating system. There are actually some simple programs that have just one file, and which do not require any installation. These standalone program files are quite rare these days, but they can be used much like old MS/DOS programs. To use the program you copy it onto the hard disc, and to run it you use the Run option from the Start menu, or locate the file using Windows Explorer and double-click on it. No installation program is used, and it is perfectly all right to remove the program by deleting the program file.

Most programs are installed onto the computer using an installation program, and this program does not simply make folders on the hard disc and copy files into them from the CD-ROM. It will also make changes to the Windows configuration files so that the program is properly integrated with the operating system. If you simply delete the program's directory structure to get rid of it, Windows will not be aware that the program has been removed. During the boot-up process the operating system will probably look for files associated with the deleted program, and will produce error messages when it fails to find them.

Matters are actually more involved than this, and there is another potential problem in that Windows utilizes shared files. This is where one file, such as a DLL type that provides additional program code, is shared by two or more programs. In deleting a program and the other files in its directory structure you could also be deleting files needed by other programs. This could prevent other programs from working properly, or even from starting up at all.

If a program is loaded onto the hard disc using an installation program, the only safe way of removing it is to use an uninstaller program. There are three possible ways of handling this.

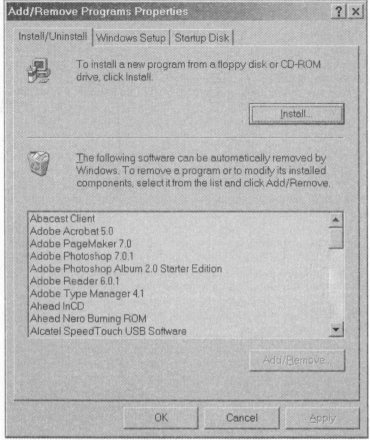

Fig.1.22 The Windows ME uninstaller

Custom uninstaller

Some programs load an uninstaller program onto the hard disc as part of the installation process. This program is then available via the Start menu if you choose Programs, and then the name of the program concerned. When you choose this option there will be the program itself, plus at least one additional option in the sub-menu that appears. If there is no uninstall option here, no custom uninstaller has been installed for that program. Uninstaller programs of this type are almost invariably

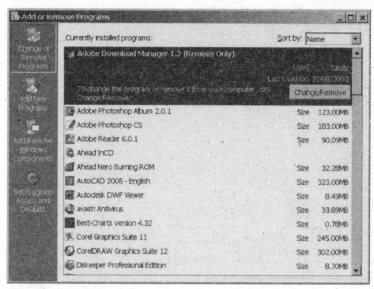

Fig.1.23 The Windows XP version of the uninstaller

automatic in operation, so you have to do little more than instruct it to go ahead with the removal of the program.

With any uninstaller software you may be asked if certain files should be removed. This mostly occurs where the program finds shared files that no longer appear to be shared. In days gone by it did not seem to matter whether you opted to remove or leave these files, with Windows failing to work properly thereafter! These days things seem to be more reliable, and it is reasonably safe to accept either option. To leave the files in place is certainly the safest option, but it also results in files and possibly folders being left on the disc unnecessarily.

Windows uninstaller

Windows has a built-in uninstaller that can be accessed via the control panel. From the Start menu select Settings, Control Panel and Add/ Remove programs. By default this takes you to the uninstaller, and the lower section of the screen shows a list of the programs that can be uninstalled via this route. Figure 1.22 shows the Windows ME version of the uninstaller, and Figure 1.23 shows the Windows XP equivalent. Although different in points of detail, these two programs are used in

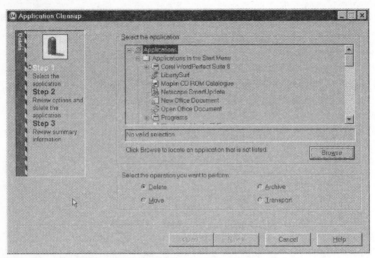

Fig.1.24 The CyberMedia Uninstaller program in action

much the same way. Removing a program is just a matter of selecting it from the list and then operating the Add/Remove button (Windows ME) or the Change/Remove button (Windows XP). Confirm that you wish to remove the program when prompted in the new window that appears, and the removal process will begin.

In theory the list should include all programs that have been added to the hard disc using an installation program. In practice there may be one or two that have not been installed "by the book" and can not be removed using this method. Some programs can only be removed using their own uninstaller program, while others have no means of removal at all. It is mainly older software that falls into the non-removable category, particularly programs that were written for Windows 3.1 and not one of the 32-bit versions of Windows. In fact it is very unusual for old Windows 3.1 software to have any means of removal.

Third-party uninstallers

There are uninstaller programs available that can be used to monitor an installation and then uninstall the software at some later time. As this feature is built into any modern version of Windows, and the vast majority of applications programs now either utilize the built-in facility or have

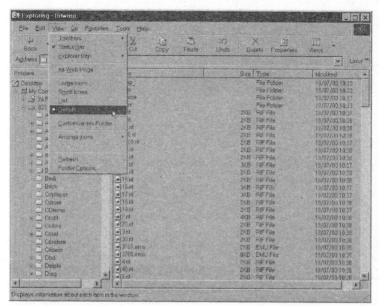

Fig.1.25 The Details option provides useful information about the files

their own uninstaller software, these programs are perhaps less useful than they once were. Most will also assist in the removal of programs that they have not been used to install, and this is perhaps the more useful role. Most uninstallers will also help with the removal of things like unwanted entries in the Start menu and act as general cleanup software, although Windows itself provides means of clearing some of this software debris. Figure 1.24 shows the CyberMedia Uninstaller program in action, but there are numerous programs of this type to choose from.

Leftovers

Having removed a program by whatever means, you will sometimes find that there are still some files and folders associated with the program remaining on the hard disc. In some cases the remaining files are simply data or configuration files that have been generated while you were trying out the program. If they are no longer of any use to you there should be no problems if they are deleted using Windows Explorer. In other cases the files could be system files that the uninstaller has decided not to

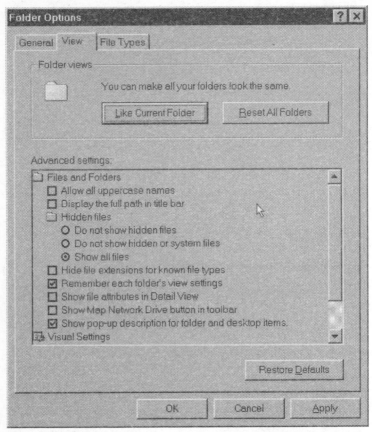

Fig.1.26 The View section of the Folder Options window

remove in case they needed by other applications. Removing files of this type, or any files of indeterminate type, is more risky and it is probably better to leave them in place.

Sometimes the folders may seem to be empty, but it is best to check carefully before removing them. An important point to bear in mind here is that not all files are shown when using the default settings of Windows Explorer. Using the default settings hidden files will live up to their name and files having certain extensions are not shown either. In normal use this can be helpful because it only results in files that are likely to be of interest being shown, while those that are of no interest are hidden. This makes it much easier to find the files you require in a folder that contains a large number of files. It is clearly unhelpful when you are looking inside folders to see if they contain any files, as it could give the impression that a folder is empty when it does in fact contain files. Windows Explorer should be set to show as much detail about the files as possible.

First go to the View menu and select the Details option (Figure 1.25). This will result in the size, type, and date of each file being shown. Then go to the View menu again, select Folder Options, and then left-click on the View tab in the new window that appears (Figure 1.26). Under the Hidden Files entry in the main section of the window select the "Show all files" option. The hidden files are certain critical system files, such as those associated with the Windows Registry, that are not normally displayed by Windows Explorer (so that they can not be accidentally altered or erased by the user). I would recommend ticking the checkbox for "Display full path in title bar". This way you can always see exactly what folder you are investigating, even if it is one that is buried deep in a complex directory structure.

Remove the tick in the checkbox next to "Hide the extension for known file types". The extension should then be shown for all file types, which makes it easy to see which one is which when several files have the same main file name. When viewing the contents of directories you can use either the List or Details options under the View menu, but the Details option provides a little more information. It provides the file type (if it is a recognised type), the date that the file was created or last altered. If the "Show attributes in Detail view" checkbox is ticked, it will also show the attributes of the file. These are the letters used for each of the four attributes:

A   Archive

H   Hidden

R   Read-only

S   System

Thus a file that has "R" as its attribute letter is a read-only type, and one that has "HA" in the attribute column is a hidden archive file. Choose the List option if you prefer to have as many files as possible listed on the screen. Details of any file listed can be obtained by right-clicking on its entry in Windows Explorer and then choosing the Properties option from the pop-up menu. This will bring up a screen of the type shown in Figure 1.27, which shows the type of file, the creation date, when it was last modified, its size, etc.

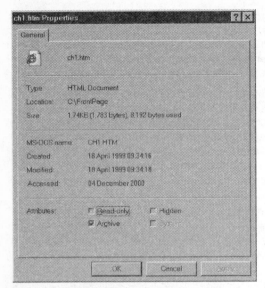

Fig.1.27 The Properties window for a file

Make sure that the checkbox for the "Remember each folder's view settings" is not ticked. Placing a tick in this box gives each folder its own settings, making it necessary to alter the settings for individual folders rather than altering them globally.

If any folders are definitely empty, there should be no problem if they are removed. The same is true of data and configuration files that are no longer needed. With other files it may not be clear what their exact purpose is, and it is a bit risky removing files of unknown function.

Unfortunately, it is not uncommon for uninstallers to leave large numbers of files on the hard disc. The uninstaller seems to go through its routine in standard fashion, and reports that the program has been fully removed, but an inspection of the hard disc reveals that a vast directory structure remains. I have encountered uninstallers that have left more than 50 megabytes of files on the disc, removing only about 10 percent of those initially installed. Other uninstallers report that some files and folders could not be removed, and that they must be dealt with manually. Some uninstallers seem to concentrate on extricating the program from the operating system by removing references to the program in the Windows registry, etc., rather than trying to remove all trace of it from the hard disc.

Softly, softly

So what do you do if the disc is left with vast numbers of unwanted files after a program has been uninstalled? The temptation, and what many people actually do, is to simply drag the whole lot into the Recycle Bin.

Sometimes this may be acceptable, but there is the risk that sooner or later Windows will look for some of the deleted files and start to produce error messages. If you are lucky, the deleted files will still be in the Recycle Bin, and they can then be restored to their original locations on the hard disc. If not, you may have problems sorting things out.

The safer way of handling things is to leave the directory structure and files intact, but change some file or folder names. If only a few files have been left behind, try adding a letter at the front of each filename. For example, a file called "drawprog.dll" could be renamed "zdrawprog.dll". This will prevent Windows from finding the file if it should be needed for some reason, but it is an easy matter for you to correct things by removing the "z" from the filename if problems occur.

If there are numerous files in a complex directory structure to deal with it is not practical to rename all the individual files. Instead, the name of the highest folder in the directory structure should be renamed. This should make it impossible for Windows to find the file unless it does a complete search of the hard disc, and it is easily reversed if problems should occur. Ideally the complete directory structure should be copied to a mass storage device such as a CD writer, a backup hard disc drive, or another partition on the hard disc. The original structure can then be deleted. If problems occur and some of the files have been cleaned from the Recycle Bin, you can reinstate everything from the backup copy.

Of course, in cases where little has been left behind by an uninstaller there is not a great deal to be gained by removing a few files of unknown function. Erasing them will not recover much disc space or give a significant increase in performance. It could cause problems in the future if one of the files proves to be important, so this type of disc tidying is probably more trouble than it is worth. The situation is very different where masses of files have been left behind, and it is then worthwhile making some tests to see if they can be removed safely.

After uninstalling a program you will often find that the shortcut icon is still present on the Windows desktop. If the installation program did not put the icon there in the first place it will not remove it. Shortcut icons that are placed on the Windows desktop manually must be removed manually. This simply entails dragging the icon to the Recycle Bin. There is no risk of this having an adverse effect on Windows operation.

An uninstaller should remove the entry in the Programs section of the Start menu when removing a program. Unfortunately, this item does sometimes seem to be overlooked, and after removing a number of programs there can be a growing band of orphan entries in the menu.

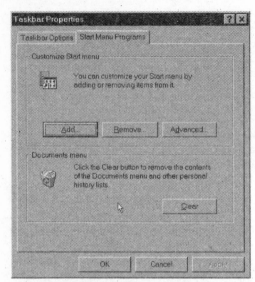

Fig.1.28 The Taskbar Properties window includes a section for the Start menu

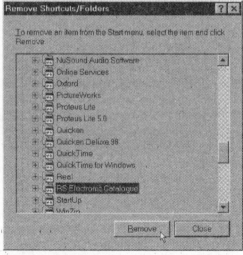

Fig.1.29 The Start menu items are listed here

Once again, removing these entries manually should not entail any risk of "gumming up" Windows, but will make it quicker and easier to use the PC.

To remove an orphan entry go to Settings in the Start menu, and then select Taskbar And Start Menu. The Taskbar menu is offered by default, so left-click the Start Menu Programs tab to bring up the Window of Figure 1.28. Next left-click on the Remove button, which will bring up a scrollable list of all the items in the Start menu. Left-click on the item you wish to remove in order to highlight it (Figure 1.29), and then left-click the Remove button. A warning message will appear onscreen to give you a chance to change your mind, and the entry will be deleted if you confirm that you wish to go ahead. A quick check of the Start menu should show that the

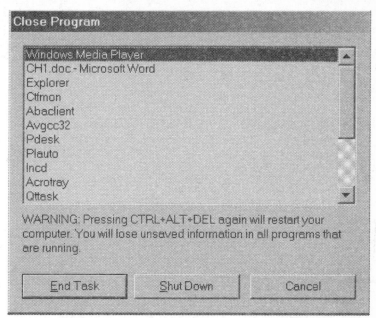

Fig.1.30 The Close Program window lists the current programs and processes

offending entry has been removed. It is actually placed in the Recycle Bin, so it can be easily reinstated if you make a mistake.

Processes

Background processes are important to modern computing and provide a number of useful tasks. For example, an antivirus program running in the background can protect your PC from infection, dealing with viruses and computer pests before they have a chance to do any harm. The problem with background processes is that too many of them running at once can hog a PC's resources. The processing time and memory used by each process will probably be quite small, but with ten processes running the overall drain on the PC's resources could be considerable. In fact having a large number of these processes running simultaneously would almost certainly slow down even the most potent of PCs.

A big problem with background processes is that many of them are installed automatically when applications programs are loaded onto a

Fig.1.31 Windows XP has a Task Manager

PC. The installation program might explain that a background process
will be installed, and there is sometimes an option to omit it from the
installation. In practice few users pay any attention to these options
when installing new software. If you simply opt for "default" or "typical"
installations it is likely that your PC will soon be running some additional
background tasks.

The exact purpose of many background processes is less than obvious,
but many of them are intended to make things happen faster when using
a certain facility of an application program. This is fine if you make

Fig.1.32 The Task Manager has the processes listed separately

frequent use of the program and facility in question, but the overhead on the PC's performance is unlikely to be justified in the case of an infrequently used feature. Where possible, it makes sense to suppress background tasks that do not "earn their keep".

Under Windows 98/ME it is possible to obtain a list of all the programs and processes that are running by pressing the Control, Alt, and Delete keys together. This produces the Close Program window (Figure 1.30), and provided there are no application programs running at the time, all the entries will be for background processes. Do not be surprised if

there are more than a dozen entries in the list. Some of these will be
processes used by the operating system rather than user processes
such as antivirus programs.

The same key combination can be used under Windows XP to launch
the Windows Task Manager, but it will be necessary to operate the Task
Manager button in the first window that appears. Holding down the
Control, Shift, and Escape keys will launch Task Manager immediately.
Either way a window like the one in Figure 1.31 will appear.

Task Manager lists application programs and processes separately, and
by default it will probably list any application programs you are running
at the time. Operate the Processes tab to produce a list of the background
processes that are running (Figure 1.32). The list will be pretty long, but
a substantial proportion of the processes will be part of Windows. For
example, all the entries marked "SYSTEM" in the User Name column
are part of the operating system. The ones that have the name of the
current user in this column are the background tasks that are probably
optional.

Identification

A process can be switched off by selecting its entry and then operating
the End Task or End Process button. However, this is a rather clumsy
way of handling things since it would be necessary to use this method
each time the PC was booted. Ideally, the unnecessary processes should
be prevented from automatically starting at switch-on. First there is the
minor matter of identifying each process and determining its function.
In some cases the names listed by Task Manager will make it clear which
programs the processes are associated with. Many of the names used
are decidedly cryptic though.

The easy way to identify processes is to use the name of the process in
an Internet search engine such as Google, together with something like
"Task Manager" or "background processes". There are a number of
sites that give details of all the background processes that they have
managed to identify, and the search will probably lead you to one of
these.

There are several sites that specialise in this type of information, or that
have a section that deals specifically with this type of thing. One of the
best known is www.answersthatwork.com (Figure 1.33). While working
on this book I found a process called wzqkpick, which was not one that
I had noticed before. Using the processes library of this site I soon

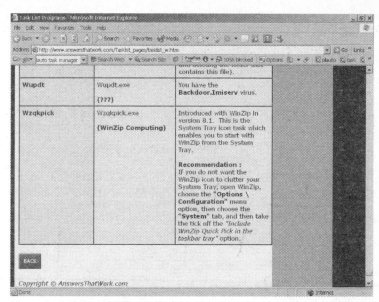

Fig.1.33 Details of wzqkpick are provided, and it turns out to be part of the WinZip program

discovered that it was part of the popular WinZip file compression and decompression program. It was part of the new version of the program that I had just installed, and had not been included with the old version installed previously. It had a matching button on the System Tray, and a check of these buttons will often help to identify background processes.

There are three basic approaches to removing a process that is not really of any great use to you. The most simple of these is to uninstall the software associated with the process. In the case of wzqkpick for example, uninstalling the WinZip program would also remove this process. The obvious problem with this method is that you will often need the program even though you have no requirement for the offending process. In this case I was certainly not prepared to uninstall WinZip.

Method number two is to look through the options available within the program to see if there is any way of switching off the unwanted process. Most programs have a menu entry such as Options or Configuration somewhere in the menu structure. In the case of WinZip it was just a matter of selecting the Configuration option and then operating the System tab. This produced the window of Figure 1.34, and removing

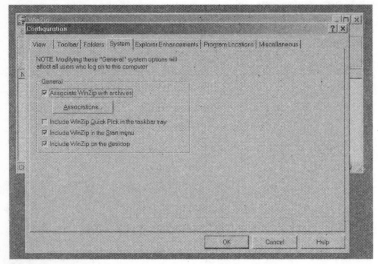

Fig.1.34 The wzqkpick process is easily switched off

the tick from the appropriate checkbox suppressed the wzqkpick process. Note that this type of change does not usually take effect until the PC is rebooted.

System Configuration

The third approach is to use the built-in facility of Windows called the System Configuration Facility. This can be launched by selecting Run from the Start menu and typing "msconfig" into the textbox of the small window that appears. Operating the OK button will then produce a window similar to the one shown in Figure 1.35. The General section will probably be shown by default, but other sections such as Services (Figure 1.36) and Startup (Figure 1.37) are the ones of interest in the current context. Figures 1.35 to 1.37 show the Windows XP version of the System Configuration Utility. The Windows ME version (Figure 1.38) is slightly different, but it provides essentially the same facilities.

These list various processes, and there is a checkbox for each one. Deleting the tick in its checkbox will result in the corresponding process being suppressed each time the PC is booted. Having made the required changes, operate the Apply and Close buttons, and then opt to restart

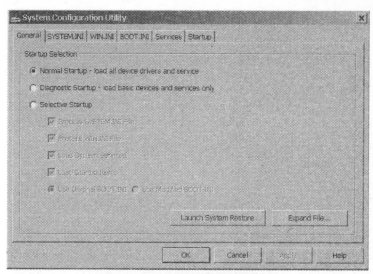

Fig.1.35 The General section of the System Configuration Utility

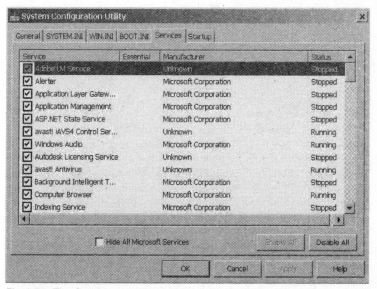

Fig.1.36 The Services section will list a number of processes

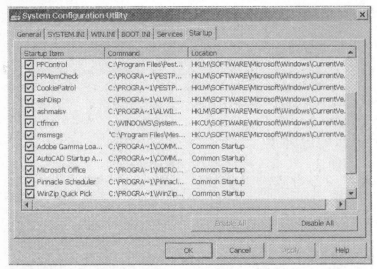

Fig.1.37 This section lists the programs automatically run at startup

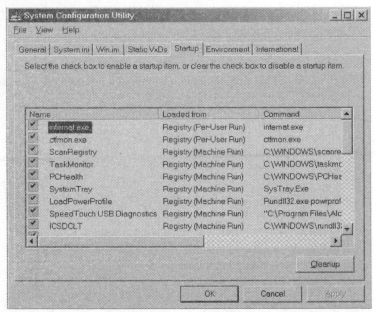

Fig.1.38 The Windows ME version of the utility is broadly similar

the computer when prompted. The computer will then reboot and the unwanted processes will be suppressed. This method of deactivating processes is really only intended for diagnostic purposes. It provides an easy means of switching off processes but it is also easy to reinstate them again if they prove to be more important than you originally thought. Where a process does turn out to be unnecessary, it is better to reinstate it in the System Configuration Utility and then find another way of removing the process.

The System Configuration Utility could be used as a means of permanently suppressing processes where no alternative can be found, but it should only be used in this way if a desperation measure is needed. Do not simply locate and delete the program file for a process in order to prevent it from running at start-up. This will actually have the desired effect, but it will also produce an error message when Windows tries to run the program and finds the executable file missing. With processes that are simply not useful rather than actually causing a nuisance, it is probably better to leave them running if no easy method of removal can be found. This is certainly better than messing up the system by using a partially successful method of removal.

Cookies

Anyone who uses the Internet to any extent will soon accumulate a fair number of cookies on their PC. A cookie is just a text file that is deposited on the hard disc drive of your PC when certain web sites are visited. In most cases the use of cookies is optional, but without them you will find

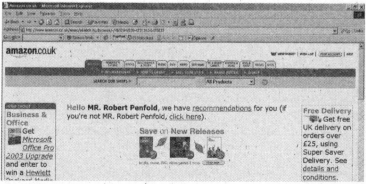

Fig.1.39 Cookies enable web sites to provide clever features

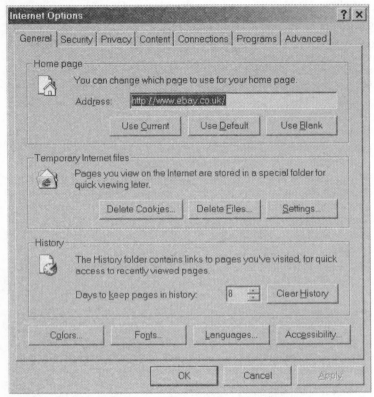

Fig.1.40 This window facilitates the deletion all cookies

that certain features of the site do not work properly. With a few sites you can only use its facilities if your PC is set to accept cookies. Since a cookie is just a small text file it should be completely innocuous. There is a special folder on the hard disc drive for cookies (usually C:\Windows\Cookies), and if you take a look at its contents there will usually be a large number of files there. On my PC I found over 1800 cookies in this directory!

The main use of cookies is to enable a site to automatically identify you on each visit. When I visit www.amazon.co.uk for example, I am greeted with the message "Hello MR. Robert Penfold" (Figure 1.39). The site identifies me by looking for a cookie left on the hard disc during a previous visit to the site. The site will not know who I am if that cookie is deleted

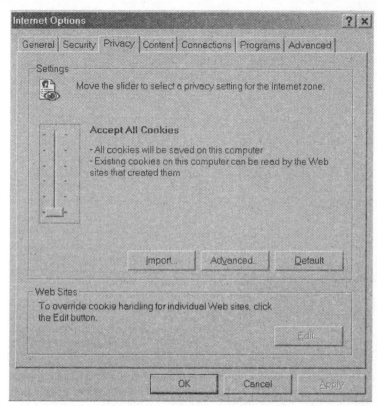

Fig.1.41 All or certain types of cookie can be blocked

or I use a different PC to access the site. Indeed, if I use a PC belonging to someone else and that person has used the Amazon site, it is the greeting for that person that I will receive.

One slight problem with cookies is that they tend to build up on your hard disc drive, especially if you use the Internet for research and visit many sites per day. I think that the importance of this tends to be exaggerated somewhat, since the files are small and will each consume whatever the minimum amount per file happens to be for your PC. Eventually some 25 to 50 megabytes could be used, which is small when compared to the capacities of modern hard disc drives. On the other hand, a few thousand cookies on the hard disc certainly adds to the general clutter.

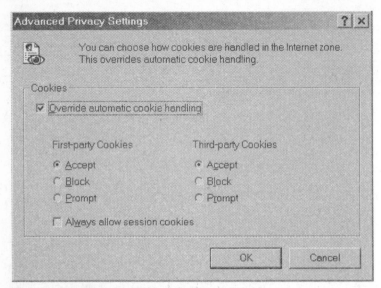

Fig.1.42 The Advanced Privacy Settings window

The "belt and braces" approach to removing unwanted cookies is to simply remove all cookies from your PC. This will clearly remove the useful ones along with the rubbish, but the useful ones will be restored on signing in to your favourite web sites again. In order to remove all cookies it is just a matter of launching Internet Explorer, selecting Internet Options from the Tools menu, and then operating the Delete Cookies button in the middle section of the window (Figure 1.40). Operate the Yes button when asked if you are sure that you wish to delete the cookies.

Cookie options

You are not obliged to accept cookies on your PC in the first place, and it is possible to prevent all or some of them from being written to the hard disc drive. Of course, by blocking cookies you will lose whatever facilities they would have provided. Cookies are controlled via the Privacy section of the Internet Options window (Figure 1.41). The cookie control has six settings from Accept All Cookies to Block All Cookies. The text to the right of the control briefly explains the effect of each setting.

This control is really intended as a means of blocking cookies that might invade your privacy. The higher the setting used, the greater the degree

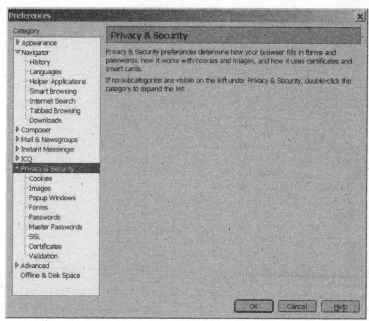

Fig.1.43 Controlling privacy and security settings in Netscape

of privacy provided, and the lower the number of cookies that will find their way onto the hard disc drive. Bear in mind though, that with the higher settings you will almost certainly find that some of the facilities at your favourite sites fail to work, and all or part of a few sites might be inaccessible.

It is possible to override automatic handling of cookies by operating the Advanced button in the Privacy section of the Internet Options window. This produces a window like the one shown in Figure 1.42, and the checkbox near the top must be ticked in order to make the other options active. First- and third-party cookies can be blocked, allowed to pass, or you can be prompted each time a site tries to use a cookie. There is a lot to be said for the prompting method, which ensures that only cookies you agree to use find their way onto the hard disc. In practice it might mean a lot of hassle though. Per-session cookies will always be allowed if the checkbox near the bottom of the window is ticked. There is probably nothing to be gained by blocking this type of cookie so it makes sense to tick this checkbox.

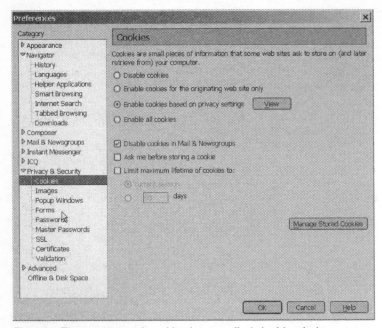

Fig.1.44 The treatment of cookies is controlled via this window

Netscape

Internet Explorer is by far the most popular browser, but there are others in use, and they have different means of controlling privacy and security settings. Netscape Navigator is the main rival to Internet Explorer, and it has some useful settings that govern privacy and security. These can be accessed by first selecting Preferences from the Edit menu, which launches the Preferences window. Then double-click the Privacy & Security entry in the list down the left-hand side of the window. This will expand the entry to show its constituent parts (Figure 1.43). You can then double-click one of these parts to bring up the appropriate options in the right-hand section of the Preferences window (Figure 1.44). It is possible to control the way in which cookies and pop-ups are handled, whether or not passwords should be remembered, and so on.

Further facilities for handling cookies are available from the Cookie Manager which is accessed via the Tools menu. In addition to the ability to accept cookies, there is a manager facility for stored cookies (Figure

1.45). This shows a list of cookies, together with the site that stored each one. This makes it easy to find and remove unwanted cookies, and there is also a button that enables all the stored cookies to be removed.

Keep it simple

A PC that has a fancy Desktop and other clever features might look quite impressive, but do the clever features actually make it any better to use? These features

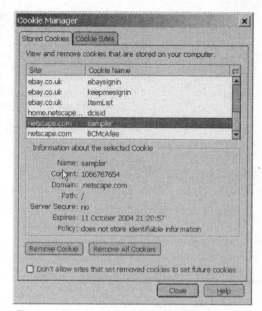

Fig.1.45 The Netscape Cookie Manager

almost invariably have an overhead in terms of reduced overall performance, so they are something to give a "wide berth" if you are seeking the greatest possible speed from you PC. In fact, the simpler the setup, the faster a PC is likely to run. Even having something other than a plain background for the Windows Desktop will use memory and thus give a slight reduction in performance.

As standard, Windows XP uses the familiar field and sky background image, but it is easy to change this to a plain background. First select Control Panel from the Start menu, which will launch the Windows Control Panel. Double-click the Display icon and then select the Desktop page in the new window that appears (Figure 1.46). Select None from the list of Desktop designs in the bottom left-hand section of the window, and then select Apply and OK to make the changes take effect. This will give the traditional plain blue background to the Windows Desktop. Also avoid using screensavers if you wish to minimise unnecessary use of the PC's resources.

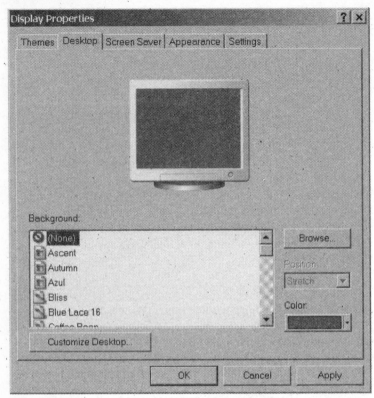

Fig.1.46 A plain Desktop helps to conserve memory

Swap file

If Windows starts to run short of real memory, or "physical" memory as it is often termed, it uses space on the hard disc drive as so-called virtual memory. Virtual memory is inevitably much slower than real memory, so it is advisable to have plenty of the real thing installed in a PC if high performance is required. It is not essential for the user to become involved with virtual memory, since Windows will handle the allocation of disc space for this task.

However, the performance of virtual memory can be improved by having a separate swap file. This means having a separate partition that is only used for the swap file. This partition can be part of the main (boot) drive

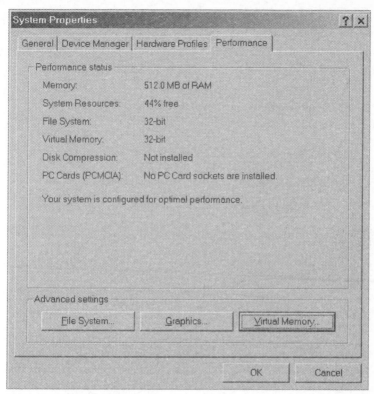

Fig.1.47 The System Properties window

or it can be provided by a second hard disc drive. There seems to be some disagreement about the effectiveness of having a separate swap file provided by a partition on the main hard disc. With many PCs having hard disc capacities that are well in excess of anything the user is likely to use, there is little to be lost by setting a few gigabytes aside as a separate partition for use as a swap file. Although hard disc drives are relatively cheap these days, installing one for swap file use will still cost a significant amount of money. It would probably be worthwhile for a PC that is used for memory intensive applications such as video or graphics editing, but is otherwise unlikely to be worth the money and effort involved.

Having created a new partition for a swap file, installed a second hard disc drive, or whatever, it is easy to use it for a separate swap file. Launch

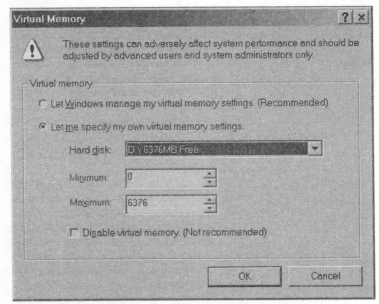

Fig.1.48 Here the drive for the swap file can be specified

the Windows Control Panel and then double-click the System icon. This produces the System Properties window, where the Performance tab is operated. This gives a window like the one shown in Figure 1.47. Next, operate the Virtual Memory button to launch the Virtual Memory window (Figure 1.48). Here you have to operate the lower radio button so that you can specify your own settings. Then the appropriate drive or partition is selected from the drop-down Hard Disk menu.

A maximum size for the swap file can be specified, but the idea is to have the disc or partition used for nothing other than the swap file. Accordingly, there is no point in using anything other than the default setting, which will use all of the disc or partition for the swap file. Operate the OK button when the changes have been made. This will probably produce a warning message, but it is safe to go ahead with the changes provided you have been careful not to make any careless errors.

Memory

The early PCs usually had a fair number of switches and jumpers on the motherboard that were used to set things such as the clock speed of the microprocessor and the amount of memory fitted. These days all or most of the configuration is handled by the BIOS and it is to a large extent automatic. It is usually possible to go into the BIOS Setup program and alter some of the settings, and in theory it is possible to "fine tune" them for optimum performance. The default settings are usually quite conservative, to make them suitable for "run of the mill" hardware. Accordingly, it is possible to speed things up slightly, provided the hardware is of sufficiently high quality.

In practice there might be nothing to be gained from tweaking the BIOS settings. The PC's manufacturer will probably have already made any necessary adjustments to optimise the settings for the particular hardware used in the PC. Alternatively, the manufacturer may have failed to do so because the default settings are the fastest ones that can be used reliably with the installed hardware. It might be possible to obtain slightly better performance by risking one or two faster settings in the hope that the hardware will be able to cope. The computer will tend to crash or fail to boot properly if the hardware is not up to the task, but you can always revert to the original settings if this should happen.

Entry

The first task when tweaking BIOS settings is to actually get into the BIOS Setup program. In the past, there have been several common means of getting into this program, but with modern motherboards there is only one method in common use. This is to press the Delete key at the appropriate point during the initial testing phase just after switch-on. The BIOS will display a message, usually in the bottom left-hand corner of the screen, telling you to press the "Del" key to enter the Setup program. The computer's instruction manual should provide details if the motherboard you are using has a different method of entering the Setup program. The most common alternative is to press the "Escape" key rather than the "Del" key, but numerous alternatives have been used over the years, and no doubt some of these are still in use.

Every PC should be supplied with a manual that has a section dealing with the BIOS. Actually, a lot of PCs are supplied with a very simple "Getting Started" manual, but this is usually augmented by the manufacturers' manuals for the main components. It is then the

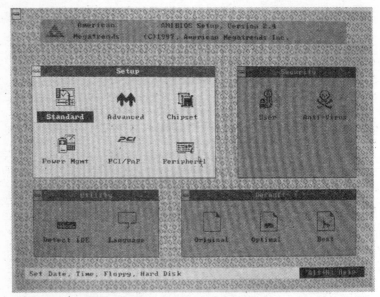

Fig.1.49 The WIMP environment of an AMI BIOS Setup program

motherboard manual that will deal with the BIOS. It is worth looking through the BIOS section of the manual before you actually go into the BIOS program. This will give you an idea of how things work, but do not bother too much about the more obscure settings. Do not expect the manual to give detailed explanations of the various settings. Most motherboard instruction manuals assume the user is familiar with all the BIOS features, and there will be few detailed explanations. In fact, there will probably just be a list of the available options and no real explanations at all. On the other hand, it should give a good idea of the features available from the particular BIOS fitted to your PC.

There are several BIOS manufacturers and their BIOS Setup programs each work in a slightly different fashion. The Award BIOS and AMI BIOS are two common examples, and although they control the same basic functions, they are organised in somewhat different ways. A modern AMI BIOS has a Setup program that will detect any reasonably standard mouse connected to the PC, and it offers a simple form of WIMP environment (Figure 1.49). It can still be controlled via the keyboard if preferred, or if the BIOS does not operate with the mouse you are using.

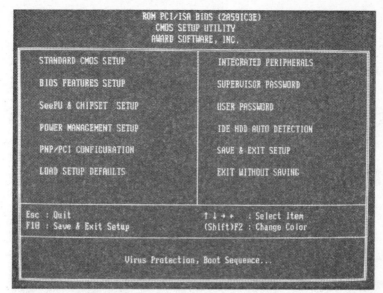

Fig.1.50 An example of an Award BIOS Setup program

The Award BIOS is probably the most common (Figure 1.50), and as far as I am aware it only uses keyboard control.

Apart from variations in the BIOS due to different manufacturers, the BIOS will vary slightly from one computer to another. This is simply due to the fact that features available on one main board may be absent or different on another board. Also, the world of PCs in general is developing at an amazing rate, and this is reflected in frequent BIOS updates.

Altering the BIOS settings is not something to be recommended unless you really know what you are doing. It is unlikely that any damage could result from daft settings, but the computer could be rendered unbootable until the correct settings are reinstated. Note though, that no settings are actually altered unless and until you select the Save Parameters and Exit option, and then answer Yes when asked to confirm this action.

This is clearly the route you should take if everything has gone according to plan. Take the Exit Without Saving option if things have not gone well. Simply switching off the PC or pressing the reset button should have the same effect. Note also that a BIOS normally has an option to load the default settings, and this should get the computer working again if the

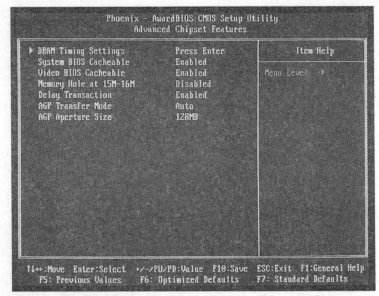

Fig.1.51 *The DRAM timing is a sub-menu of the Advanced Chipset Features menu*

settings become seriously scrambled. There might also be an option to revert to the previous settings.

Memory timing

The usual BIOS tweak is to alter the CAS latency setting for SDRAM memory. This setting is also known as C latency, latency, or just CL. When a memory chip places new data onto the computer's data bus, it takes a short time for the signal to settle at the correct level. In this context a short time means a matter of nanoseconds, and certainly well under a millionth of a second. It is important that the processor does not read the memory chips until the signal levels have had time to settle at the correct levels. A long latency delay makes the computer operate more slowly, but it gives better reliability. Using a shorter hold-off gives greater speed but could seriously compromise reliability.

With a modern BIOS it is usually necessary to delve quite deeply for the setting you require. The main menu has a number of options, but many of these lead to further menus. The Phoenix-Award BIOS of the PC used

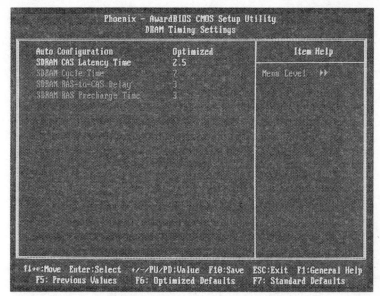

Fig.1.52 This page includes a setting for the CAS latency timing

in this example has an Advanced Chipset Features option in the main menu, and this page (Figure 1.51) has an option that gives access to the DRAM timing settings (Figure 1.52). The figure for the SDRAM CAS Latency Time is the one that is of interest here, and it is usually adjustable from about 2 to 3.5 in increments of 0.5. A modern BIOS might have a more restricted range, with just two options of 2 and 2.5 for example. I assume that this figure is the delay in terms of system clock cycles. Anyway, lower values equate to faster memory operations.

The general idea is to set the timing one step lower than its original setting, where this is possible. Then save the new settings and exit the BIOS Setup program. Next, try the PC with the new settings to see if it will operate reliably. There are test programs that can be used to check reliability by repeatedly checking parts of the system. An alternative to one of these is to use the computer for something unimportant, such as surfing the Internet for a while. Do not use the PC for producing anything important until you are sure that it is functioning reliably. Go back into the BIOS Setup program and revert to the original latency setting if there are any signs of unstable operation.

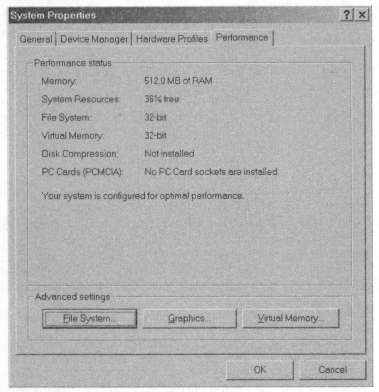

*Fig.1.53 The Performance section of the System Properties window.
Here the File System button is operated*

Faster memory modules can be installed if the existing memory modules
are unable to run reliably using a lower latency setting. These faster
modules are guaranteed to provide stable operation with a specified
latency figure, but they are obviously more expensive than "bog standard"
memory modules. It is probably not worthwhile changing to faster
modules, since the increase in performance would probably not justify
the expense. It might be worthwhile abandoning the existing modules
and opting for a faster type when undertaking a substantial upgrade to
the amount of memory. This is clearly dependent on being able to get
the new memory modules at a reasonable price.

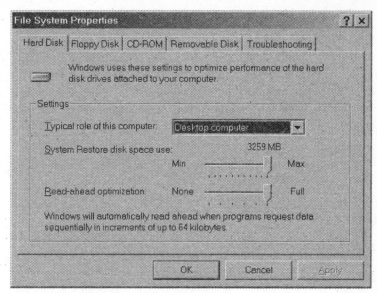

Fig.1.54 The File System Properties window

System Restore

The System Restore facility of Windows ME and Windows XP is a very useful one, but it requires compressed copies of old system files to be retained so that the operating system can be returned to an earlier state. Automatically adding restoration points obviously takes up time, and the copies of old system files can eventually take up a large amount of disc space. Despite the usefulness of the System Restore facility, some users prefer to switch it off in order to conserve system resources. This does remove an escape route if the operating system becomes seriously damaged, but the System Restore feature is far from essential where a full backup of the main drive is available.

In order to switch off the System Restore feature in Windows ME, it is first a matter of going to the Windows Control Panel. Double-click the System icon and then operate the Performance tab when the System Properties window appears (Figure 1.53). Next, the File System button is operated, and this produces the File System Properties window of Figure 1.54. Operating the Troubleshooting tab produces a page that has a number of checkboxes (Figure 1.55). In this case it is the one at

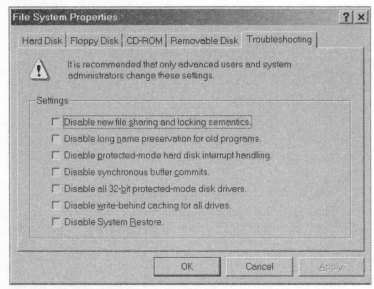

Fig.1.55 The Troubleshooting section has a number of checkboxes

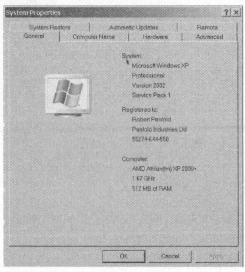

Fig.1.56 The XP System Properties window

the bottom that is of interest, and ticking this box disables the System Restore feature. Operate the OK button to make the change take effect.

In Windows XP it is again a matter of first going to the Control Panel and double-clicking the System icon. This produces a System Properties window like the one in Figure 1.56. Operate the System Restore tab to produce the page shown in Figure

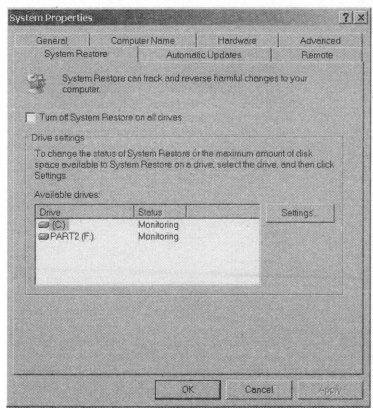

Fig.1.57 The required checkbox is in the System Restore section

1.57. Tick the checkbox near the top of the window and then operate the Apply and OK buttons to make the change take effect.

Drivers

In an ideal world the manufacturers of computer hardware such as video and audio cards would supply the perfect drivers with their products. In the real world very little hardware seems to be launched complete with fully tested, working, and optimised drivers. In fact it seems to be quite normal for equipment to be launched even though the drivers are not fully operational. Video card manufacturers seem to be particularly bad offenders in this respect.

Consequently, it is worthwhile searching the Internet for newer and better versions of the hardware drivers for your PC. The web site of the computer's manufacturer will often have updated drivers for the hardware used in their PCs. Failing that, it is a matter of going to the web sites of the companies that produced the individual components. Note that drivers are often needed for hardware that is part of the main board, so it is worthwhile investigating the web site of the main board's manufacturer. If you use the Windows Update facility this will often have updates for drivers in addition to the usual security patches, etc.

When looking for new hardware drivers it is necessary to exercise due care. Manufacturers of computer hardware tend to produce a number of products under similar names, making it easy to download the wrong drivers. Installing the wrong hardware driver could make the computer unusable, although reverting to the original drivers should solve the problem. This can be more difficult than one might expect, and it is certainly something that should be avoided.

Modem efficiency

If you have Internet access via a dialup connection it is unlikely that you will be satisfied with the connection speed. There are programs that enable large downloads to be handled more efficiently, and others that will tweak certain Windows Registry settings in an attempt to provide speedier downloads. There is also the option of tweaking the Windows Registry yourself in an attempt to optimise results, but direct editing of the Registry is not something to be undertaken lightly. Get it wrong and you could end up with a PC that operates unreliably or will not boot into Windows at all.

The two Registry tweaks that are normally used to improve results with modems are the MTU and MSS settings. MTU stands for Maximum Transmission Unit, and it sets the maximum size for a packet of data. It is normally set at 1500 bytes, which is fine for a local area network (LAN). It can be too high for use with a dial-up modem, giving reduced performance. Although the packet size may seem to be of no great consequence, you have to bear in mind that with this type of link it is not unusual for errors to occur. The system includes error checking, and this does not give problems with corrupted data. If a packet contains errors that can not be corrected, the whole packet is sent again. Taking an extreme example, with a packet size of one million bytes, an error-free packet might never be received. At the other extreme, taking things

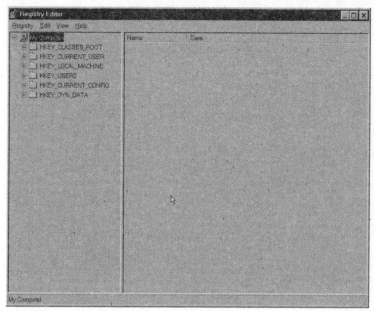

Fig.1.58 The initial window of the Regedit program

on a byte by byte basis would waste a lot of time regulating the flow of data. What is needed is a good compromise between these two extremes.

Another train of thought about MTU is that setting it too large results in packets of data to or from your PC being larger than the packet size used by your Internet service provider. This results in the packets being broken down into smaller packets and then reassembled at the destination, which reduces efficiency. Whichever way you look at it, a smaller packet size can be beneficial.

The MSS (Maximum Segment Size) value controls the maximum amount of data that can be sent in a packet. At first sight it may seem that this is the same as the MTU value, but you have to bear in mind that each packet actually contains more than the data. For example, it contains addresses that enable it to find its way from the server to your PC. Consequently, the MSS value is slightly smaller than the one for the MTU setting.

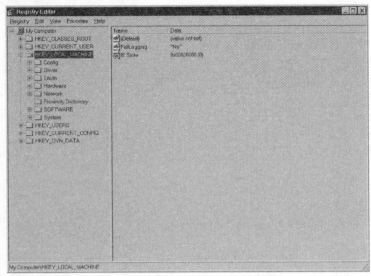

Fig.1.59 Expanding the HKEY_LOCAL_MACHINE folder

Tweaking

You can tweak these registry values using either the Windows Regedit program or a special utility program. The Regedit method has the advantage of avoiding the need to buy any additional software, but you do have to proceed very carefully in order to avoid damaging the system. Any alterations to the Registry are made at your own risk. It is always a good idea to make backup copies of the existing registry files before making any changes.

The first task is to find the section of the registry that deals with the dialup adapter. Start the Registry Editor program by selecting Run from the Start menu. Then type "regedit" into the text box and operate the OK button. This will launch the Regedit program, which will have an initial window like the one on Figure 1.58.   Next left-click on the HKEY_LOCAL_MACHINE folder. This should result in something like Figure 1.59. Then expand the Enum, Root, and Net folders so that you have something like Figure 1.60. Every PC is different, so the exact Registry entries may be different on your PC, but there should be several subfolders of the Net folder with names like 000, 0001, 0002, etc.

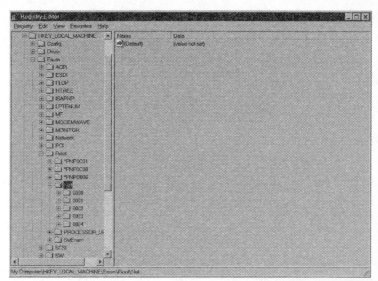

Fig.1.60 Next the Enum, Root, and Net folders are expanded

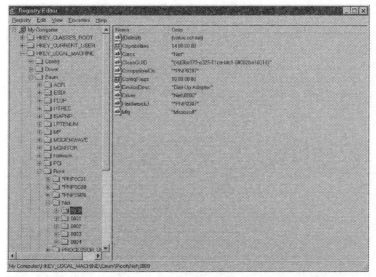

Fig.1.61 Find the subfolder with "DeviceDesc" in the Name field

1 The built-in facilities

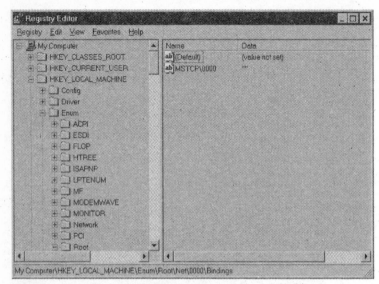

Fig.1.62 Here there should be an entry that starts "MSTCP"

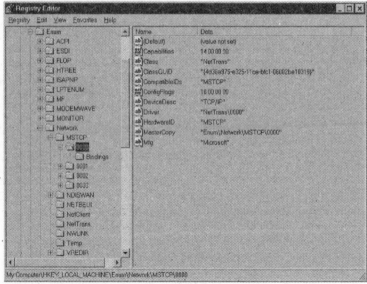

Fig.1.63 Here, it is the Driver entry that is of interest

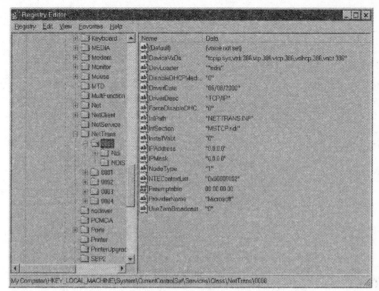

Fig.1.64 At last, this page is where the changes are made

Now left-click on each of these folders in turn, and look at the data that appears in the right-hand section of the window. You are looking for the entry that has "DeviceDesc" in the Name field and "Dial-Up Adapter" in the Data field. This will probably be found in the first of the folders (Figure 1.61). The folder that contains this entry should have a subfolder called Bindings, which should now be expanded. This subfolder should contain an Entry in the name field that starts "MSTCP/", followed by a four-digit number. Make a note of this number, which will probably just be 0000 (Figure 1.62). Next go to:

HKEY_LOCAL_MACHINE\Enum\Network\MSTCP\xxxx

Here xxxx is the four-digit number noted previously. In this folder there should be a Value entry called Driver, and its Data entry will be something like "NetTrans0000" (Figure 1.63). It is the four-digit number in the Data entry that is required.

Close the subfolders to remove the clutter in the left-hand side of the screen and return to the basic keys. To make the changes to the Registry go to HKEY_LOCAL_MACHINE again and go down the directory structure through System, CurrentControlSet, Services, Class, NetTrans, and 000x.

Here 000x is the number of the dialup adapter that you determined previously, or 0000 in this example. This should give you something like Figure 1.64. Right-click in the right-hand section of the screen to produce

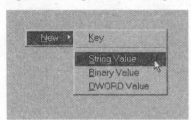

a small popup menu (Figure 1.65) and select the String Value option. A new Value entry then appears in the list (Figure 1.66), and this is edited to read "MaxMTU". Then double-click on the new entry to produce the window of Figure 1.67 where a value of 576 should be entered. Repeat this process, but the second time use "MaxMSS" for the Value field and 536 as the Data value. Next

Fig.1.65 Use this menu to create a new string value

choose Exit from the File menu to close Regedit and then reboot the computer so that the changes can take effect. Run Regedit again and check that the changes are present and correct (Figure 1.68). Close Regedit and go online to see if the new settings have the desired effect.

There are no entries for MTU and MSS already present in the Registry because the default values are built into the Windows program code

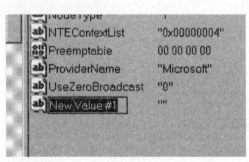

and are not normally controlled by way of the Registry. Thus the entries first have to be generated and then given data values. If you find entries for MTU and MSS already present, either someone has already added them manually or an accelerator program has put them there.

Fig.1.66 The newly created entry

Note that tweaking MTU and MSS must be repeated for each dialup adapter if there is more than one installed. There will almost certainly be more than one if you are using two or more Internet service providers. Additional adapters will be found in the keys called 0001, 0002, etc., when initially searching the Registry for the main dialup adapter's entry.

Internet advice

There are endless Windows and hardware tweaks detailed on the Internet, and it is worthwhile searching for the latest tweaks. Many of these tweaks are specific to certain hardware such as a particular graphics card. This is fine if you happen to be using the appropriate hardware, but it clearly means that many of the ideas will

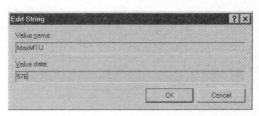

Fig.1.67 Setting the Data part of the new entry

not be relevant to your particular PC. Bear in mind that many of the ideas for tuning items of hardware involve some form of over-clocking. If you should happen to "fry" some of the chips in your PC there will be no prospect of getting replacements under guarantee. You do this type of thing entirely at your own risk.

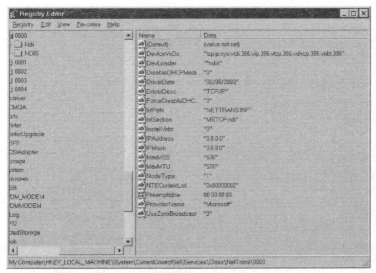

Fig.1.68 The two new entries in position on the correct page

It is important to bear in mind that some of the advice available on the Internet is less than totally reliable. In some cases the advice is just poorly explained, rendering it either useless or even potentially harmful. There is also a percentage that is deliberately misleading, and this type of thing will usually attempt to make users do something that will damage their PCs. It is not advisable to take anything on the Internet at face value, and this is certainly the case with PC tweaks.

Points to remember

Windows includes some useful tools and facilities for keeping a PC running efficiently. The Disk Cleanup utility is a quick way of removing certain types of clutter from the hard disc. As with any cleanup utility, it is possible to remove something useful from the disc. This is not likely to occur with the Disk Cleanup program, but a certain amount of care should be exercised when using it.

One of the main causes of a PC gradually slowing down is fragmentation of the files on the hard disc. Windows includes a defragmenter program, and running this occasionally should keep the hard drive operating efficiently.

It is worth running Scandisk (Windows ME) or Check Disk (Windows XP) when a PC seems to take an eternity each time the hard disc is accessed. There could be a flaw in the filing system which these utilities will detect. In most cases any errors can be automatically corrected.

Over a period of time, it is quite normal for a PC to have more and more programs installed. This can lead to a gradual slowing down, and it is advisable to uninstall any unused programs if a PC suffers a serious case of software bloat. Always use a proper uninstaller to remove unwanted programs and do not simply delete their folders.

Background processes can seriously slow down a PC. Each process will probably consume only a small amount of memory and processor time, but the cumulative effect of several processes can be very significant. Some processes perform vital tasks, but there are usually a few that can be switched off without any ill effects.

Cookies are small text files used by some web sites to provide facilities such as logging in automatically. Huge numbers of them can accumulate on the hard disc and it is advisable to clear them from time to time. Deleting all the cookies might result in a loss of facilities at some web sites, but it should not take long to reinstate these facilities.

Applications that use a lot of memory, and eventually resort to virtual memory, will run faster if a separate swap file is used. Ideally this should be on a separate hard drive to the system files, etc., and used for nothing else. Failing that, its own partition on drive C should suffice.

Tweaking a couple of Registry entries can give a slight improvement in the speed of dialup Internet access. However, directly editing the Registry is not a good idea unless you have a reasonable understanding of what you are doing. Do not expect Registry tweaks of this type to produce large improvements in performance.

2

Third-party programs

Be realistic

There are plenty of third-party tuning programs for those that feel the built-in tuning facilities of Windows are inadequate. It is only fair to point out that some of the claims for these programs are a bit unrealistic. In fact the claims for some of them totally lack credibility. If you decide to invest in this type of software it is important to be realistic in your expectations and avoid programs that offer "the earth".

There is also something to be said for sticking with the well-established programs from well-known software houses. A badly written tuning program can easily result in Windows being brought to a halt rather than speeded up. In fact one careless error in an otherwise well-written program could have dire results for a Windows installation. The popular programs are well tried and tested, and should be free from any significant bugs.

Better defragmenting

The benefits of defragmenting a hard disc were covered in Chapter 1. Defragmenter programs are available if you feel that something more potent than the built-in utility is required. Probably the most popular of these is Diskeeper, and Figure 2.1 shows the initial screen obtained when running Diskeeper 8. This program is essentially the same as the one supplied with Windows XP, and it will actually install itself in place of the built-in defragmenter when it is installed on a Windows XP system.

The basic defragmenting routine is presumably the same as the one used in the built-in program, but the user interface is rather different. There are buttons towards the top right-hand corner of the window that provide shortcuts to some facilities. The bottom section of the window

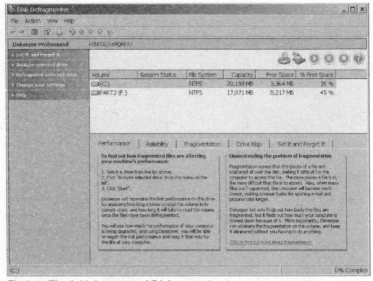

Fig.2.1 The initial screen of Diskeeper 8

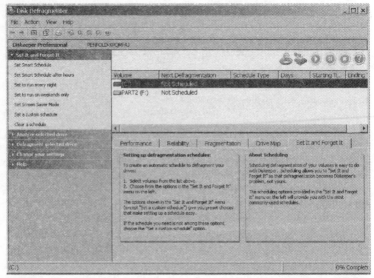

Fig.2.2 The program can be scheduled to run automatically if required

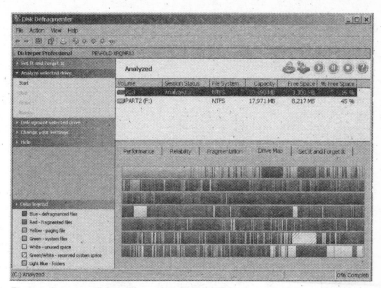

*Fig.2.3 It is possible to have the disc analysed at any time, with the
results displayed in graphic form*

provides more information than in the basic program, and some extra
features are available from the menu near the top left-hand corner of the
window. One of these is the Set and Forget facility (Figure 2.2), which
enables the program to run automatically at nights, weekends, etc. It is
also possible to analyse the disc at any time (Figure 2.3) and to
defragment it on demand. As with the basic version, the disc will be
placed in efficient working order without necessarily fully defragmenting
the disc (Figure 2.4).

Buying a disc defragmenter is perhaps a more worthwhile proposition
for those running Windows ME than it is for those using Windows XP. A
program such as Diskeeper 8 is a large step up from the Windows ME
defragmenter, but it has relatively little advantage for Windows XP users.
Whether you opt for the built-in program or a third-party add-on, make
sure that you do actually use the program and avoid letting the disc get
badly defragmented. A fragmented disc is more or less guaranteed to
slow down any program that requires frequent disc accesses.

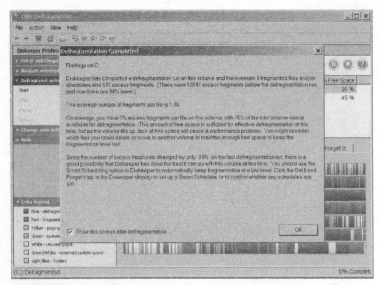

*Fig.2.4 The report produced after the program has been run will
probably indicate that a small amount of fragmentation remains*

Speedier Internet

Pop-up advertisements, or just pop-ups as they are often called, were
originally used as a means of advertising porn and other sites at the less
than respectable end of the market. Some sites were deliberately
misleading and lured users via search engines using popular search
terms. On arriving at a site of this type users found nothing of interest,
but would find that numerous pop-up advertisements appeared. The
owners of the web sites were paid a small amount for each pop-up that
their site produced, and they presumably made large sums of money in
this way.

This type of trickery has not totally disappeared from the Internet, but it
is nothing like as prevalent as it used to be. This is not to say that pop-
ups are now something of a rarity. If you surf the Internet for a few minutes
you will almost certainly encounter several pop-up advertisements, and
could encounter dozens. Pop-ups have moved upmarket, and they are
now to be found on many of the more respectable sites on the Internet.
The usual banner advertisements tended to pass unnoticed by most
users, rendering them largely ineffective. Flashing lettering and moving
graphics gave these advertisements a new lease of life, but they were

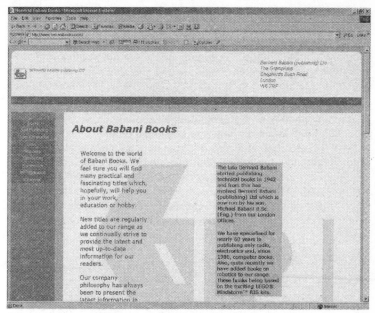

Fig.2.5 The new toolbar is added beneath the existing toolbars

still not effective enough for many advertisers. Hence the move to pop-up advertisements that the user can not overlook.

Pop-up blockers

The main objection of most users is that pop-ups are irritating and a bit of a nuisance, but they can also tend to slow things down when surfing the Internet. There are programs that will block pop-up advertisements, but some of these are more successful than others. Unfortunately, some of these programs seem to let most of the pop-ups through while blocking a proportion of your normal Internet activity. Two main approaches are used by these programs, and one it to block the JavaScript code that is normally responsible for generating the pop-ups. The other approach is to block access to a list of known advertising sites. A mixture of the two methods is often utilised.

One of the best pop-up blockers I have encountered is the one that comes as part of the toolbar that is available from the popular Google search engine (www.google.co.uk). It is a reasonably small download and it has the advantage of being completely free, so there is not a lot to lose by trying it. Once installed, the toolbar appears below the other toolbars in Internet Explorer (Figure 2.5). Like any normal toolbar in Internet Explorer, it is easily switched off. Just select Toolbars from the View menu followed by Google from the submenu. Do the same again in order to reinstate the toolbar.

There is no need to switch off the entire toolbar in order to permit pop-ups. They can be toggled on and off simply by operating the pop-up button in the toolbar. It is also possible to temporarily enable them by holding down the Control key while clicking on a link. There might seem to be no point in allowing pop-ups, but they are sometimes used to perform useful functions, so you might actually need them from time to time. On the other hand, I have been using the Google toolbar for several months and have not yet found it necessary to enable pop-ups.

Banner blockers

Things can be taken a stage further, and some programs try to identify the banner advertisements on a web page and then block them. This can substantially reduce the amount of data that is downloaded and hence speed up Internet surfing. This feature is often offered in addition to a pop-up blocking facility. The early attempts at banner blocking were somewhat less than entirely successful. Some programs were overcautious and failed to block most banner advertisements. Most suffered from the opposite problem and were a bit overzealous. They often removed ordinary content from web pages.

Modern banner blockers mostly operate between these two extremes and provide much better results. This type of thing is unlikely to give perfect results every time though. Figure 2.6 shows AdsCleaner in action, and it has done quite a good job on this page. The blank areas are where the banner advertisements have been removed from the page. The graphs have been left in place, and there is no sign of the page's normal contents having been "zapped".

The toolbar at the top of the page indicates that 33.65 kilobytes of data have been blocked, which would typically add about seven seconds to the download time using a dialup connection. This type of program is probably less worthwhile for broadband users. With a 512k ADSL connection the time saved on downloading this page could be less than half a second, although it would be much more than this with a slow server.

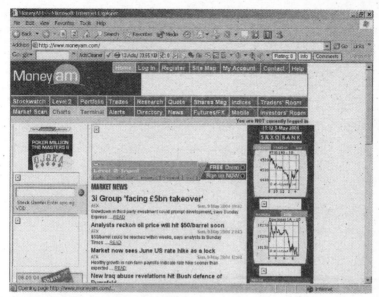

Fig.2.6 AdsClean has successfully removed the advertisements

Easy tweaking

Tweaking the MTU and MSS settings in the Windows Registry was covered in Chapter 1. If you do not wish to delve into the Windows Registry directly, and I would certainly not recommend it, the easy alternative is to use one of the many programs that make it easy to change the default values. Here the popular TweakDUN program will be used as an example of this type of acceleration program. This should be available from any of the large software download sites or the manufacturer's site at:

www.pattersondesigns.com.

Unregistered versions of the program are only partially operational, but do enable the MTU and MSS settings to be changed. When first run there is a splash screen followed by a menu that permits the desired adapter to be selected (Figure 2.7). The adapters listed here will obviously depend on the set-up of your PC. Left-click on the entry for the adapter you wish to modify and then operate the Select button. The program then moves to the main screen (Figure 2.8) where the MTU value of 576

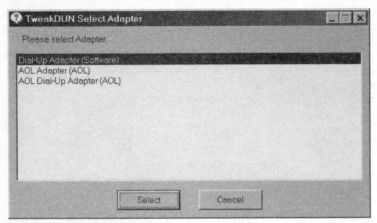

Fig.2.7 Here the appropriate adapter is selected

can be selected using the appropriate radio button. Operate the OK button to implement the changes and then the Yes button when asked if you wish to restart the computer. Once the computer has rebooted the changes will have taken effect and it is ready for testing online. This method is certainly a lot easier than manually delving around in the Windows Registry, and it should be equally effective.

Download accelerators

If you have an Internet connection via a standard telephone line and you regularly achieve something close to the theoretical maximum data transfer figures, there is no point in trying to obtain significantly faster connection speeds other than by changing to a faster method of connection such as ADSL. Even if you were to achieve theoretically perfect results the improvement in performance would be minimal. If downloads seem to go rather slowly, with frequent restarts, a download manager could help to speed things up.

One function of a download manager tries to make sure that the rate at which data is downloaded is as close as possible to the maximum rate that your modem supports. There are two main approaches, and one of these is to test the various sources of the file so that the fastest server or servers can be used. The other is to use settings that are likely to give optimum results when downloading large files. A program that only adjusts settings (such as TweakDUN) is usually called an optimiser or accelerator rather than a download manager. However, the terminology of these programs is rather loosely applied, so you need to read the "fine print" in order to determine the exact facilities provided by any programs of this genre.

A download manager can also be used to carry on where you left off if the connection to the server is lost. Normally there is no way of continuing with a download if the

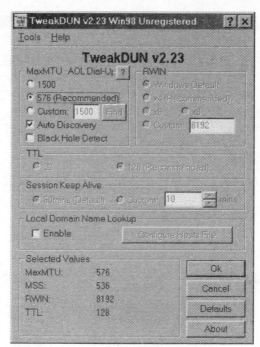

Fig.2.8 The main screen of TweakDUN

connection is lost. Establishing the connection again and continuing with the download will almost invariably result in the process starting "from scratch", and the part of the file downloaded previously will be lost. Even if there were only a few bytes of a 100-megabyte file left to go when the connection went down, the part of the file that was downloaded will be lost!

With large files and unreliable servers it may only be possible to download large files with the aid of a download manager. Without one you might never get more than half the file downloaded. In less severe instances it can still save a lot of wasted time, since you will not keep downloading the same data over and over again until the complete file is eventually downloaded in one lump. The ability to resume downloads is probably the most important one provided by download managers.

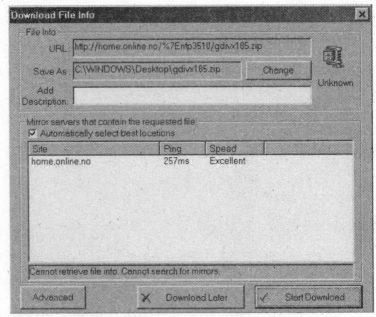

Fig.2.9 On this occasion only one download site has been found

The right connections

A download manager that searches for the best download sites and/or can resume where it left off, is normally set to pop up automatically when a download is about to commence. Figure 2.9 shows Accelerator Plus in operation, and in this case it has not been able to find any information about alternative download sites, or "mirror" sites as they are termed. This gives no option but to download the file from the original site. The chance of finding mirror sites depend on the popularity of the file you are trying to download. With a very popular download there could be dozens of alternative sites available. Figure 2.10 shows the result when trying to download the popular Winzip program. In this case there are so many mirror sites that the list has gained a scrollbar.

Pinging

The list includes a ping time for each site and a rating of that ping time. Pinging is sending a small packet of data to a server and back again.

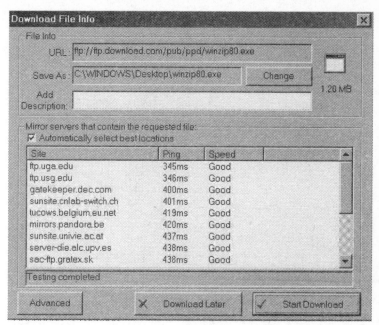

Fig.2.10 With a more popular file about 20 sources have been found

The shorter the time this takes, the faster the download is likely to be. It tends to be assumed that the rate at which data can be downloaded is purely dependent on the quality of the connection to the Internet service provider and the speed at which the server can send data. However, data is not downloaded from the server in the form of one continuous stream of data. It is sent in smaller chunks called "packets", and a dialogue is needed between your PC and the server in order to ensure that everything works smoothly. Time is lost each time your PC and the server try to establish contact.

Pinging is used to measure how quickly (or otherwise) your PC and the server can establish contact, rather than just measuring the rate at which data can be transferred between the two. With a short ping time there is relatively little time wasted trying to establish contact so that messages or packets of data can be exchanged efficiently. Of course, if the rate of data flow is very low, this will also produce a long ping time.

The obvious approach is to use whichever site gives the shortest response time, but many download managers take things a step further. The fastest site is used initially, but if this site fails to live up to expectations another

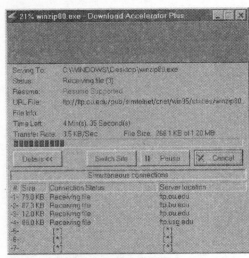

fast site will be tried instead. There may be an option to manually select the sites to use, but automatic selection is easier and likely to yield the best results. Operating the Start Download button gets things underway, and a small window then appears. This shows how things are progressing (Figure 2.11) and also indicates if it is possible to resume a broken download,

Fig.2.11 *The program has found and is using four download sites*

which it normally is. Where appropriate, the bottom section gives details of how the data is being downloaded using simultaneous connection to several sites.

Multiple threads

Some download managers try to obtain increased download speeds by using multiple threads. In other words, the program instigates several connections to the server with each one downloading a different part of the file. Figure 2.12 shows FlashGet 1.6 in operation, and a popup window offers a number of options. The one of interest here is the Split parts field, where a value of 1 to 10 can be used. This controls the number of threads used for the download, and the default value is 5. Figure 2.13 shows a download in progress, and the lower section of the window shows the amount of data downloaded by each of five threads.

The multiple thread approach can greatly speed up downloads, make no difference, or produce a download rate anywhere between these two extremes. With an ordinary dialup connection it is unlikely to make any difference. The limiting factor on the download speed will almost invariably be the speed of the Internet connection rather than the server.

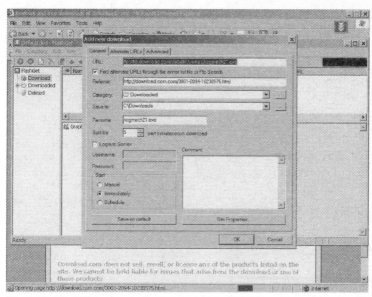

Fig.2.12 FlashGet can use from one to ten threads

The situation is different with a broadband connection that can download at 60 kilobytes or more per second. Many servers will be able to match this rate, but some will have a lower transfer rate, particularly at times of high demand. With a maximum rate of (say) 10 kilobytes per second from the server, using five threads would increase the download rate to 50 kilobytes per second. In practice the extra loading on the server would probably reduce this slightly, but the actual download rate would still be much higher than the one obtained from a single thread.

Note that some servers do not permit multiple threads, and that many FTP servers only permit one or two. Repeated attempts to use an excessive number of threads could get you banned from one of these sites. Another point to bear in mind is that using multiple threads could be regarded as antisocial behaviour. If your download speed is increased, the download rate for other users will probably be decreased.

A download manager can be very useful when downloading files from FTP sites. A modern version of Internet Explorer can actually handle many FTP sites, but by no means all of them. Most download managers are better at accessing and downloading files from the more difficult FTP sites. Surprisingly perhaps, Internet Explorer and the built-in

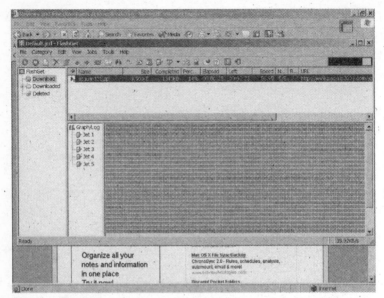

Fig.2.13 The display shows how things are progressing on each thread

downloading facility of Windows do sometimes succeed where some download managers fail. It can therefore be worth trying Internet Explorer or a dedicated FTP program in cases where a download manager is unable to make a connection or produces erratic results.

Tweaking

There are numerous programs that allow the user to tweak a particular aspect of a PC's performance, and there are also a number of all-in-one programs that cover many aspects of a PC's performance. The second category is by far the most popular, and it is certainly more practical to use one far-ranging program than a number of small utilities. On the face of it, specialist programs could provide a performance advantage over a "jack of all trades" program, but in practice the two types of program perform essentially the same tasks. Consequently, any improvement in performance is likely to be much the same whatever program is used to provide the tweaking.

The "Tweak....." series of programs is extremely popular, and Figure 2.14 shows the opening screen of Tweak-XP Pro. This is a general tune-up

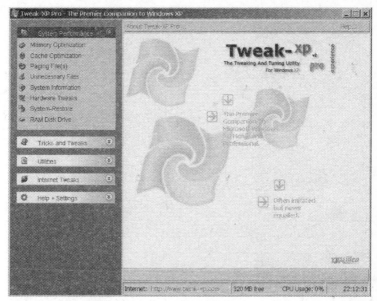

Fig.2.14 The opening screen of Tweak-XP Pro

program for computers running Windows XP. The range of facilities on offer is so wide that it is broken down into four groups that are accessed via the large menu down the left-hand side of the window. The fifth group gives access to the Help system and the program's own settings. Some of the facilities offered by this program are things such as file shredders that are not anything to do with tuning a PC, but a full range of tuning utilities is also included.

A Registry Cleaner option is available in the Utilities section (Figure 2.15), and this is a useful feature that is to be found in many general tune-up programs. Selecting this option changes the window to look like Figure 2.16, and operating the Start Search button initiates a scan of the registry. Eventually a list of suspected errors will be listed in the lower section of the window, and in this example 33 suspected problems were found. Why does the Registry need cleaning, and what sort of errors will be found?

In theory, there should be no need for any maintenance of the Registry. When software is installed on a PC it makes additions to the Registry. In the days of MS-DOS it was normal for each program to have a folder in

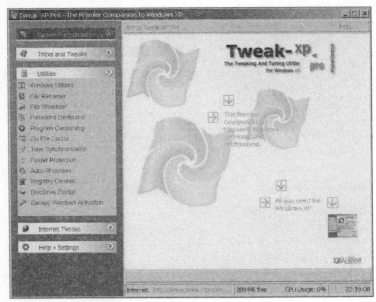

Fig.2.15 The Utilities section includes a Registry cleaner

which it stored a configuration file or files. A configuration file is a database that contains default settings for the program, such as the screen colours and the default font details. Normal configuration files are rarely used with modern versions of Windows. Instead, the configuration information is stored in the Registry files, which is where the configuration information for Windows itself is also stored.

Programs should only place valid entries in the Registry during installation. In the real world mistakes are made, and there can be entries that refer to files that do not exist, files that are not in the specified location, and this type of thing. Probably the majority of errors occur when a program is uninstalled. All the Registry entries for a program should be removed when it is uninstalled, but in practice it is quite normal for some entries to be left behind. Sometimes this is done deliberately so the program can use the old configuration settings if it is ever reinstalled. In other cases it is due to deficiencies in the uninstaller program. Either way, there can be entries that serve no useful purpose and simply bloat what is likely to be a huge Registry.

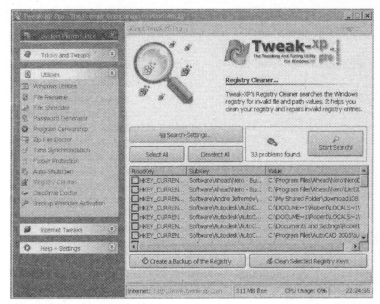

Fig.2.16 A list of erroneous entries is produced

Safety first

Great care needs to be taken when making changes to the Registry manually, since an error could prevent an application program from running properly. Worse still, an error could give problems with the operating system or even prevent the computer from booting at all. Manually searching the Registry for errors is difficult and time consuming, even if you know what you are doing. Without expert knowledge it is not really a practical proposition and would be more or less guaranteed to end in disaster. The only practical approach is to use programs that can automatically search the Registry for errors and fix them.

Commercial programs that clean up the Registry almost invariably insist on making a backup copy first. If major damage to the registry should result from the changes made, it is then reasonably easy to revert to the old Registry. With Windows ME and Windows XP systems a restoration point might be made instead of, or in addition to backing up the Registry. If the Registry should be rendered unusable by the changes made, the Windows Restore program can be used to take things back to their original state. It is definitely not a good idea to use any program that

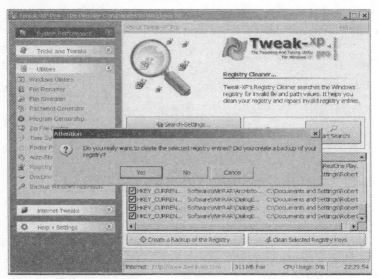

Fig.2.17 The usual warning message is produced before anything is deleted

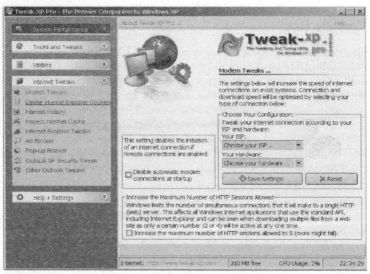

Fig.2.18 The program can tweak the Internet connection

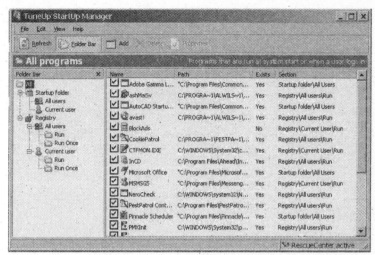

Fig.2.19 The Start-Up manager of the TuneUp program

alters the Registry unless there is some easy way of reversing the changes.

Returning to Tweak XP Pro, the "orphan" entries are shown in the lower part of the window so that the user can look through them and check that they do not refer to any currently installed software. In this example the entries all referred to either old versions of programs or to software that had been removed from the system. The checkbox is ticked for each entry that is to be removed. Operating the Select All button will add a tick in all the checkboxes, but only after a warning message has been acknowledged. Operate the Clear Selected Registry Keys to go ahead and remove the selected entries. These entries will be deleted once another warning message has been received (Figure 2.17). The PC is then rebooted to make the changes take effect.

Some programs search more thoroughly for incorrect Registry entries. Trying TuneUp Utilities on the same PC produced well over four hundred entries that the program considered erroneous in some way. Of course, the more deeply a program delves into the Registry, and the greater the number of changes made, the larger the risk you take in permitting the changes. However, letting the TuneUp Utilities program make the additional changes did not produce any problems. Remember that you can always resort to a backup copy of the Registry if major problems are experienced with the "cleaned" version.

2 Third-party programs

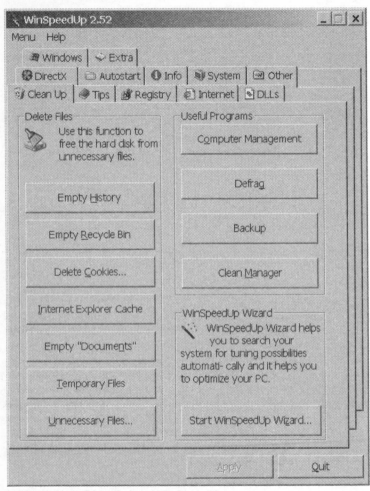

Fig.2.20 The initial screen of WinSpeedUp

There are many other facilities available in Tweak XP Pro, such as for tweaking the Internet connection (Figure 2.18). This enables optimum performance to be obtained without having to resort to any manual editing of the Registry. Some of the facilities on offer are really just the ones that are available from within Windows. In fact some of the simpler tuning programs seem to do little more than act as a convenient user interface

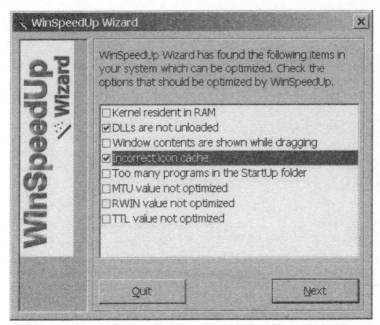

Fig.2.21 The WinSpeedUp Wizard produces a list of improvements

for launching the built-in Windows disc utilities, etc. Most programs take things at least one stage further and try to provide more convenient versions of the standard Windows utilities. Figure 2.19 shows the StartUp Manager of the TuneUp program. By default this shows all the programs that are run at start-up, so that it is easy to go down the list and remove the tick from the checkbox of any program that you wish to suppress. It is still possible to look at a single category by selecting the appropriate folder in the left-hand section of the window.

Automatic tuning

Many tuning programs can analyse the system and provide suggestions for improving performance. The initial screen of WinSpeedUp (Figure 2.20) provides access to the usual facilities for clearing the Internet history, emptying the Recycle Bin, and so on, but it also has an automatic analyser. This is in the form of a wizard that can be called up via the menu system. It provides a list of items that can be optimised (Figure 2.21), and a tick is placed in the checkbox for any that you wish to go ahead with. It is merely necessary to operate the Next button to go ahead and make the changes. The changes will not take effect until the computer has been rebooted, and there is the option of rebooting immediately (Figure 2.22).

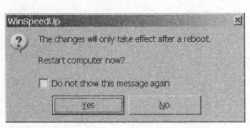

Fig.2.22 There is the option of rebooting immediately

The TuneUp program has facilities to analyse various parts of the system and suggest changes. In Figure 2.23 it has come up with some suggested changes to the system's configuration. As usual, there is a checkbox for each suggestion so that you can opt not to go ahead with

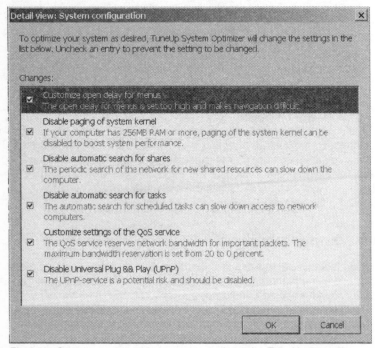

Fig.2.23 Some suggested improvements from the TuneUp program

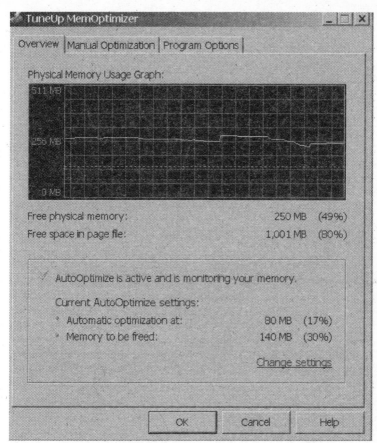

Fig.2.24 The memory optimiser has a display that shows memory usage versus time

any changes that would alter or remove features that you require. Although there is an obvious attraction in using a program that alters the system in a fully automatic fashion, this is not really something that could be recommended. Similarly, you should not simply let the program get on with it and implement all its suggested changes without bothering to review any of them. It is advisable to check each suggestion, and only go ahead with changes that will definitely not nobble a feature that you require.

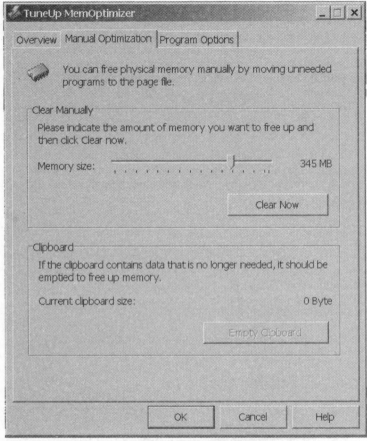

Fig.2.25 It is possible to manually clear a certain amount of memory

Memory

It is quite common for tuning programs to include a utility that is intended to provide more effective use of a PC's memory. Separate utilities of this type are also available. When a PC runs out of conventional memory it resorts to using the swap file on a hard disc drive instead. This works, but applications will normally slow down quite significantly when the swap file is used. A memory optimiser tries to prevent the memory from being used up, and it achieves this by removing anything stored in memory that is not considered to be sufficiently important.

Figure 2.24 shows the memory optimiser of the TuneUp program in operation. The display shows how the use of memory changes with time, but this window is normally minimised and the program then runs as a background application. It can be set to optimise the memory usage when a certain key combination is used, and it will then use the manual optimisation setting. This feature is also available from within the program by operating the Manual Optimisation tab followed by the Clear Now button (Figure 2.25). The slider control is used to set the amount of memory that will be cleared. If the Windows Clipboard is in use, operating the button in the lower section of the window clears the data stored on the Clipboard.

Of course, a memory optimiser can not work miracles and there is a limit to the effectiveness of any program of this type. If an application program needs large amounts of memory in order to run efficiently, a small amount of memory plus a memory optimiser is unlikely to give really good results. However, a good memory optimiser will avoid problems such as memory not being freed properly when a program is terminated. It should ensure that good use is made of whatever amount of memory is fitted to the PC. The optimiser program will itself consume system resources, but it should "earn its keep".

Points to remember

There are plenty of third-party programs that can be used to boost the performance of a flagging PC, but be wary of the inflated claims for some of this software. These programs can help to keep a PC operating at top performance, but they will not turn a 2 gigahertz processor into a 3 gigahertz one.

Third-party disc defragmenters are available, but they will not necessarily do a better job than the built-in program. This is definitely the case with Windows XP, which comes complete with a version of the excellent Diskeeper program. Users of Windows ME perhaps have more to gain by switching to a third-party defragmenter.

Download accelerators and managers are useful with any type of Internet connection because they will usually permit an interrupted download to be resumed. They can be especially useful with broadband connections. By using multiple threads a download accelerator can boost download speeds with some slow servers, but note that not all servers permit the use of multiple threads. Using multiple threads is unlikely to be of any benefit with an ordinary dial-up Internet connection.

Pop-up and banner advertisement blockers can greatly speed up surfing the Internet by reducing the amount of data downloaded per page. It is better to use one that lets through a few advertisements rather than one which tends to overdo things and block some of the main content on pages.

Many of the more simple tuning programs seem to do little more than act as a convenient front-end for the built-in facilities of Windows. If you buy this type of software, it is advisable to invest in one that offers extra facilities even if this means paying a somewhat higher price.

Registry cleaning programs remove erroneous entries in the Windows Registry. Before using any program that will alter the Registry it is advisable to either make a backup copy of the Registry and (or) create a new restoration point. If the worst should happen it is then relatively easy to return to the original Registry.

Although there are plenty of programs that can provide largely automatic tuning of a PC, the fully automated approach is not the best one. You really need to review the changes that will be made and remove any that will have a detrimental effect on any feature that is of importance to you. You could otherwise end up with an efficient PC that lacks one or two features which you find very useful.

A memory manager or optimiser runs as a background application and helps to avoid memory wastage. However, it is no substitute for a large amount of memory when running memory intensive applications.

Viruses and
other pests

Spanner in the works

If a PC gradually slows down over a period of time, it is likely that this is caused by the dreaded software bloat. The situation is different when a PC suddenly slows down for no apparent reason. If some new software has been added, it could simply be that this is using the PC's resources and is slowing things down. Bear in mind that many programs insist on loading clever little utilities during the boot process. This obviously extends the boot process as there is more to load. Although the utilities simply run in the background doing very little most of the time, they still use up the computer's resources such as memory and processing time.

If no new software has been added, it is possible that the Windows installation has been damaged. The usual Windows troubleshooting techniques can be used in an attempt to cure the problem, the System Restore facility can be used to take the system back to a setup where it functioned properly, or Windows can be reinstalled. System Restore and reinstalling Windows are covered in the next two chapters of this book.

Another possible cause of the slow-down is that the computer has been infected with some form of computer pest. This is a very real possibility if the PC is used on the Internet. It is important to realise that things have moved on from what might be termed the traditional computer virus. An ordinary virus attaches itself to other files and tries to propagate itself across the system and on to other systems if the opportunity arises. At some stage the virus will make its presence obvious by placing a message on the screen and/or starting to damage files. Not all viruses try to do any real damage, but a substantial percentage of them will do so unless they are removed first.

A virus is unlikely to produce any noticeable reduction in speed with a modern PC, although this is something that can not be totally discounted.

However, there are other forms of pest that certainly will reduce some aspects of performance. This will often be in the form of a greatly extended boot-up period, and there can also be some general loss of speed thereafter. Disc accesses will often take longer than expected when a computer has been infected by a pest.

It is important to understand the differences between the various types of computer pest that are currently in circulation. Computer security has become more important with the rise in use of the Internet and Email. The original viruses were designed to spread themselves across any system whenever the opportunity arose. In most cases the purpose was to damage the file system of any infected computer. Many of the recent pests are more sinister than this, and in many cases will not actually try to cause significant damage to the file system. Instead, they aid hackers to hijack your PC, extract information such as passwords from it, or something of this nature. If a computer pest is causing your PC to run slowly this could be the least of your problems! The next sections describe the various types of computer pest currently in circulation.

Virus

The non-technical press tend to call any form of software that attacks computers a virus. A virus is a specific type of program though, and represents just one of several types that can attack a computer. Initially, someone attaches the virus to a piece of software, and then finds a way of getting that software into computer systems. These days the Internet is the most likely route for the infection to be spread, but it is important not to overlook the fact that there are other means of propagating viruses. Indeed, computer viruses were being spread around the world long before the Internet came along.

Programs (and possibly other files) can carry viruses regardless of their source. If someone gives you a floppy disc, CD-ROM, or DVD containing software it is possible that the contents of the disc are infected with a virus. In the early days of personal computing the main route for viruses to spread was by way of discs containing illegally copied programs. Discs containing pirated software are still used to propagate viruses. Avoid any dodgy software if you wish to keep your PC virus-free.

A later development was pirated software placed on bulletin boards so that it could be downloaded by computer users having PCs equipped with a modem. A modem was an expensive piece of equipment in those days, but once someone had downloaded a piece of software they would usually make several copies and distribute them to friends who would in turn make and distribute further copies. Although the old bulletin board system was crude compared with the modern Internet, it was actually remarkably quick and efficient at spreading viruses. The main way in which viruses are now spread is much the same as the bulletin board method, but with the Internet acting as the initial source. Due to the popularity of the Internet, it is possible for viruses to rapidly spread around the world via this route.

Anyway, having introduced a virus into a system via one route or another, it will attack that system and try to replicate itself. Some viruses only attack the boot sector of a system disc. This is the part of the disc that the computer uses to boot into the operating system. Other viruses will try to attach themselves to any file of the appropriate type, which usually means a program file of some sort. The attraction of a program file is that the user will probably run the program before too long, which gives the virus a chance to spread the infection and/or or start attacking the computer system.

At one time there were only two possible ways in which a virus could attack a computer. One way was for the virus to attach itself to a program file that the user then ran on his or her computer. The other was for someone to leave an infected floppy disc in the computer when it was switched off. On switching the computer on again the floppy disc was used as the boot disc, activating the virus in the disc's boot sector.

Script virus

These days you have to be suspicious of many more types of file. Many application programs such as word processors and spreadsheets have the ability to automate tasks using scripts or macros as they are also known. The application effectively has a built-in programming language and the script or macro is a form of program. This makes it possible for viruses or other harmful programs to be present in many types of data file. Scripts are also used in some web pages, and viruses can be hidden in these JavaScript programs, Java applets, etc. There are other potential sources of infection such as Email attachments.

I would not wish to give the impression that all files, web pages, and Emails are potential sources of script or macro viruses. There are some types of file where there is no obvious way for them to carry a virus or other harmful program. A simple text file for example, should be completely harmless. Even in cases where a harmful program is disguised as a text file with a "txt" extension, the file should be harmless. The system will treat it as a text file and it can not be run provided no one alters the file extension. Similarly, an Email that contains a plain text message can not contain a script virus. Do not get caught by files that have a double extension such as file.txt.exe. A file such as this is an executable (exe) type and not a text (txt) file.

It is probably best to regard all files and Emails with a degree of suspicion. As explained later in this chapter, even though simple text can not carry a true virus, it can carry a virus of sorts. A virus could conceivably slow down a PC, but it is unlikely to have a significant effect until it starts to attack in earnest. A lengthening of the boot process is a more likely symptom.

Benign virus

It tends to be assumed that all viruses try to harm the infected computer system. As already pointed out, this is not correct and many viruses actually do very little. For example, you might find that nothing more occurs than a daft message appears onscreen when a certain date is reached, or on a particular date each year. Viruses such as this certainly have a degree of nuisance value and could slightly slow down the PC, but they are not harmful. I would not wish to give the impression that most viruses are harmless. Many computer viruses do indeed try to do serious damage to the infected system. If in doubt, you have to assume that a virus is harmful.

A virus that does attack the system will often go for the boot sector of the hard disc drive, and this will usually make it impossible to boot the computer into the operating system. Other viruses attack the FAT (file allocation table) in an attempt to effectively scramble the contents of the disc. Another way of attacking the files on the disc is to take the direct approach and simply alter all or part of their contents. Renaming or simply deleting files are other popular ploys.

Worm

A worm is a program that replicates itself, usually from one disc to another, or from one system to another via a local network or the Internet. Like a virus, a worm is not necessarily harmful. In recent times many of the worldwide virus scares have actually been caused by worms transmitted via Email, and not by what would normally be accepted as a virus. The usual ploy is for the worm to send a copy of itself to every address in the Email address book of the infected system. A worm spread in this way, even if it is not intrinsically harmful, can have serious consequences. There can be a sudden upsurge in the amount of Email traffic, possibly causing parts of the Email system to seriously slow down or even crash. Some worms compromise the security of the infected system, perhaps enabling it to be used by a hacker for sending spam for example. This can obviously cause a major reduction in the speed at which programs run.

Trojan horse

A Trojan horse, or just plain Trojan as it is now often called, is a program that appears to be one thing but is actually another. In the early days many Trojans were in the form of free software, and in particular, free antivirus programs. The users obtained nasty shocks when the programs were run, with their computer systems being attacked. Like viruses, some Trojans do nothing more than display stupid messages, but others attack the disc files, damage the boot sector of the hard disc, and so on.

Backdoor Trojan

A backdoor Trojan is the same as the standard variety in that it is supplied in the form of a program that appears to be one thing but is actually another. In some cases nothing appears to happen when you install the program. In others the program might actually install and run as expected. In both cases one or two small programs will have been installed on the computer and set to run when the computer is booted.

One ploy is to have programs that produce log files showing which programs you have run and which Internet sites you have visited. The log will usually include any key presses as well. The idea is for the log file to provide passwords to things such as your Email account, online bank account, and so on. Someone hacking into your computer system will usually look for the log files, and could obviously gain access to important information from these files. Another ploy is to have a program that makes it easier for hackers to break into your computer system, and this is a backdoor Trojan. A backdoor Trojan does not attack the infected computer in the same way as some viruses, and it does not try to spread the infection to other discs or computers. Potentially though, a backdoor Trojan is more serious than a virus, particularly if you use the computer for online banking, share dealing, etc.

Spyware

Spyware programs monitor system activity and send information to another computer by way of the Internet. There are really two types of spyware, and one tries to obtain passwords and send them to another computer. This takes things a step further than the backdoor Trojan programs mentioned earlier. A backdoor Trojan makes it easier for a hacker to obtain sensitive information from your PC, but it does not go as far as sending any information that is placed in the log files. Spyware is usually hidden in other software in Trojan fashion.

Adware

The second type of spyware is more correctly called adware. In common with spyware, it gathers information and sends it to another computer via the Internet. Adware is not designed to steal passwords or other security information from your PC. Its purpose is usually to gather information for marketing purposes, and this typically means gathering and sending details of the web sites you have visited. Some free programs are supported by banner advertising, and the adware is used to select advertisements that are likely to be of interest to you.

Programs that are supported by adware have not always made this fact clear during the installation process. Sometimes the use of adware was pointed out in the End User License Agreement, but probably few people bother to read the "fine print". These days the more respectable software companies that use this method of raising advertising revenues make it clear that the adware will be installed together with the main program. There is often the option of buying a "clean" copy of the program. Others try to con you into installing the adware by using the normal tricks.

Provided you know that it is being installed and are happy to have it on your PC, adware is not a major security risk. It is sending information about your surfing habits, but you have given permission for it to do so. If you feel that this is an invasion of privacy, then do not consent to it being installed. The situation is different if you are tricked into installing adware. Then it does clearly become an invasion of your privacy and you should remove any software of this type from your PC. Note that if you consent to adware being installed on your PC and then change your mind, removing it will probably result in the free software it supports being disabled or uninstalled.

Dialers

A dialer is a program that uses a modem and an ordinary dial-up connection to connect your PC to another computer system. Dialers probably have numerous legitimate applications, but they are mainly associated with various types of scam. An early one was a promise of free pornographic material that required a special program to be downloaded. This program was, of course, the dialer, which proceeded to call a high cost number in a country thousands of miles away. In due course the user received an astronomic telephone bill.

A modern variation on this is where users are tricked into downloading a dialer, often with the promise of free software of some description. A user goes onto the Internet in the usual way via their dial-up connections, and everything might appear to be perfectly normal. What is actually happening though is that they are not connecting to the Internet via their normal Internet service provider (ISP). Instead, the dialer is connecting them to a different ISP which is probably thousands of miles away and is costing a fortune in telephone charges. Again, the problem is very apparent when the telephone bill arrives.

The increasing use of broadband Internet connections has largely or totally removed the threat of dialer-related problems for many. If there is no ordinary telephone modem in your PC, there is no way the dialer can connect your PC to the Internet or another computer system via a dial-up connection. There is a slight risk if your PC is equipped with a telephone modem for sending and receiving faxes. The risk is relatively small though, since you would presumably notice that the modem was being used for no apparent reason.

Hoax virus

A hoax virus might sound innocuous enough and just a bit of a joke, but it has the potential to spread across the world causing damage to computer systems. The hoax is usually received in the form of an Email from someone that has contacted you previously. They say that the Email they sent you previously was infected with a virus, and the Email then goes on to provide information on how to remove the virus. This usually entails searching for one or more files on your PC's hard disc drive and erasing them.

Of course, there was no virus in the initial Email. The person that sent the initial Email could be the hoaxer, or they might have been fooled by the hoax themselves. The hoax Email suggests that you contact everyone that you have emailed recently, telling them that their computer could be infected and giving them the instructions for the "cure". This is the main way in which a hoax virus is propagated. The files that you are instructed to remove could be of no real consequence, or they could be important system files. It is best not to fall for the hoax and find out which.

These hoax viruses demonstrate the point that all the antivirus software in the world will not provide full protection for your PC. They are simple text files that do not do any direct harm to your PC, and can not be kept at bay by software. Ultimately it is up to you to use some common sense and provide the final line of defence. A quick check on the Internet will usually provide details of hoax viruses and prevent you from doing anything silly.

Note that there are other scams that involve hoax Emails. Recently there have been several instances of Emails being sent to customers of online financial companies. These purport to come from the company concerned, and they ask customers to provide their passwords and other account details. A link is provided to the site, and the site usually looks quite convincing. It is not the real thing though, and anyone falling for it has their account details stolen. The success of this scam has been limited, but some accounts have been plundered.

Likely candidates

Several types of computer pest have the ability to slow down a PC and/ or extend the boot-up time. One of my PCs recently suffered from the slow boot-up problem and it also seemed to be slow when any disc accesses were involved. A good starting point if you suspect that there could be an "intruder" present in your PC is to use the Control-Alt-Delete key combination to bring up the Task Manager. You can then look for any programs or processes that should not be there. If you are not sure about any of them it is easy to find details using a search engine such as Google. Use the name of the process plus the word "process" as the search string, and several links to sites giving basic details of it will be found.

It could well be that the suspect process is perfectly legitimate. In this case I was concerned about one called "Plauto", but the Internet search showed that this was actually part of the downloader for the Casio camera I use with the PC (Figure 3.1). Of course, it is more than a little suspicious if the process is one associated with software or hardware you are not using. It is likely that some form of pest is masquerading as a legitimate

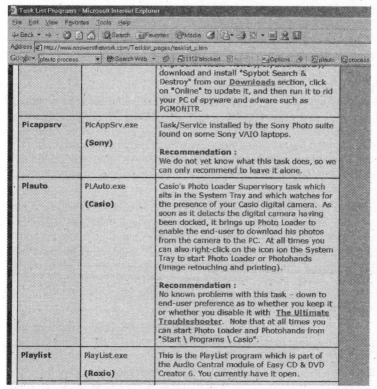

		download and install "Spybot Search & Destroy" from our Downloads section, click on "Online" to update it, and then run it to rid your PC of spyware and adware such as PGMONITR.
Picappsrv	PicAppSrv.exe (Sony)	Task/Service installed by the Sony Photo suite found on some Sony VAIO laptops. **Recommendation :** We do not yet know what this task does, so we can only recommend to leave it alone.
Plauto (Casio)	PLAuto.exe	Casio's Photo Loader Supervisory task which sits in the System Tray and which watches for the presence of your Casio digital camera. As soon as it detects the digital camera having been docked, it brings up Photo Loader to enable the end-user to download his photos from the camera to the PC. At all times you can also right-click on the icon ion the System Tray to start Photo Loader or Photohands (image retouching and printing). **Recommendation :** No known problems with this task – down to end-user preference as to whether you keep it or whether you disable it with The Ultimate Troubleshooter. Note that at all times you can start Photo Loader and Photohands from "Start \ Programs \ Casio".
Playlist (Roxio)	PlayList.exe	This is the PlayList program which is part of the Audio Central module of Easy CD & DVD Creator 6. You currently have it open.

Fig.3.1 An Internet search showed that Plauto was a perfectly innocent background process

process. You may find that the search engine provides links to pages dealing with viruses, Trojans, and the like, which again indicates that there is probably some form of infection present. One of the web pages will probably indicate the type of pest involved, or even the precise culprit.

In this example it was the lack of a process that indicated that there was a problem. The AVG antivirus software installed on the PC normally has two processes running in the background. One of them (AVG9) was present, but the other (AVG32) was missing. For obvious reasons, Trojans and viruses often search for and try to "nobble" firewall and antivirus programs. In this case a backdoor Trojan had found its way onto the system and was automatically loading at start-up. It would then check the other programs that were launched at start-up. The AVG antivirus program was one that it was designed to disable, which it duly did. This additional activity was presumably responsible for the extended boot time.

Basic measures

Ideally you should try to avoid getting into the position where some form of computer pest is installed on your PC. By the time you discover and remove the pest it is possible that harm of some form will have already been done. The obvious way of protecting a PC from viruses and other harmful programs is to simply keep it away from possible sources of infection. Unfortunately, the quarantine approach is not usually a practical one.

If you use a PC to (say) produce letters that are printed out and then sent by post, then the quarantine method should work. Once the computer has been set up ready for use it should not be necessary to put any discs into the floppy or CD-ROM drives, and there is no need for it to connect to the Internet or any other network. It might be necessary to have a CD/RW disc or two for backup purposes, but provided these discs are not used in any other computer there is no significant risk of them introducing a virus into the computer.

Unfortunately, little real world computing is compatible with this standalone approach. I use my PC to produce letters that are sent through the post, but I probably send about 50 times as many Emails. Large numbers of Emails are also received in my Email accounts. My PC is used mainly for generating work that is sent off on CDR discs, but I also receive data discs occasionally, and these have to be read using my computer. I have to use the Internet extensively for research, and I sometimes download software updates. Isolating my computer from the outside world would render it largely useless to me.

Totally removing the threat of attack is not usually possible, but the chances of a successful attack can be greatly reduced by using a few basic precautions.

Email attachments

Some individuals operate a policy of never opening Email attachments. I do not take things that far, but I would certainly not open an Email attachment unless I knew the sender of the Email and was expecting the attachment. Bear in mind that some viruses and worms spread by hijacking a user's Email address book and sending copies of the infected

Email to every address in it. The fact that an Email comes from someone you know, or purports to, does not guarantee that it is free from infection. Another point to bear in mind is that Email attachments are now the most common way of spreading viruses and computer worms.

Selective downloading

Downloading software updates from the main computer software companies should be safe, as should downloading the popular freebies from their official sources. Downloading just about anything else involves a degree of risk and should be kept to a minimum.

Pirated software

Pirated software has become a major problem for the software companies in recent years. In addition to casual software piracy where friends swap copies of programs, there is now an epidemic of commercial copying. Apart from the fact that it is illegal to buy and use pirated software, unlike the real thing, some of it contains viruses, spyware, etc.

Virus protection

Some programs, and particularly those from Microsoft, have built-in virus protection that is designed to block known macro/script viruses. If you have any programs that include this feature, make sure that it is enabled.

P2P

P2P (peer to peer) programs are widely used for file swapping. Even if you use this type of software for swapping legal (non-pirated) files, it still has to be regarded as very risky. In most cases you have no idea who is supplying the files, or whether they are what they are supposed to be. Also, you are providing others with access to your PC, and this access could be exploited by hackers.

Switch off

Some PC users leave their computers running continuously in the belief that it gives better reliability. It did in the days when computers were based on valves, but there is no evidence that it improves reliability with modern computers. It will increase your electricity bills, and it also increases the vulnerability of your PC if it has some form of always-on Internet connection. No one can hack into your computer system if it is switched off.

Prevention

The old adage "prevention is better than cure" certainly applies to computer viruses. In addition to some basic security precautions, equip your PC with antivirus software and keep it up-to-date. No antivirus software can guarantee one hundred percent protection, but the popular programs of this type will usually detect and deal with viruses before they have a chance to spread the infection or do any damage to your files.

Particularly when using some form of broadband connection that is always active, the use of a firewall is considered to be highly desirable these days. Although some people seem to think that a firewall and antivirus programs are the same, there are major differences. There is often some overlap between real world antivirus and firewall programs, but their primary aims are different.

An antivirus program is designed to scan files on discs and the contents of the computer's memory in search of viruses and other potentially harmful files. Having found any suspect files, the program will usually deal with them. A firewall is used to block access to your PC, and in most cases it is access to your PC via the Internet that is blocked. Bear in mind though, that a software firewall will usually block access via a local area network (LAN) as well. Some broadband modems have a built-in hardware firewall, and they are also available as add-ons.

Of course, a firewall is of no practical value if it blocks communication from one PC to another and access via the Internet. What it is actually doing is preventing unauthorised access to the protected PC. When you access an Internet site your PC sends messages to the server hosting that site, and these messages request the pages you wish to view. Having requested information, the PC expects information to be sent from the appropriate server, and it accepts that information when it is received. A firewall does not interfere with this type of Internet activity provided it is set up correctly.

It is a different matter when another system tries to access your PC when you have not instigated the initial contact. The firewall will treat this attempted entry as an attack and will block it. Of course, the attempt at accessing your PC might not be an attack, and a firewall can result in legitimate access being blocked. Something like P2P file swapping is likely to fail or operate in a limited fashion. The sharing of files and resources on a local area network could also be blocked. A practical firewall enables the user to permit certain types of access so that the computer can work normally while most unauthorised access is still blocked. However, doing so does reduce the degree of protection provided by the firewall.

A software firewall is usually very good at dealing with backdoor Trojans and other pests that try to send information from the PC via the Internet. The pest program will not have authorisation to access the Internet, and it should therefore be blocked by the firewall when it tries to do so. In most cases the firewall program will also alert the user to the fact that a mystery program has tried to access the Internet. Some hardware firewalls operate in the same fashion, but note that the firewalls built into modems are often designed to block unauthorised external access. They will not block programs running on the PC from using the Internet. For maximum protection this type of firewall should be backed up by a software firewall.

ZoneAlarm

There are plenty of software firewalls to choose from, and most of them are capable of providing your PC with a high degree of security. Black Ice Defender is a popular program that has the advantage of requiring little setting up before it is ready for use. ZoneAlarm is another popular firewall, and it exists in free, trial, and full commercial versions. It is quite easy to set up and use, and the free version represents a good starting

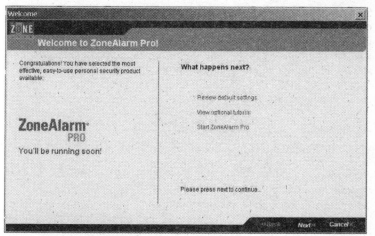

Fig.3.2 The initial screen of ZoneAlarm Pro

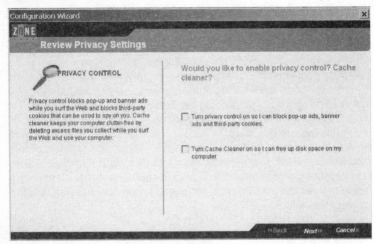

Fig.3.3 Two optional extras are available

point for private users wishing to try a good quality firewall at minimum cost. All versions of this program are reasonably easy to set up. ZoneAlarm Pro will be used for this example, and this program has a few more facilities than the basic (free) version.

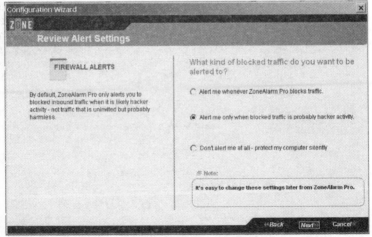

Fig.3.4 Here you select the level of alerts that will be produced

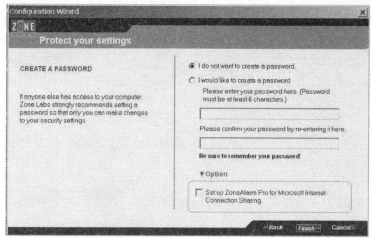

Fig.3.5 If required, the program can be password protected

Figure 3.2 shows the initial window produced once the installation process has been completed. This simply explains that there are a few processes to complete before the program is ready for use. The options available at the next screen (Figure 3.3) are for two of Zone Alarm Pro's optional extras. One of these is a routine that blocks pop-up advertisements and third-party "spy" cookies. Pop-ups are now so widespread on the Internet that they have become a major nuisance. Apart from being irksome, they can slow down your Internet connection by increasing the amount of data that has to be downloaded. This can be a serious drag on your surfing if you do not have some form of broadband connection. A pop-up blocker is therefore a very useful feature.

Cache cleaning is the other option. Copies of many Internet files are kept on a PC so that they do not have to be downloaded again when the relevant pages are revisited. Anyone undertaking a lot of surfing is likely to end up with many megabytes of cached Internet files on their PC's hard disc. These files should eventually be removed by Windows, but the cache cleaner provides a neater solution by preventing a massive build-up from occurring in the first place.

Things then move on to a window (Figure 3.4) where you choose the types of Internet access that will produce alerts. You can opt to have an onscreen message appear when any access is blocked, or for no alerts to be issued. Note that the program will still continue to block Internet

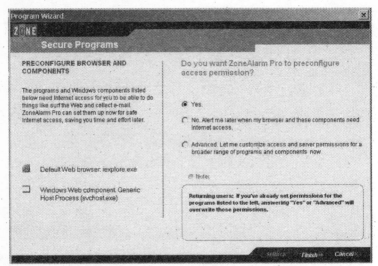

Fig.3.6 Now or later, you can choose which programs are granted Internet access

access as and when it sees fit, even if the alerts are completely switched off. The middle option results in an alert being produced when the program considers that attempted access is probably the result of an

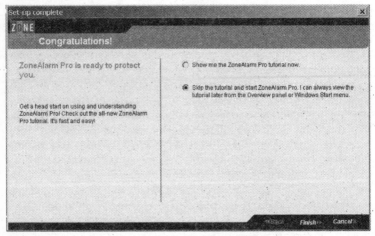

Fig.3.7 You can start the program or view a tutorial

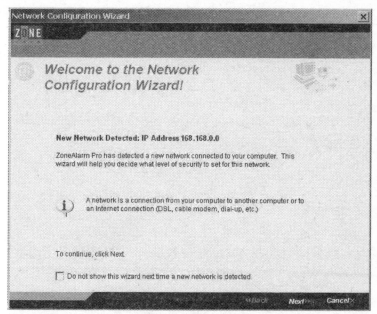

*Fig.3.8 The program has detected a network, and it must be
configured so that ZoneAlarm will permit file sharing*

attack by a hacker. This is the default option and is probably the best
choice.

The next window (Figure 3.5) enables the program to be password
protected. This is only necessary if someone else has access to your
PC. This is followed by the screen of Figure 3.6. Here ZoneAlarm lists
programs that it thinks will need Internet access. The list will include the
default browser and any other programs that are required for normal
Internet access. By default, these programs will be given Internet access,
but other programs will produce a warning message if they attempt to
use the Internet. Access will then be allowed only if you give permission.
You might prefer to choose which programs will be granted access during
the setting up process rather than dealing with it later as programs try to
access the Internet. As most programs do not require Internet access, it
is probably easier to grant access as and when necessary.

The next window (Figure 3.7) gives the option of starting the program or
viewing a quick tutorial. It is definitely a good idea to look at the tutorial,
but it can be viewed at any time by running ZoneAlarm Pro and operating
the Tutorial button.

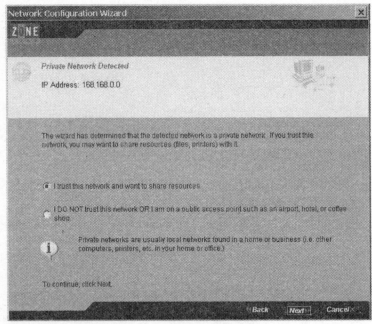

Fig.3.9 The network can be enabled or blocked

Network

The PC used for this demonstration has its Internet connection provided by a broadband modem that has a built-in router, with two other PCs connected to the router. This network was detected by ZoneAlarm Pro (Figure 3.8), and the Network Configuration Wizard was launched. Remember that a firewall will block any network access, including the LAN (local area network) variety, unless instructed otherwise. At the next screen (Figure 3.9) you have the option of enabling this network or blocking it. Obviously it must be enabled in order to permit the system to go on working properly.

The window of Figure 3.10 enables the network to be given a name of your choice, or you can simply settle for the default name. The next window (Figure 3.11) simply shows the settings you have chosen and provides an opportunity to go back and change them. Finally, the program is run (Figure 3.12). In normal use the program runs in the

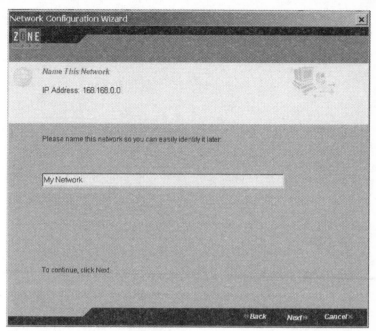

Fig.3.10 Here you can give the network a name or accept the default

background and it is only necessary to go to this screen if you need to make changes to the setup or to view the statistics produced by the program.

Operating the Firewall tab switches the window to look like Figure 3.13, and the degree of security in each zone can then be adjusted via the slider controls. Unless there is good reason to change the setting for the Internet Zone, it should be left at High. The other tabs permit easy control of other aspects of the program, such as alerts (Figure 3.14). Therefore, if you find any of the initial settings unsatisfactory it is easy to change them.

In use, it is likely that the program will initially query potential problems that are really just a normal part of the PC's operation. In the example of Figure 3.15 an alert has been triggered by an image editing program trying to access the Internet. Although there is no obvious reason for such a program requiring the Internet, many programs these days use the Internet to regularly look for program updates. Operate the Yes button to permit Internet access or the No button to block it. Tick the checkbox

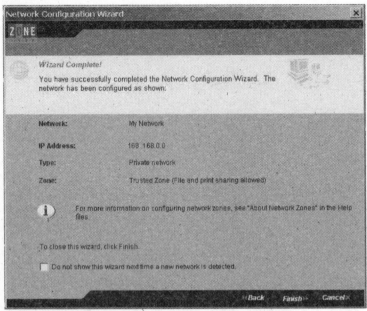

Fig.3.11 Use this window to review the selected settings

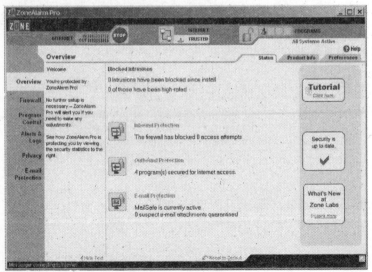

Fig.3.12 Finally, the program is operational

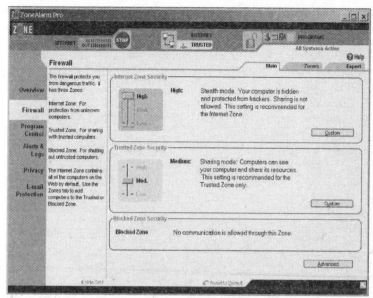

Fig.3.13 Here the Firewall tab has been operated

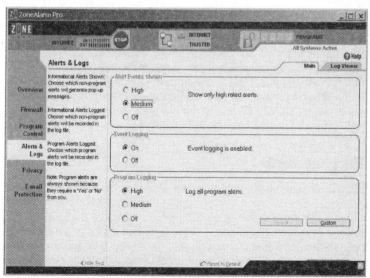

Fig.3.14 You are not stuck with the settings selected during installation

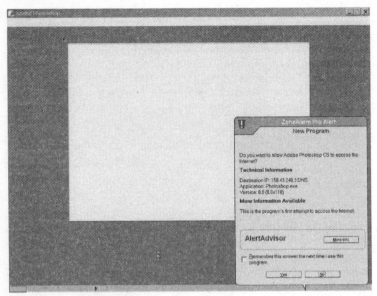

Fig.3.15 An alert produced by a program trying to access the Internet

if you would like this answer to be used automatically each time the program tries to access the Internet.

Sometimes the alert will genuinely show something that is amiss. In Figure 3.16 the alert shows that a file called msbb.exe has tried to access the Internet. Some delving on the Internet revealed that this is part of the Ncase adware program, which was supposedly uninstalled from the PC a few weeks earlier. Clearly it had not been successfully uninstalled, and some further work was needed in order to banish it from the system.

Be prepared

Many computer users take the view that they do not need antivirus software until and unless a virus attacks their PC. This is a rather short-sighted attitude and one that is asking for trouble. By the time that you know a virus has infected your PC it is likely that a substantial amount of damage will have already been done to the system files and/or your own data files. Using antivirus software to help sort out the mess after a virus has struck is "shutting the stable door after the horse has bolted". The

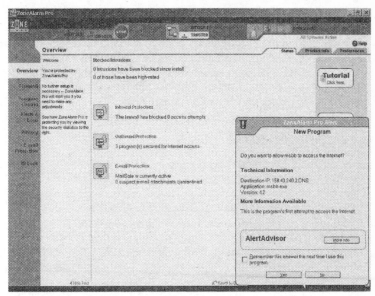

Fig.3.16 This alert was produced by an adware component

virus may indeed be removed by the antivirus software, but there may be no way of correcting all the damage that has been done.

Another point to bear in mind is that your PC could be rendered unbootable by the virus. Many viruses attack the operating system and will try to make the system unbootable. If the system is not bootable, you can not install antivirus software. Most antivirus programs do some basic checks as part of the installation process. The program will not be installed if any hint of a virus is detected. The reason for this is that the installation process involves copying numerous files onto the hard disc and making changes to some of the Windows system files. This can provide an opportunity for the virus to spread and do further damage.

Many antivirus programs can be used once a virus has attacked a PC, and even if the PC can not be booted into Windows. One approach is to either have a set of boot floppy discs supplied as part of the package, or for these rescue discs to be produced during installation. If the PC becomes unbootable at some later date and a virus is thought to be the cause, the PC is booted from the first disc in the set. A series of checks are then performed, with the other discs being used as and when required.

A more modern alternative to this method is for the installation disc to be bootable. The basic facilities provided are generally much the same as when using a set of boot discs, but there is no need to keep changing discs. Also, the high capacity of a CD-ROM means that more facilities are easily included in the program suite, if required. The drawback of both methods is that the discs will never be fully up-to-date, and may not be able to handle some of the more recent viruses.

Background tasks

Most antivirus programs run as background tasks. An antivirus program does not have to run as a background task, but it does have to do so in order to be as effective as possible. You could simply use the program to periodically scan the drives of your PC, and antivirus programs invariably have this mode of operation. In fact, most can be set up to provide automatic scans at a certain time on a given day of each week. This way of handling things has a big limitation though. It is possible for a virus to be on the system for nearly a week before the discs are scanned and there is any possibility of it being detected. In that time the virus could become well entrenched and would probably start to attack the files on the hard disc drive. More frequent scans could be scheduled, but the computer would then spend much of its time looking for viruses. This would probably be inconvenient, and would significantly reduce the operating life of the hard disc drive.

Most antivirus programs have two or three different modes of operation. In addition to the scanning mode, most can operate in real-time, and many have some form of rescue mode that tries to cure problems if a virus should find its way onto the hard disc. It is the real-time mode that is probably the most important. Like a firewall, the program runs in the background and monitors Internet activity. In fact most programs do rather more than that, and also monitor the interchangeable disc drives such as the floppy and CD-ROM drives.

The general idea is to have the program spot a virus as soon as it enters the system, and to then alert the user to its presence before it has time to spread. This greatly reduces the chances of the PC coming to grief, but there is a slight downside with both software firewalls and real-time antivirus programs. They both operate continuously in the background and utilise some of the computer's resources. In particular, they take up a certain amount of the PC's processing time and memory. This tends to make the computer run application programs a little slower.

In the past this problem was certainly more of an issue than it is now. The best PCs of ten years ago were far less powerful than even an inexpensive PC of today. There was often a very marked loss of performance when a firewall or antivirus program was installed on a PC. These days it is unlikely that a noticeable reduction in performance will occur, but there will be some reduction in speed. Another problem with many of the early antivirus programs was that they tended to take over the PC. Most were more than a little intrusive in operation, and some produced over-protective warnings whenever you tried to do practically anything. Fortunately, most modern antivirus programs are much more discreet and remain unseen in the background most of the time.

Real-world programs

There are a number of "big name" antivirus programs, and any of these should provide your PC with excellent protection against viruses and other harmful files. These programs provide broadly the same functions but are different in points of detail. We will consider a few representative examples here. It is worth emphasising the point that it is not a good idea to have more than one of these programs installed on your PC at any one time. Antivirus programs are less intrusive than they used to be, but they still operate continuously in the background monitoring the PC's activity.

Having two of the programs operating simultaneously can easily produce conflicts that result in the PC crashing. With many of the older antivirus programs you never actually managed to get that far. Having two of them installed on a PC usually resulted in it failing to boot into Windows. It might seem reasonable to have two or three antivirus programs installed, since this gives a better chance of a virus being detected. In practice it does not work very well when applied to real-time monitoring.

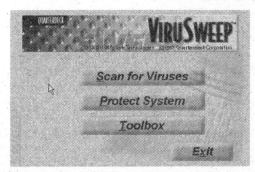

Fig.3.17 The ViruSweep startup screen

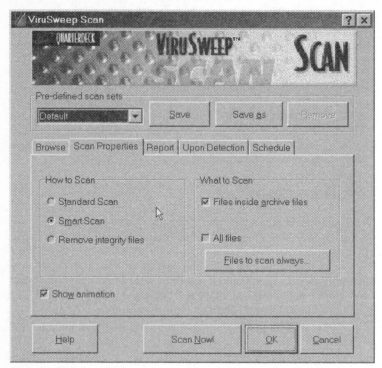

Fig.3.18 The first ViruSweep screen after scanning for viruses

It can be useful to have the ability to scan using two or three antivirus programs in succession, but having more than one operating at a time is definitely something to be avoided.

Figure 3.17 shows the startup screen for the Quarterdeck ViruSweep program, and operating the "Scan For Viruses" button takes the user into further screens that permit various options to be selected. The first screen (Figure 3.18) permits the user to select the parts of the system that will be checked. Viruses can exist in memory as well as in disc files, so checking the memory is normally an option. Further screens enable the type of scan to be selected (Figure 3.19), and the action to be taken if a virus is detected (Figure 3.20). Most anti-virus software has the option of removing a virus rather than simply indicating that it has been detected. Note though, that in some cases it might not be possible to automatically "kill" a virus. The program will then usually give details of how to manually remove the virus.

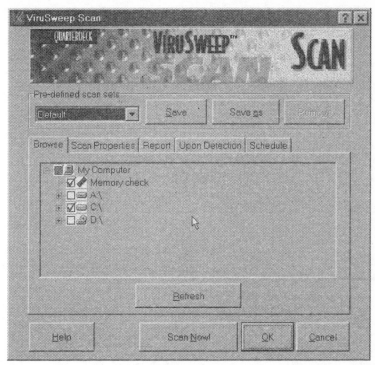

Fig.3.19 This screen enables the type of scan to be selected

Things are likely to be very difficult if you do not use anti-virus software and your PC becomes infected. On the face of it, you can simply load an anti-virus program onto the hard disc and then use it to remove the virus. As explained previously, it is definitely not advisable to try this method, and most software of this type will not load onto the hard disc if it detects that a virus is present. There would be a very real danger of the antivirus program itself spreading the infection and becoming damaged itself.

Boot disc

The method offered by many (but not all) anti-virus suites is to boot from a special floppy disc that contains anti-virus software. With this method there is no need to load any software onto the hard disc, and consequently

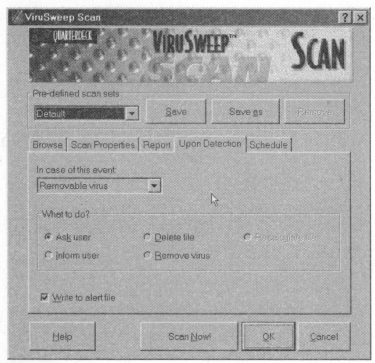

Fig.3.20 This screen gives control over the action to be taken when a virus is detected

there is no risk of the anti-virus software causing the virus to be spread further over the system. With the Norton Antivirus program a boot disc plus four support discs are made during the installation process (Figure 3.21). If boot problems occur at a later date, the PC can be booted using the Norton boot disc, and with the aid of the other discs a comprehensive range of virus scans can be undertaken (Figure 3.22). In some cases the virus can be removed automatically, and it might also be possible to have any damage to the system files repaired automatically as well.

With recent versions of many antivirus programs it is possible to boot from the installation CD-ROM. Figure 3.23 shows the initial screen produced when booting from the Panda Antivirus CD-ROM. This requires the appropriate language to be selected. After negotiating two more screens the scanning process commences (Figure 3.24) and eventually

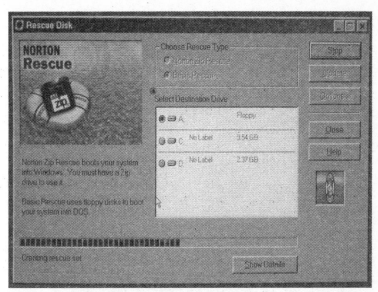

Fig.3.21 *Many antivirus programs can make recovery discs. Norton Antivirus makes a set of five recovery discs*

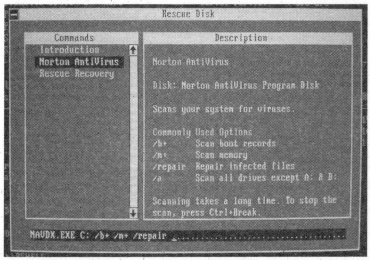

Fig.3.22 *Virus scanning using the Norton Antivirus recovery discs*

Fig.3.23 The initial screen when booting from the Panda Antivirus CD-ROM

a report giving details of any detected viruses is produced. The advantage of booting from a CD-ROM rather than a floppy disc is that the capacity of a CD-ROM is many times higher than that of a floppy disc. This enables more sophisticated software to be used, and avoids the need for multi-disc sets.

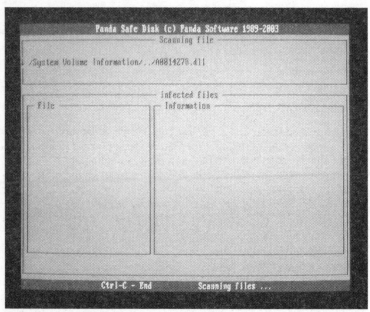

Fig.3.24 Virus scanning using the program on the Panda Antivirus CD-ROM

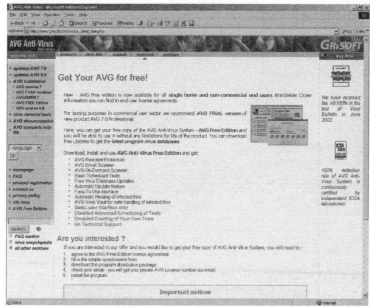

Fig.3.25 AVG 6.0 is available from the Grisoft web site

Free check-up

A good antivirus program can be quite inexpensive. It does not have to cost anything at all since there are various free options available if you would prefer not to buy one of the mainstream commercial products. The best source for this type of software is undoubtedly the cover mounted discs provided "free" with computer magazines. There seems to be a steady stream of antivirus software provided on these discs. Read the "fine print" though, as some of these programs are actually only time-limited trials that are no good for long-term use.

There is also a catch with many of the others in that the program is free, but a subscription has to be paid in order to keep the virus database up to date. Note that even with full commercial products the updates are usually only available free of charge for one year. After that time you either have to buy the new version of the program or subscribe to updates. Of course, you can simply continue to use out-of-date antivirus software,

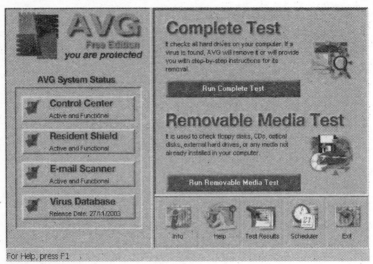

Fig.3.26 The main screen of AVG 6.0

and it will still detect many viruses. However, if a new virus infects your PC it is unlikely that an out-of-date antivirus program will be able to detect it.

There are one or two totally free antivirus programs available on the Internet, where you do not even have to pay for monthly online updates to the database. AVG 6.0 from Grisoft is one that is certainly worth trying. The Grisoft site is at:

www.grisoft.com

On the home page there should be a link in the list down the left-hand side called something like "AVG Free Edition". Activating this link will bring up a page like the one in Figure 3.25. This gives some information about the free version of the AVG antivirus program and provides a link that enables it to be downloaded. You do have to go through a registration process, but it is worth the effort. Monthly updates to AVG are available free of charge. This program has a reputation for being very efficient, and it certainly detected a couple of backdoor Trojan programs on my system that a certain well-known commercial program had failed to detect. It is one of the best freebies on the Internet.

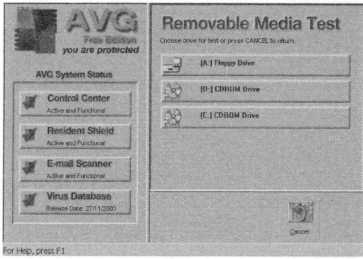

Fig.3.27 Removable media can be scanned for viruses

It does have one major limitation, which is that it does not have a rescue mode of the type provided by Norton Antivirus and some other programs. There is a facility to backup important system files so that they can be restored if the originals become damaged by a virus. There is no facility to boot from a floppy disc or CD-ROM drive and run virus checks. The program works effectively in the background detecting the vast majority of viruses, Trojans, etc., so there is little likelihood of a rescue mode being required. However, if you should get unlucky it might be necessary to resort to another antivirus program in order to clear an infection.

AVG does have a range of useful facilities and in other respects it is a very capable program. In common with most antivirus programs you can set it to scan the system on a regular basis, and it also has an automatic update facility. Manual scanning is also available, and this is another standard feature for this type of software. If you suspect that there might be a virus infection somewhere in the PC you can get the program to do a scan of the entire system. Another standard option is to scan one or more of the interchangeable disc drives such as a floppy or CD-ROM drive. This is useful in cases where you suspect that a disc someone has given you might contain a virus.

AVG normally runs automatically at start-up and then runs in the background until the PC is shut down, but it can be started in the normal

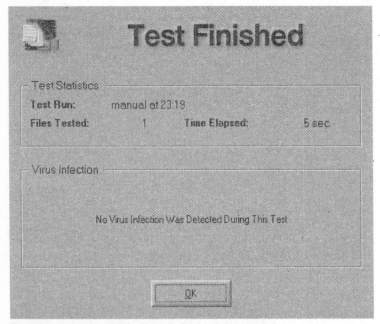

Fig.3.28 *The test results after checking a floppy disc*

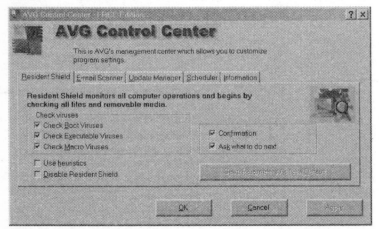

Fig.3.29 *Many of AVG's settings can be changed via the Control
Center*

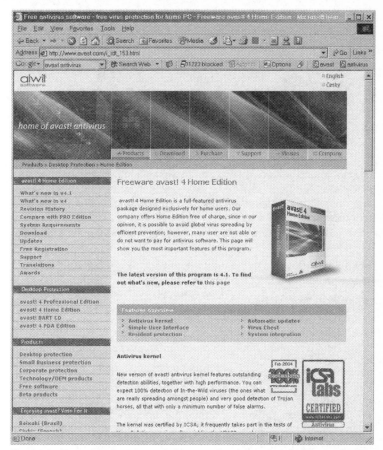

Fig.3.30 Avast Antivirus is available as a free download for home users

way from the Start menu. It then appears in a window like the one shown in Figure 3.26. One of the large buttons gives access to the full system scan and the lower one permits the removable media to be checked. Operating the lower button changes the window to look something like Figure 3.27, which has a button for each removable disc fitted to the computer. Operating one of the buttons runs a check on the appropriate drive, and a window showing the results (Figure 3.28) is produced when the process has been completed.

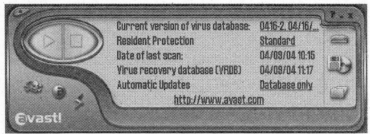

Fig.3.31 Avast Antivirus has an unconventional user interface

The test results will show what action was taken if one or more viruses were detected. The action taken depends on how the program is set up and precisely what it finds. It will leave the infected file unchanged, delete it, or quarantine the file by moving to the secure folder that is called the "Virus Vault" in AVG terminology. Alternatively, it will do nothing and ask the user to select the required option.

When running in the background, the program is represented by a small button on the toolbar at the bottom of the Windows desktop. Double-clicking the button brings up the control window of Figure 3.29, and this is typical of the way antivirus programs operate. Using this it is possible to alter a number of settings, including the types of scan that are provided. Unless there is good reason to do otherwise it is probably best to leave the default settings. It is definitely not a good idea to reduce the types of scan that are provided since this could obviously leave security holes in the system.

Fig.3.32 The Tools menu

There are other free antivirus programs available, and Avast 4 Home Edition (www.avast.com, Figure 3.30) is worthy of consideration. This program runs as a background program, but it can be run as a normal application so that it can be used to provide a full system scan. The user interface is not exactly conventional (Figure 3.31), but it is quite easy to use. Registration is free for home users, and although registration expires after 14 months it can be renewed indefinitely.

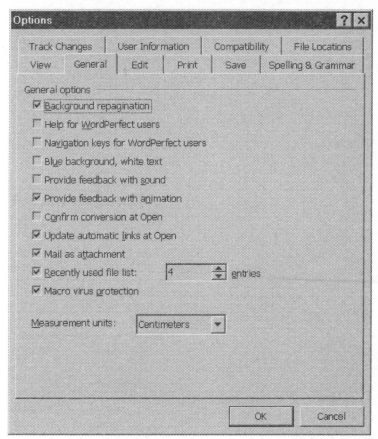

Fig.3.33 Make sure that the box for Macro Virus Protection is ticked

Attachments

Viruses transmitted via P2P file swapping and other downloads are still a common problem, but viruses, worms, etc., transmitted via Email has been a more prevalent problem in recent times. Although they are not the only threat, attachments remain the most likely route for a serious Email virus attack. In recent years a number of Email viruses have rapidly spread around the world. These Email viruses utilise the automation features that are built into Microsoft Office and other programs. These

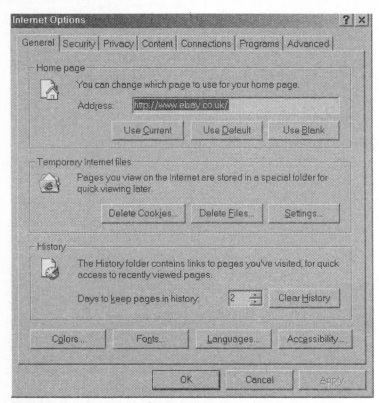

Fig.3.34 The Internet Options window

facilities are intended to provide a means of doing clever things that make life easier for users, but they can also hand over control of the PC to a virus.

If you do not need these facilities, disabling them is a simple but effective means of removing this threat to your PC. Microsoft has a useful download for Outlook 98 and 2000 that provides protection against viruses such as ILOVEYOU and Melissa. It disables the ability to download attachments that could contain a virus. The download and further information are available from this web page:

http://office.microsoft.com/downloads/2000/Out2ksec.aspx

Another tactic is to turn off the automatic running of scripts in Word, Access, and Excel. First select Options from the tools menu (Figure

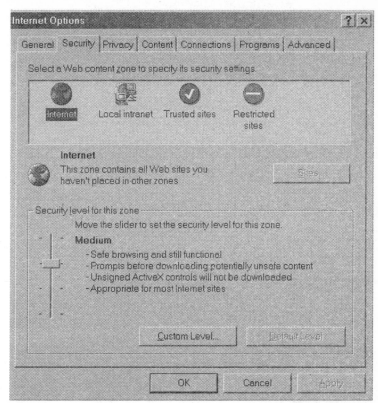

Fig.3.35 The Security options

3.32), and then operate the General tab in the window that appears (Figure 3.33). Make sure that the checkbox for Macro virus protection is ticked. It makes sense to have the security settings of Internet Explorer as high as possible, or failing that as high as possible without preventing the programs from providing the functions you require. This is a simple aspect of Internet security that many users seem to overlook, so make sure that you use the most secure settings that do not block or seriously hinder the facilities you wish to use.

The easy way of altering the security settings of Internet Explorer is to run the program and then select Internet Options from the Tools menu. This produces a window like the one of Figure 3.34, and by default the General tab will be selected. The General section is used for altering the

3 Viruses and other pests

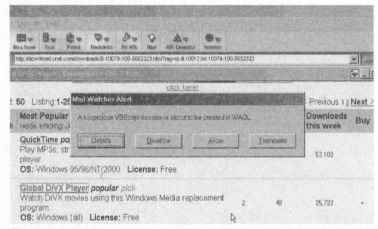

Fig.3.36 A warning message is produced by suspicious events, but many of these are just part of the PC's normal operation

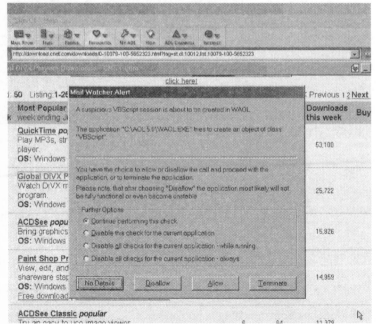

Fig.3.37 More details of the current operation can be obtained

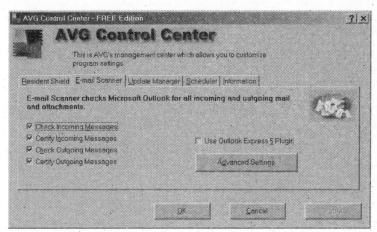

Fig.3.38 Antivirus programs often include Email scanning facilities

homepage and other basic tasks, but it is the Security page that is of interest in the current context. Selecting the Security tab produces a window like the one in Figure 3.35. The degree of security is selected by way of the slider control, which has four settings. These settings are Low, Medium-Low, Medium, and High. The text next to the slider control gives brief details of each setting, but in practice it is really a matter of using the "suck it and see" method. Use the highest level of security that does not result in any features you use being disabled.

Email anti-virus

There are protection programs designed specifically to deal with Email viruses and other infections carried by scripts. Obviously this type of program has to run in real-time, and it produces a warning if it detects something suspicious happening. Figure 3.36 shows a warning message produced by Mail Watcher from Computer Associates, which detects attempts to access the Email system. Since many of the events detected by the program are perfectly legitimate it does not block them, but instead provides a simple control panel. The Terminate button is pressed if it is felt that the detected action is possibly a virus. Operating the Allow button enables things to proceed normally. Left-clicking the Details button opens a new window (Figure 3.37) that gives more details of the current operation and the options for dealing with it.

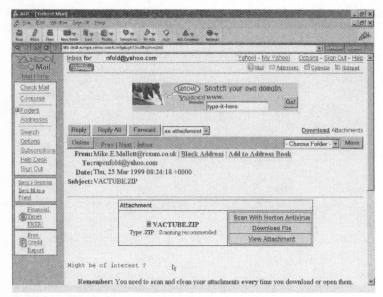

Fig.3.39 This Email has a ZIP file attached

Most antivirus suites now include a program that can check Emails or have this facility built into the main program. AVG 6.0 has a built-in Email scanning facility, and it is possible to select the required checks from the Email section of its Control Center (Figure 3.38). This type of thing is fine if you are using Outlook or Outlook Express as the Email client, but these days many people use Internet based Email services such as those provided by Hotmail or Yahoo!. These do not usually make use of Outlook, Outlook Express, or any similar program, but instead have their facilities built into the system. An antivirus program such as AVG does not usually provide any protection with a fully Internet based Email service.

This is not to say that no protection is available for users of these services. Some Email service providers have facilities for checking attachments prior to downloading them. Figure 3.39 shows an Email that is being viewed using the Yahoo.com Email service. This has a ZIP file attachment, and one option for dealing with the attachment is to simply download it regardless of the risk. Another option is to scan it using the system's built-in Norton antivirus program. The scanning process is very rapid because the file is being checked while it is still on the server. The Email,

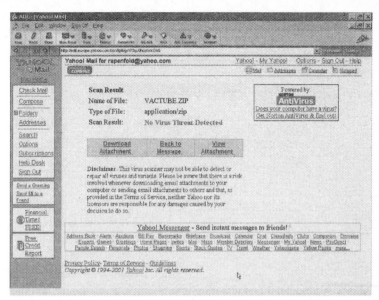

Fig.3.40 On this occasion the scan has not found an infection

complete with its attachment, can be erased if a problem is discovered. In this way the file never reaches your PC and can not infect it. Usually everything will be all right and a reassuring message will appear (Figure 3.40).

A third option is available, and this enables the attachment to be viewed so that you can check that it is genuine and not an impostor. Obviously this is not of much use with all types of file, but it is useful with something like a Word DOC file that could contain a macro virus. The system will accurately interpret the document so that it appears much the same as it would when viewed using Word itself (Figure 3.41). This method does not guarantee that the attachment is virus-free, but you can at least check that it is a proper document from someone you know.

If you need to work on the document in Word it must be downloaded, but this is not necessary if you only need to read its contents. Having viewed and read the contents the Email and attachment can be deleted. Another possibility is to cut and paste the text from the Email viewer to Word. Select the required text and press the Control and C keys to copy the text to the clipboard. Open Word and then press the Control and V

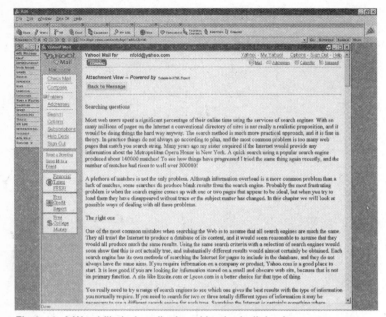

Fig.3.41 A Word file being displayed by the built-in viewer program

keys to copy the text into Word from the clipboard. With this method any clever tricks in the original document will be lost, but so will any macro virus.

If you need to exchange formatted text documents via Email attachments it is worth considering the Rich Text Format. Documents in this format can have the usual types of Windows formatting including alignment, different fonts, text colours, etc. It does not support any type of macro language, so files that use this format can not contain a macro virus. Plain text files are also safe, but have no formatting capability. Of course, these files are only safe when they are what they purport to be. Any data file needs to be checked for authenticity before you download it.

Many people now take the "belt and braces" approach of simply refusing to open any Email attachments. I suppose that this is a practical approach for anyone that has no real need to exchange anything other than plain text by Email, but it is not practical if you need to receive images, formatted documents, etc., via this route. It still makes sense not to open attachments if you do not know the sender and/or are not expecting an

Email with an attachment. Where necessary, check that the Email and attachment genuinely come from the supposed sender, and only open the attachment once you have verified their authenticity. Unfortunately, these days anything received via Email has to be treated with a degree of suspicion.

Online scan

If you suspect that a virus or other pest has infected your PC, online scanning facilities could be useful. If the PC does not have built-in antivirus protection, the online route offers a means of checking for viruses and dealing with them. In cases where the PC does have an antivirus program, online scanning offers an easy way of obtaining a second opinion. It is possible that the built-in software has missed something that one of the online scanning services will detect.

There are various companies that offer online virus scanning facilities, and most of these services are free. Although online scanning might seem an attractive option in cases where a PC has a virus infection but you have no antivirus software, there is a drawback to their use in this situation. Obviously the PC must be largely operational before it can go online and be used with this type of scanning. Assuming it can get that far, the main problem is that online scanning is not exactly online scanning.

The name suggests that a program running at the server scans your PC for viruses, but in most cases very little of the software runs at the other end of the Internet link. The usual arrangement is for an antivirus program to be downloaded to your PC, temporarily installed, run, and then erased. The problem with this method is that it is not really much different to installing an antivirus program and running it in the usual way. The file copying provides opportunities for any virus to propagate, and going online provides spyware and backdoor Trojans with an opportunity to "do their thing".

If you suspect that there could be a problem with a virus but have no definite proof, then it might be worth the risk if you do not have a better alternative. Online testing is also worthwhile if you do not intend to use normal antivirus software, but you need to be aware of its limitations. A program such as AVG 6.0 will monitor your PC and provide real-time protection. Any virus entering the system is likely to be detected immediately. With only occasional online scanning there could be a significant gap between the infection occurring and the virus being

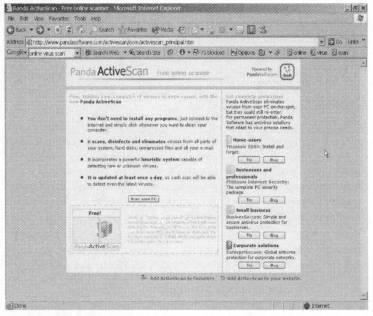

Fig.3.42 Panda Software offer a free online virus scan via their
ActiveScan system

detected. Even a few days or hours could be long enough for the virus
to spread and damage your files.

I suppose online testing might be worthwhile if you are at the stage where
you are desperate enough to try anything, but as far as possible it is best
to avoid getting into that situation. Installing a free antivirus program on
your PC is far better than getting into difficulties and then trying to recover
the situation.

An important point if you do try online virus scanning is to make sure
that you use the services of a reputable company. In the early days of
computer viruses it was quite common for infections to be spread via
antivirus software that was actually a Trojan. This method has rather
gone out of fashion, but the possibility of someone coming up with an
online version can not be ruled out. Only using the services of a "big
name" company should ensure that the scanning detects and removes
any viruses rather than adding a few!

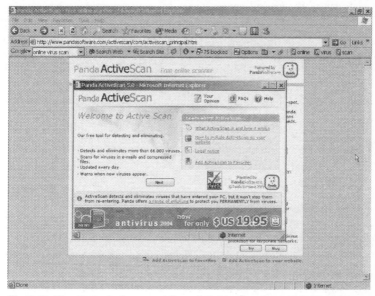

Fig.3.43 The first window provides a brief explanation of ActiveScan

ActiveScan

Panda Software is well known for its security oriented software suites, and they offer online scanning in the form of the ActiveScan facility (Figure 3.42). Operating the Scan Your PC link brings up the initial window of Figure 3.43, which briefly explains what ActiveScan does. Operating the Next button moves things on to the window of Figure 3.44 where you have to enter your Email address. If you do not wish to use your normal Email address for this type of thing, it is just a matter of setting up an account with Hotmail, Yahoo, or one of the other online Email providers. This account can then be used when obtaining free online services, which almost invariably require a valid Email address.

At the next window (Figure 3.45) you have to state your country and (possibly) area within that country. Things then move on to the stage where the software is downloaded, and the security warning of Figure 3.46 might appear. Operate the Yes button to go ahead with the download. The window of Figure 3.47 appears once the program has been downloaded and temporarily installed. The buttons near the top left-hand corner of the screen enable various parts of the system to be tested,

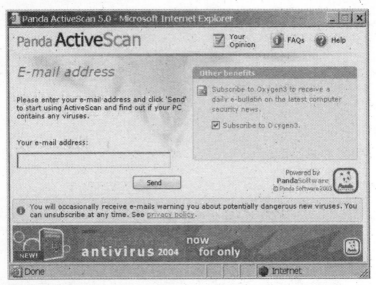

Fig.3.44 An Email address must be provided in order to proceed

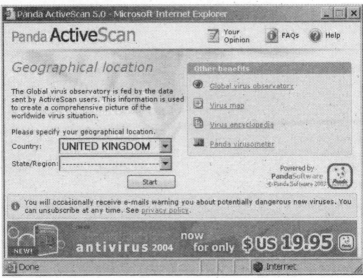

Fig.3.45 The simple registration process also requires your location

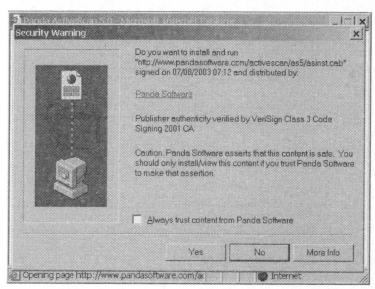

Fig.3.46 A download is required in order to carry out the scan

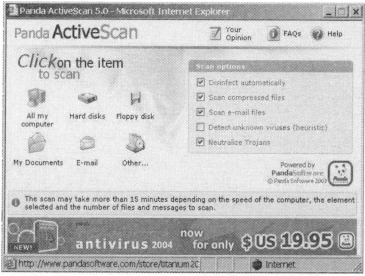

Fig.3.47 The required type of scan is selected using this window

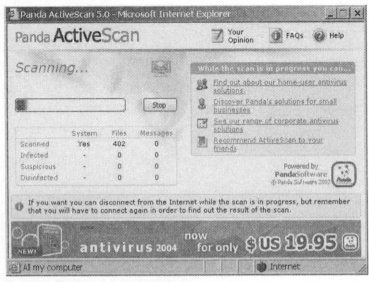

Fig.3.48 Finally, the scan is under way

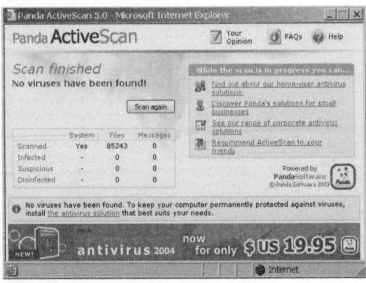

Fig.3.49 The list of results produced by the scan

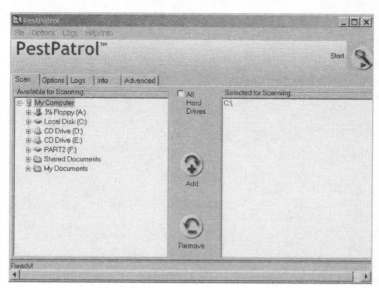

Fig.3.50 The first task is to select the drives to be scanned

and for this example the All My Computer option was used. The checkboxes in the right-hand section of the window give some control over the type of scan that is undertaken. You can opt to have Trojans neutralised for example.

A window like the one in Figure 3.48 is produced once the scan is under way. This has a bargraph display to show how far the scan has progressed. A table of results is included, and this shows things like the number of files tested, and any actions taken by the program. Note that it is not necessary to remain online while the scanning takes place, but that the PC must be online before the final results can be produced. As with any antivirus scanning, it can take some time if there is a large and almost full hard disc drive to check. Eventually the scan will be completed (Figure 3.49) and a full set of results will then be shown.

The program is much like an ordinary antivirus program in operation, and this is essentially what it is. However, when you exit the program it will effectively be uninstalled, and it can not be run in the usual fashion.

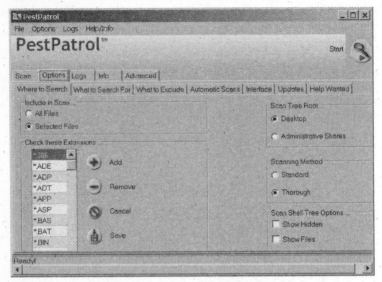

Fig.3.51 You can control the types of file that the program will seek

Non-virus pests

Antivirus programs, as their name suggests, are primarily concerned with the detection and removal of viruses. Most will actually detect a wider range of threats, including most Trojans, spyware, and backdoor Trojans. How well these types of threat are detected varies somewhat from one program to another. Antivirus programs are not usually designed to detect what could be termed nuisance programs, such as adware programs and their related files. However, there are programs that are designed to deal with this type of thing, and they will mostly detect some of the more serious threats such as spyware.

PestPatrol is one of the best known programs of this type, and it is the one that will be used as the basis of this example. The initial screen of PestPatrol is shown in Figure 3.50, and the first task is to select the drives that will be scanned. This is just a matter of selecting the required drives in the panel on the left using the standard Windows methods. The Add button is then left-clicked in order to add the drives to the list in the right panel. A drive can be removed from the list by selecting its entry and operating the Remove button. Simply tick the checkbox if you wish to check all the hard drives.

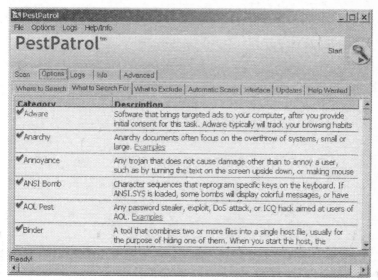

Fig.3.52 You can control the types of "pest" that the program seeks

Operating the Options tab produces a further row of tabs, and these give access to a range of options that control the way PestPatrol scans the disc. There are standard and thorough options for example (Figure 3.51), and you can also set the program to look for only certain types of "pest" (Figure 3.52). It is by no means essential to do any "fine tuning" though, and the program should work well enough if it scans the discs using the default settings. To go ahead with a scan it is just a matter of operating the Start button in the top right-hand corner of the window.

You are presented with a scrollable list of results once PestPatrol has finished the scan (Figure 3.53). It is essential to look down the list, item by item, even in cases where there are a large number of entries. What you and PestPatrol consider to be "pests" could be rather different. Remember that removing adware files could result in any programs supported by that adware becoming inoperative. You are unlikely to get away with installing supported software, disabling the associated adware, and then continuing to use the supported software. Blocking adware with a firewall does sometimes leave the supported application fully operational, but this is a morally dubious practice.

Having decided the fate of the various entries, it is just a matter of selecting each batch and then operating the appropriate button. In this example

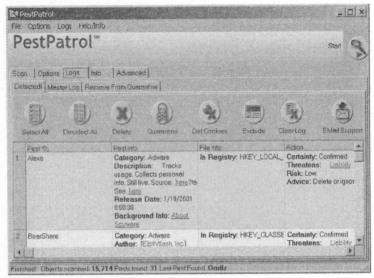

Fig.3.53 A list of "pests" is produced once the scan has been
completed

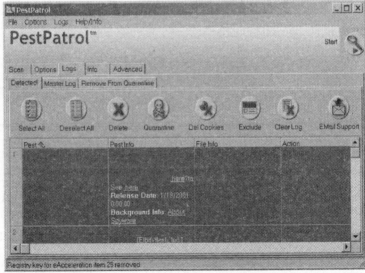

Fig.3.54 PestPatrol confirms that the selected files have been erased

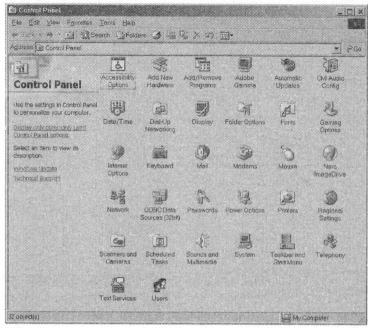

Fig.3.55 The Windows Control Panel

none of the detected files were required, so they were all deleted. The list changes to show what has been done to each file (Figure 3.54). Note that the program may be unable to delete some files and folders. It will then show the location of the relevant files or folders and recommend manual deletion.

Manual removal

When some form of infection occurs on a PC there is a natural tendency to look for a program that will remove it for you. Being realistic about it, a program such as a virus or Trojan is not going to be removable via the normal route, because it will not install itself into Windows as a normal program. It will do its best to stay hidden, and you will probably need some help in order to locate and remove the relevant file or files. However, with some of the more minor problems it is not necessary to resort to some form of antivirus or "pest control" program.

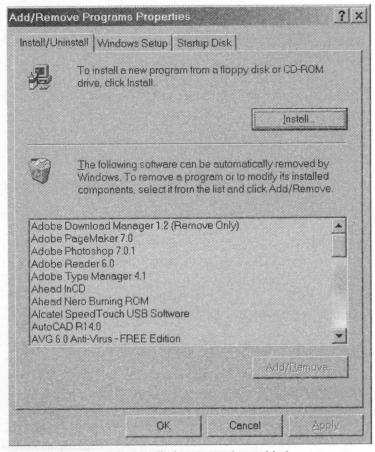

Fig.3.56 A full list of the installed programs is provided

For example, many adware programs are installed without it being made clear to the user that they are being added to the system, but most of them are installed in the normal way. Consequently, they can be uninstalled in the usual way. This means going to Settings in the Start menu and selecting Control Panel in the submenu that appears. The exact appearance of the Control Panel depends on how the computer is set up, but it will probably look something like Figure 3.55. Double-click the Add/Remove Programs icon or text entry, as appropriate.

This launches a new window like the one of Figure 3.56, which includes a scrollable list of all the programs installed on the computer. Look down this to see if the program that is giving problems is installed, or if there is anything that should not be there. To uninstall a program it is necessary to first left-click its entry in the list to select it. Then operate the Add/ Remove button and go through the additional steps needed to remove the program. These tend to be slightly different from one program to another, but it is usually just a matter of confirming that you wish to remove the program.

In the case of adware it is likely that there will be a warning to the effect that the software it supports will not operate properly if the program is removed. Unfortunately, in most cases the supported program will not be named, but you will probably be able to deduce this for yourself. It is up to you whether to remove the program anyway or put up with it. You might get a warning message saying that shared files are no longer needed by other applications and asking whether you wish to remove them. In theory it should be all right to operate the Yes button, but the no button is the safer option. Leaving shared files in place should still result in the program being properly uninstalled and rendered inoperative.

Points to remember

It is important to have antivirus software installed on a PC before it succumbs to an infection. Installing antivirus software on an infected PC is inadvisable because it entails file copying and changes to system files. Both of these can help a virus to spread across the hard disc drive. With good antivirus software installed it is unlikely that a virus will manage to take hold in the first place.

Some antivirus suites include a set of bootable floppy discs or a bootable CD-ROM so that antivirus checks can be made on a PC that does not have antivirus software installed. Using this type of software, checks can be made on a PC even if it can not be booted into Windows. One drawback of this method is that the antivirus software will not be fully up-to-date.

A Trojan is a program that purports to be one thing but is actually something else. Some Trojans attack the system, much like viruses, but can not replicate and spread like a virus. A backdoor Trojan helps hackers to penetrate your computer system, either with a view to causing damage or to steal information.

A worm looks for security "holes" in other systems in an attempt to attack that system and spread from it. Some of the worst computer attacks in recent times have been from worms that are spread by Emails, and replicate by sending copies of themselves to every address in the address book of the attacked system.

Antivirus software usually scans for more than viruses, so other harmful files such as Trojans and spyware will usually be found. Things such as adware will not be detected though, as they are often installed legitimately. Programs such as PestPatrol will scan for adware and the like, and will remove them if required.

Provided you are using up-to-date software there should be little risk of you PC being infected if you open and read an Email. Opening attachments is a different matter, and they are now a common means of trying to spread viruses.

Do not take Emails at face value, even if they supposedly come from an address that you normally deal with. With the aid of some common sense, you have to act as the first line of defence against malicious and scam Emails.

Where possible, check your Email attachments for viruses before downloading them to your PC. Never open Email attachments if the sender is unknown to you, or you are not expecting a file from that particular person. You can always Email the supposed sender of the file to check its authenticity.

Programs for scanning Emails are available and this facility is included in many antivirus suites. These programs work with Outlook and Outlook Express but do not normally work with fully Internet based Email services. However, these services sometimes have built-in virus scanning facilities.

4

Backup and Restore

Back to basics

One way of speeding up a bloated Windows installation is to reinstall everything from scratch. This takes things back to a lean installation that lacks the numerous unnecessary files that tend to build up on the hard disc drive, and it will usually produce a less cluttered registry. It is also an opportunity to completely "lose" any installed software that has proved to be something less than useful. A major drawback of this once popular approach to speeding up a PC is that it can be very time consuming. Modern PCs often have a number of major applications programs installed, together with a selection of small utilities.

Another factor to bear in mind is that most users customise Windows and some of the applications programs. Reinstalling everything from scratch involves redoing any customisation. If you use only a fairly simple setup, then reinstalling everything from scratch remains a practical approach. It is likely to be too time consuming if you use a complex installation that has a great deal of customisation. Reinstalling Windows XP and Windows ME from scratch is covered in Chapters 5 and 6 respectively.

In this chapter a quicker approach is considered, which is to provide a full backup of a basic installation. In other words, Windows and all the application software is loaded onto the hard disc, and any customisation is completed. A backup of the hard disc is then taken and this provides a quick means of reverting to the basic installation. Once restored, this installation has all your normal applications and utility programs, all the hardware drivers loaded, and any customisation included. It might be necessary to add or update one or two programs, and any recently produced data will also have to be added, but the total time taken to get back to a fully operational and fast system should be relatively small.

Image

Simply copying all the files on the hard disc to CDRs or another form of mass storage will not enable the system to be restored to its original condition. The files can be copied back to the hard disc, but they will not be in the same places on the restored disc. As a result of this the PC will not be able to boot from the disc. In order to precisely restore a disc to its previous state it is necessary to produce what is termed an image of the disc. It requires special software to produce the image file and restore the disc from this file. Power Quest's Drive Image and Norton's Ghost are two popular programs of this type. There is a rather less sophisticated backup and restore feature included as part of the Windows operating system.

With the current low cost of hard disc drives it is quite common for a large drive to be divided into several partitions. In effect, a large disc becomes two or more smaller discs. One partition is often used to store a backup of the main (boot) partition. Another method is to have a second physical drive, which is a clone of the main drive. Either way, any new data placed on the main drive is copied to the backup partition/ drive. If the Windows installation is seriously damaged or simply becomes sluggish, it is just a matter of restoring everything from the relevant partition of the backup drive. The PC should then perform much as it did before the problem occurred, complete with your data.

Having a second physical drive gives even greater security because it guards against a catastrophic failure of the main drive. If the main drive should fail it is just a matter of installing a new one and installing the backup image onto it. As an emergency measure it is possible to set the backup drive to operate as the boot disc, and you can then go on using the PC while a new disc is obtained.

There is an advantage in having the image files stored in some form of external storage such as CDRs. This ensures that you have a backup of the system should some form of catastrophic failure result in the hard disc or discs being zapped. It also guards against attack from viruses and other computer pests. Even the most sophisticated of computer viruses is unable to attack files that are on CDRs stored in drawer or cupboard.

Bear in mind though, that a backup on CDR discs will only provide a so-called "snapshot" of your PC at the time the backup copy was made. Going back to the system stored on the CDRs will not restore any data made since the backup was taken. It is therefore important to take copies of data produced since the main backup was taken, so that the data can

Fig.4.1 The initial window of the Backup and Restore Wizard

be copied onto the hard disc once the basic setup has been restored. The program used to make the image of the hard disc might have facilities to backup data made thereafter. If not, it is up to you to ensure that copies of any important data are made onto CDRs or some other form of external storage.

Windows Backup

Using backup programs it is possible to save selected files, directories, directory structures, or the entire contents of the hard disc drive. It should also be possible to make an image of the hard drive so that an exact and bootable copy of it can be restored at a later date. I think I am correct in stating that every version of Windows is supplied complete with a backup program that has the imaginative name of Backup. Although basic compared to some programs of this type it does the job well enough for many users. Its lack of popularity possibly stems from the fact that the equivalent facility in Windows 3.1 was something less than user friendly, causing many users to look elsewhere for a backup utility.

4 Backup and Restore

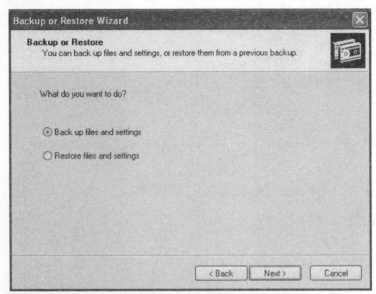

Fig.4.2 This window provides backup and restore options

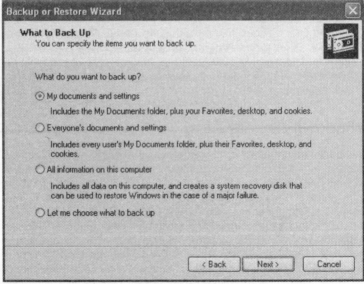

Fig.4.3 Use this window to choose what you wish to backup

156

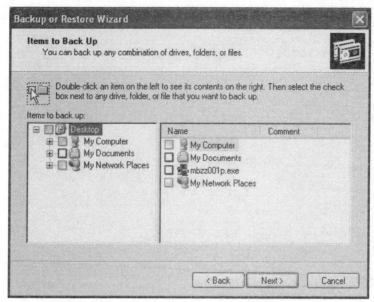

Fig.4.4 Select the files or folders you would like to backup

Perhaps the problem is simply that the Backup program is a part of Windows that has often been easy to overlook. Anyway, the Windows XP version is more user friendly and powerful than previous versions, and it is definitely there if you seek it out. With the Professional version of Windows XP it is installed by default, but with the Home Edition it will probably have to be installed from the Valueadd\Msft\Ntbackup folder on the installation CD-ROM.

Backup Wizard

Once installed, the Backup program is run by selecting All Programs from the Start menu, followed by Accessories, System Tools, and then Backup. By default the Backup Wizard (Figure 4.1) runs when this program is launched, and initially it is probably best to use the wizard. Operate the Next button to move on to the first stage (Figure 4.2). Here you have the choice of backing up or restoring data, but it is obviously necessary to produce a backup disc before anything can be restored. Therefore, initially the Backup radio button has to be selected.

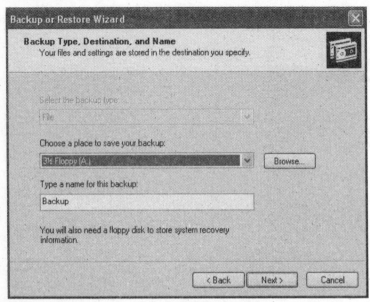

Fig.4.5 Use this window to select the backup drive

The next window (Figure 4.3) is used to select the data to be backed up. The top option produces a backup of the My Documents folder plus some system settings and cookies. The second option is similar, but it provides a backup of the documents and settings for all users. Using the fourth option produces a file browser (Figure 4.4) so that the user can select the files and folders that will be backed up. The third option is the one that is of most use if the system becomes seriously damaged or the hard disc becomes unusable. It permits the whole system to be backed up, and it also produces a recovery disc that enables it to be easily restored again. In fact the restoration process is almost totally automated. It is the third option that will be considered here.

The next window (Figure 4.5) enables the backup drive to be selected, and a variety of drive types is supported. These include Zip discs, local hard drives, and some tape backup systems. Unfortunately, CD writers are not supported. Sometimes there are ways of working around this limitation, but it is probably best to opt for a third-party backup program if you wish to use CD-R or CD-RW discs to hold the backup files. Use the menu or the Browse option to select the correct drive. If you select a device that is not supported by the Backup program, an error message

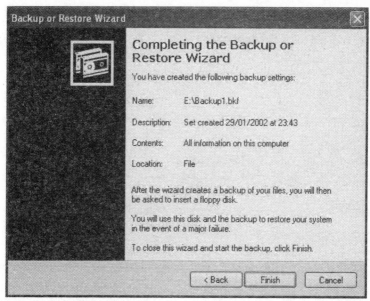

Fig.4.6 *The selected options are shown before the backup is started*

will be produced when Windows tries to create the file. This will simply state that the backup file could not be produced.

In the current context the best option is to have a second drive as the backup device. It is not essential to keep the second drive connected once the backup has been made, and the backup drive can have its power and data leads disconnected once the backup has been completed. Of course, the power should be switched off before the drive is disconnected. The drive is reconnected again if you need to restore the backup copy at some later time. Disconnecting the drive avoids wear and tear, and also keeps the contents safe from viruses. Of course, it also prevents new data from being backed up on the second drive. If you produce large amounts of data it might be worthwhile keeping this drive connected and in operation.

By default, the backup file is called "Backup", but the name in the textbox can be changed to any valid filename. Operating the Next button moves things on to a window like the one in Figure 4.6. This shows the options that have been selected, and provides an opportunity to change your mind or correct mistakes. Use the Back button if it is necessary to return

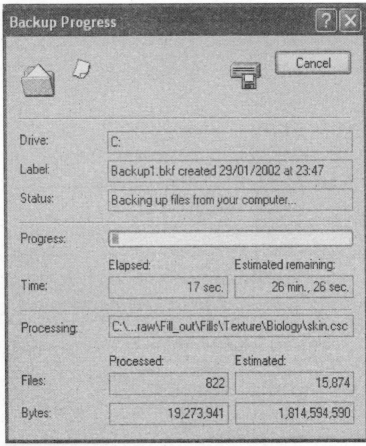

Fig.4.7 This window shows how the backup is progessing

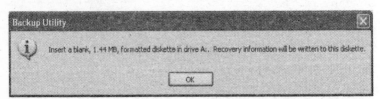

Fig.4.8 The floppy disc is inserted into drive A: when this message appears

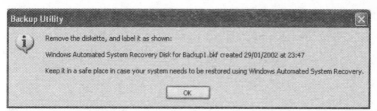

Fig.4.9 This message indicates that the backup has been completed

to earlier windows to make changes, or operate the Finish button to go ahead and make the backup file.

A window like the one shown in Figure 4.7 will appear, which shows the progress made by the Backup program. It provides an estimate for the

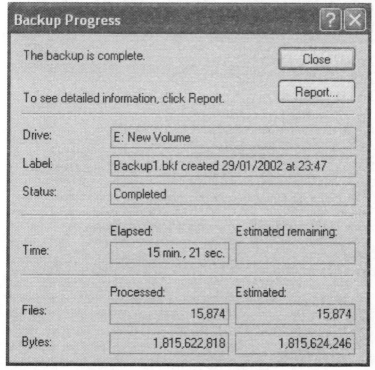

Fig.4.10 The Backup Progress window provides some statistics

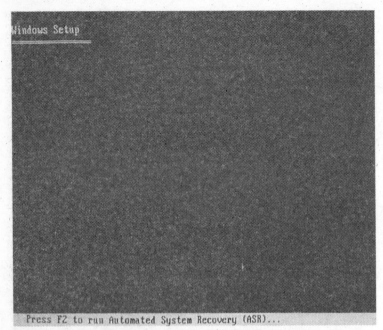

Fig.4.11 Press the F2 key as soon as this message appears at the bottom of the screen

time remaining until the task is completed, and this will vary massively depending on the amount of data to be saved and the speed of the backup device. With many gigabytes of data to back up it is definitely a good idea to use a fast backup device such as a second hard disc drive. With a slow backup device the process can take many hours. Where appropriate, you will be prompted when a disc change is necessary. With multiple disc backups, always label all the discs clearly. You will then be able supply the right disc each time when restoring the backup copy. Do not worry if the size of the backup file is substantially less than the total amount of data on the hard disc. The backup file is probably compressed, or perhaps no backup copies are made of standard files that are available from the Windows XP installation disc. Anyway, it is quite normal for the backup file to be significantly smaller than the source.

The message shown in Figure 4.8 will appear towards the end of the backup process. The floppy disc is needed to make an automatic recovery disc. This disc is needed in order to restore the system from the backup disc, and the backup is relatively little value without the

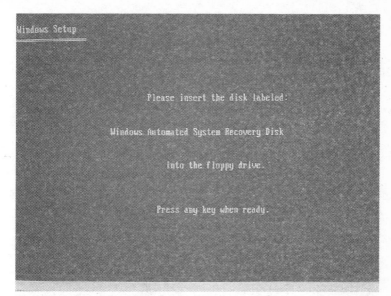

Fig.4.12 Insert the backup disc in drive A: when this prompt appears

recovery disc. Insert a 1.44-megabyte floppy disc into drive A: and operate the OK button. The message of Figure 4.9 appears once the recovery disc has been completed. Label the disc as indicated in the message and store it safely. The automatic recovery process is not possible without this disc. Finally, you are returned to the Backup Progress window (Figure 4.10), which should indicate that the backup has been completed successfully.

Booting from CD-ROM

There is little point in having a means of restoring the backup that requires the computer to boot normally into Windows XP, since this will often be impossible when the restoration feature is needed. The Windows XP method of restoring a full system backup is more straightforward than the Windows 9x equivalent. In fact the Windows XP method makes the process about as simple as it is ever likely to be. It is termed the Automated System Recovery, and it certainly lives up to the automated part of its name.

The first task is to boot from the Windows XP installation CD-ROM. Note that the BIOS must be set to boot from the CD-ROM drive before it tries

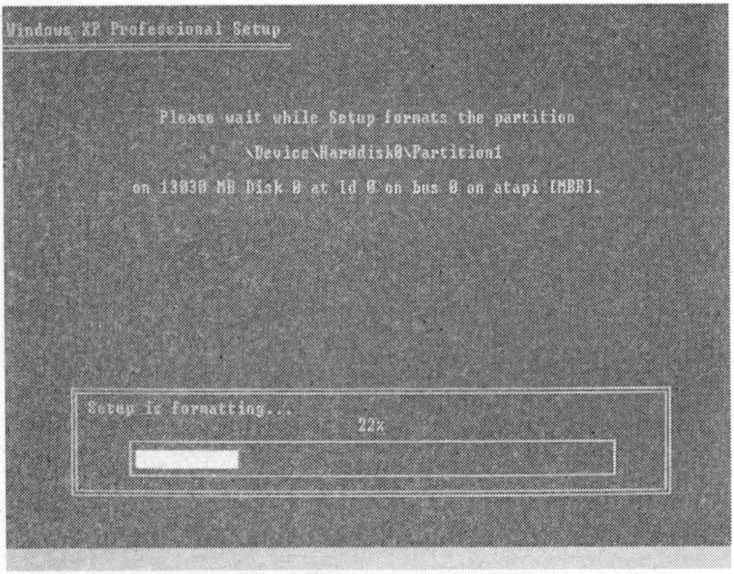

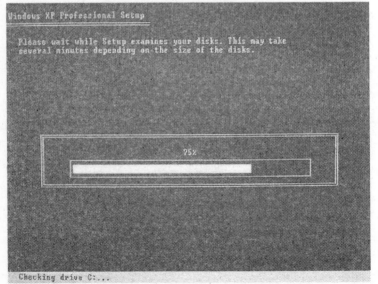

Fig.4.13 *Formatting erases all the data stored in the disc partition*

Fig.4.14 *The Setup program briefly examines the disc drives*

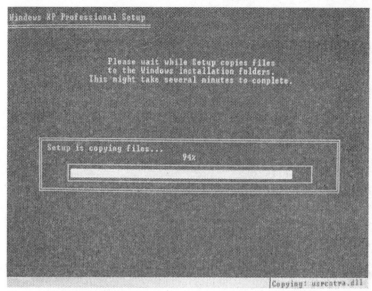

Fig.4.15 It takes a few minutes for the installation files to be copied

to boot from the hard disc drive. If the boot sequence is the other way around, the computer will probably start to boot from the hard drive and the CD-ROM drive will be ignored. With the installation disc in a CD-ROM drive and the correct BIOS settings, a message saying "Press any key to boot from CD-ROM" will appear for a few seconds at the beginning of the boot process. Press any key while this message is displayed or the computer will revert to booting from the hard disc drive.

Messages appear along the bottom of

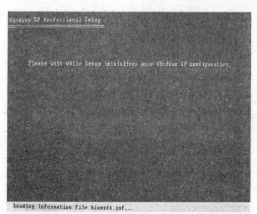

Fig.4.16 More files are loaded

the screen when the computer starts booting from the CD-ROM. Look for the one that says "Press F2 to run Automated System Recovery (ASR)", as in Figure 4.11. This message only appears briefly, so press F2 as soon as it appears. After some disc activity the message of Figure 4.12 will appear, and the floppy disc

Fig.4.17 The computer will reboot automatically if the Return key is not operated

produced when backup was made must be placed in drive A:. Then press any key to continue. The restoration process requires little intervention from the user, but it is as well to keep an eye on things in

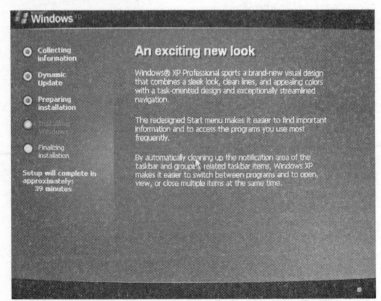

Fig.4.18 Installation starts in earnest once the computer has rebooted

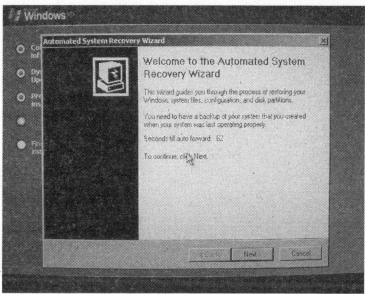

*Fig.4.19 The Automatic System Recover Wizard runs once Windows
XP has been reinstalled*

case something goes wrong. First, the partition used by the system is
formatted, which effectively wipes all data from it. If there is any data on
the disc that has not been backed up, it is lost forever at this stage. The
formatting will take several minutes, and an onscreen "fuel gauge" shows
how far the formatting has progressed (Figure 4.13).

A similar gauge is used at the next screen (Figure 4.14), where the
program examines the disc drives. This is usually much quicker than
formatting the restoration partition, and this screen may only appear for
a second or two. A further gauge appears on the next screen (Figure
4.15), and here the program copies some files to the hard disc. Next the
program loads some more files (Figure 4.16). The computer is then
rebooted, and it will reboot after several seconds even if you do not
press Return to restart the computer (Figure 4.17). Note that the
Automated System Recovery disc in drive A: must be removed at this
stage. The computer might try to boot from this disc if it is left in the
drive, and this would probably prevent the computer from rebooting
properly. If the reboot should stall because the disc is left in drive A:,
removing it and pressing any key should get things underway again.

4   Backup and Restore

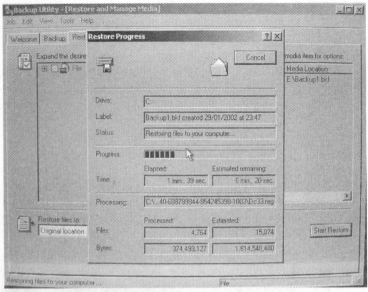

Fig.4.20 The Restore program copies files to the hard disc

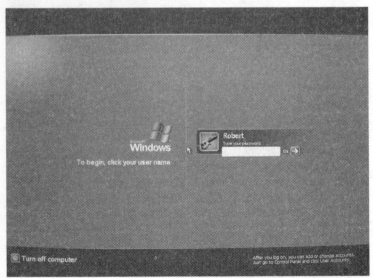

Fig.4.21 Login normally once the files have been restored

Fig.4.22 Windows XP should now look and work as before

Windows is installed on the appropriate partition when the computer has rebooted, and a screen like the one in Figure 4.18 shows how the installation is progressing. Once Windows has been installed, the Automated System Recovery Wizard runs (Figure 4.19). This does not require any input from the user though, and you can just sit back and watch while your files are restored to the hard disc (Figure 4.20). Once this has been completed, the usual login screen (Figure 4.21) appears. You login using your normal password, and the computer then goes into Windows XP (Figure 4.22). This should look the same and have the same settings that were in force when the backup was made. Any programs, data, etc., on the partition that was backed up should be included in the restored installation.

In practice there might be one or two minor differences to the system. In particular, any passwords or other data hidden on the disc in "invisible" files will not have been placed on the backup disc. Files of this type are very secure, but they are "invisible" to the Backup program. It is therefore unable to save them in the backup file. This should not be of any major consequence, because the relevant applications can be run, and the passwords (or whatever) can be stored on the hard disc again. Of course,

4 Backup and Restore

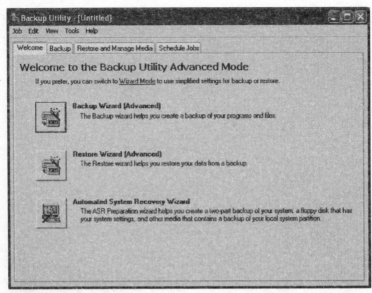

Fig.4.23 Three options are offered when Advanced Mode is selected

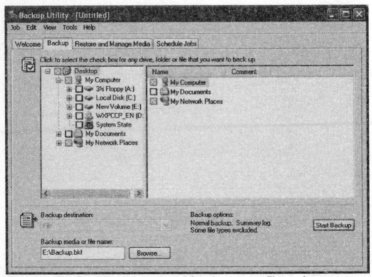

Fig.4.24 The Backup program enables the source files to be selected easily

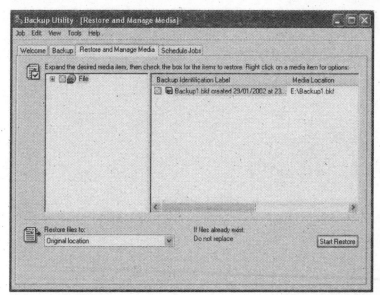

Fig.4.25 The Restore program enables the backup file and destination to be selected

any data files produced after the backup was made will not be automatically restored to the hard disc. They must be restored manually, and it is essential to make sure that any recent data files are backed up before you start the restoration process.

Advanced mode

Use of the Backup Wizard is not mandatory, and the Backup program can be controlled directly by the user. Start running the program in the usual way, but left-click on the "Advanced mode" link. This produces a window like the one in Figure 4.23, and two of the buttons give access to more advanced versions of the Backup and Restore wizards. The third button provides another route to the Automated System Recovery Wizard. The tabs near the top of the window provide manual operation of the Backup and Restore programs, and access to scheduled backups.

Figure 4.24 shows the window for the Backup program. The files and folders to be backed up are selected in the upper section of the window, while the backup drive and filename are entered in the textbox near the

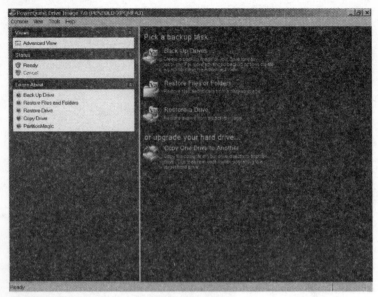

Fig.4.26 The initial screen of Drive Image

bottom left-hand corner of the window. The usual Browse facility is available here. Once everything has been set up correctly, the Start Backup button is operated. The Restore program's window is shown in Figure 4.25. The upper section of the window is used to locate and select the backup file, and the lower section is used to select the destination of the restored backup. This will usually be the original location, but it can be restored to an alternative location. Once everything has been set correctly, the Start Restore button is operated.

The Backup and Restore programs are not difficult to use, and are certainly more user friendly than the equivalent functions in some previous versions of Windows. However, except where some very simple backup and restore operation is required, it is probably best to use the wizards. These should ensure that you do not overlook anything, and that backup files can always be successfully restored. The Automated System Restore facility is invaluable, and is well worth using. In the past it has been slow, difficult, and expensive to implement this type of backup system. With this facility and an inexpensive hard disc added to the PC, the entire system can be backed up quite rapidly and restored again with ease.

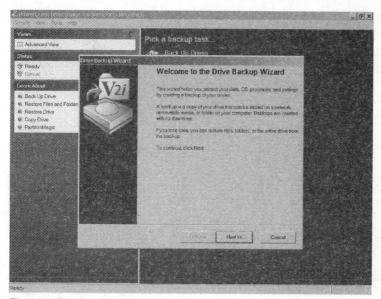

Fig.4.27 *The Backup Wizard makes it easier to produce the backup file*

Alternatives

Ideally a backup should be made onto CD-R or CD-RW discs, but this needs a third-party backup program. CD-RW discs have the advantage that they can be reused, but they are more expensive than CD-R discs. Another point to bear in mind is that an ordinary CD-R can be read using any form of CD-ROM drive without the need for any special drivers. The same is not true for CD-RW discs. Most other forms of high capacity disc also need special driver software in order to get the disc drive functioning properly.

This is no problem when you have a fully working computer that is running Windows, but it might be problematic if you have a computer that will not boot into Windows. You need to do some careful checking before using any form of backup that relies on anything other than a standard form of disc for storage. There is no point in carefully producing sets of backup discs if the image they contain can never be restored to the PC. If in doubt, stick to standard disc types, which really means a hard drive or CD-Rs.

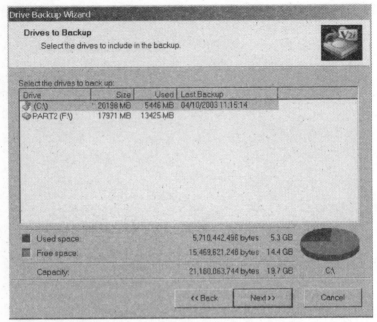

Fig.4.28 The first step is to select the drive to be backed up

Power Quest's Drive Image 7 is used in this example of producing a backup to CD-Rs and restoring it. There are other backup programs that no doubt work very well, and I am using Drive Image 7 here simply because it is the one installed on my PC. When this program is run under Windows XP it is possible to produce a backup from within Windows. With other backup programs and other versions of Windows it is often necessary to exit Windows and reboot into MS/DOS or an equivalent written specifically for the backup program. This ensures that Windows does not restrict access to any files on the disc, but is obviously not very convenient. However, with most modern backup programs the reboot into a basic operating system is taken care of by the program, and the process may well be completely automatic.

Launching Drive Image 7 produces the initial screen of Figure 4.26, and the Backup Drives option is selected in order to start the backup process. Making the backup is made easier by the use of a wizard (Figure 4.27). Operating the Next button moves things on to the window of Figure 4.28 where the drive to be backed up is selected. Actually, in a multi-drive

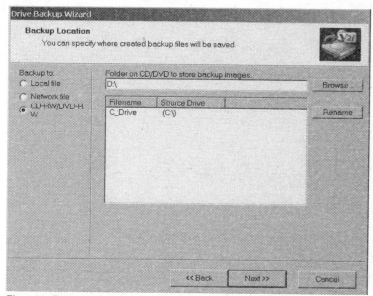

Fig.4.29 This window is used to select the destination for the file

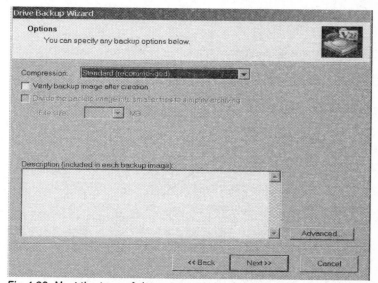

Fig.4.30 Next the type of data compression is selected

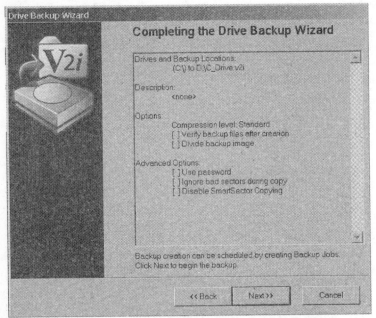

Fig.4.31 This window shows a summary of the selected options

system it is possible to select more than one drive if desired. In this example only the boot drive (drive C) will be backed up, because the other hard drive is itself a backup drive.

The destination for the backup is selected at the next window (Figure 4.29). The Local File option is used when the backup will be onto another hard disc drive. Obviously the Network option is used where the PC is on a local area network (LAN) and the backup will be placed elsewhere on the network. In this case the backup will be made to a CDRW drive, so it is the third option that is selected. The required drive can be selected using the usual file browser if the Browse button is operated.

The required type of compression is selected at the next window (Figure 4.30). Data compression enables more data to be placed on each disc in the backup set. When making a backup to CDR or CDRW discs the compression has the beneficial effect of reducing the number of discs required. With a relatively slow backup device it can also reduce the time take to create and restore a backup. Some types of data compress

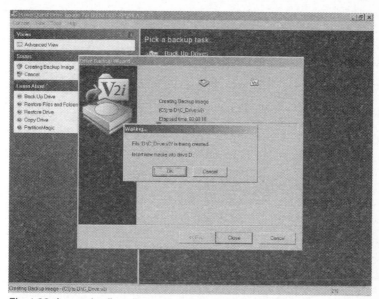

Fig.4.32 Insert the first disc and get the backup under way

more readily than others. Some files on the disc may already be in compressed form and will not be amenable to further compression. On the other hand, things like program and simple text files will often compress by a factor of three or more. In practice, compression roughly halves the number of discs required. Opt for the Standard method of compression. If required, a description can be added in the textbox in the bottom section of the window (e.g. "Full backup of drive C").

The next window (Figure 4.31) simply provides a summary of the options that have been selected. If necessary, use the Back button to return to an earlier window so that a correction can be made, then use the Next button to return to this window. When the right options have been selected, operate the Next button to start making the backup. Eventually a message like the one in Figure 4.32 will appear, and the first disc is then placed in the CDR drive and the backup process starts.

A full backup is likely to require about six to twelve discs, and could obviously require substantially more than this if a large and almost full disc is being backed up. The program will prompt you each time a change of disc is required. Carefully number each disc because they must be used in the correct order when the backup is used to restore

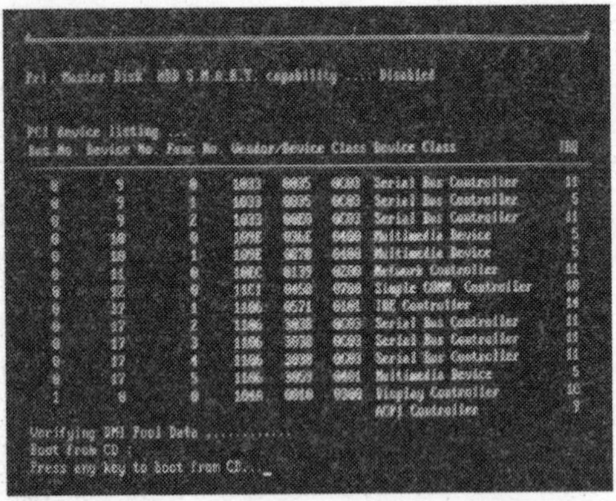

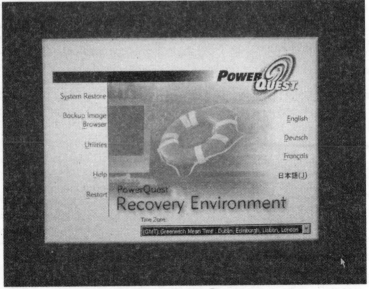

Fig.4.33 Press F2 if this message appears

the contents of the hard disc drive. Eventually the program will indicate that the backup has been completed, and you are then returned to the main screen of Drive Image 7.

Restoring

There are facilities in the main Drive Image program for restoring data, but this route is not usable in the current context. Instead, the computer is booted using either a set of boot discs made using the program or via the Drive Image installation CD. These days, practically any PC can be booted from a

Fig.4.34 The options available from the Recovery program

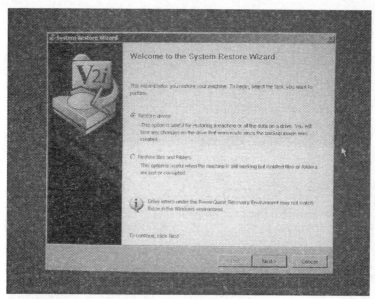

Fig.4.35 A full or partial restoration can be selected

suitable CD-ROM, and it is probably best to use this method where the option is available. Note that this option is not available with earlier versions of Drive Image and with some other backup programs. With some PCs it might be necessary to alter the BIOS settings in order to boot from a CD-ROM. The computer's operating manual should explain how to do this. Using a set of bootable floppy discs is one way around the problem if you do not feel confident about dealing with the BIOS Setup program.

The computer will usually start booting from the CD-ROM or bootable floppy disc without any preamble. Depending on the BIOS used in your PC, it might instead try to boot into the damaged operating system on the hard disc unless you press a key at the right time. If a message like the one in Figure 4.33 appears at the bottom of the screen, immediately press F2 or whatever key the message indicates. The PC should then boot into the operating system contained on the bootable CD-ROM or floppy disc.

This will usually be MS-DOS or something similar, but the Restore program usually includes a simple Windows style user interface. Some

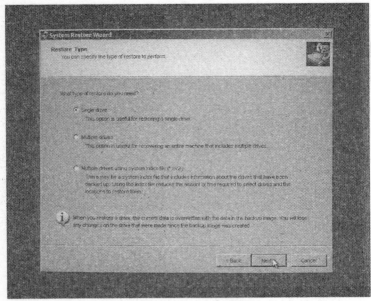

Fig.4.36 One or multiple drives can be restored

messages will probably appear on the screen giving a brief explanation of what the program is doing. When using the floppy disc method there will usually be a boot disc and one or more program discs. Change discs when prompted. The boot process can be quite long, because the Restore program will probably scan the PC's hardware so that it can operate with the mouse, etc., you are using. Where appropriate, networking might be activated so that the hard disc can be restored from an image file stored on another PC on the network.

Eventually the boot and loading processes should come to an end and a screen like the one of Figure 4.34 will then be obtained. A number of options are available, but it is the System Restore facility that is needed in this case. Selecting this option moves things on to the screen of Figure 4.35 where the radio buttons provide two options. One is used to restore only certain files or folders, and the other is used to restore a complete drive. It is obviously the latter that is required here. The next screen (Figure 4.36) provides the option of restoring one drive or multiple drives. In this example it is only drive C that is being restored, so the single drive option is selected.

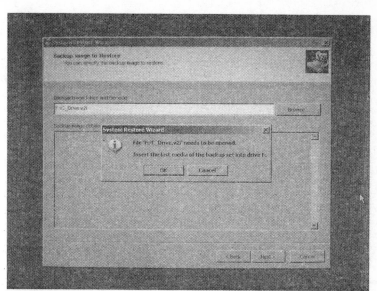

Fig.4.37 Initially the first and last discs in the set are required. This is quite normal for programs that use multi-disc sets

At the next screen the backup file is selected, and a file browser is available via the Browse button. Having pointed the program to the drive containing the first disc in the backup set, a message like the one in Figure 4.37 will appear. It is normal for programs that use multi-disc sets to require the first and last discs in the set before proceeding. After the program has read from the last disc you will be prompted to replace the first disc in the drive. You should then have something like Figure 4.38, with the screen showing the location of the backup file and some basic information for it.

Figure 4.39 shows the next screen, and here you must select the drive to be restored. You must be careful to choose the right disc if there is more than one hard drive or partition, as restoring the image to the wrong drive or partition will erase all the data it contains. It is then just a matter of following the onscreen prompts, and changing discs when necessary. The discs in the backup set must be numbered so that you can provide them in the correct order. The program will detect the error if you should get the discs muddled-up, and it will not proceed until the right disc has been placed in the drive.

4 Backup and Restore

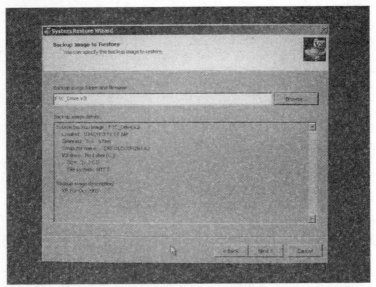

Fig.4.38 This screen shows the backup's location, etc.

Fig.4.39 Be careful when selecting which drive to restore

182

Once the restoration has been completed, remove the boot CD-ROM or floppy disc from the drive and reset the computer. It should then boot into the newly restored operating system. The PC should them operate exactly as it did at the time the backup was made. There can be minor problems such as stored passwords being lost, and automatic login facilities failing to work in consequence. This is due to the password being concealed on the disc in a hidden file that the backup program misses. You have to login manually and then reinstate the automatic facility. Of course, any data or programs added since the backup was made must be reinstated in order to bring the installation fully up to date.

Points to remember

Apart from providing an easy way back to an efficient system, backing up data and system information to another drive guards against a serious attack from a virus, a hard disc failure, or other major catastrophe. Backing up system information to the main hard drive is only sufficient to guard against problems with the operating system.

Floppy discs are inadequate to cope with the large amounts of data produced by many modern applications. A CD writer, Zip drive, additional hard disc, or some other form of mass storage device is required. A mass storage device is also required in order to make a full backup of the main hard disc drive. Note that some backup programs (including the Windows XP Backup program) are not compatible with CD writers.

In order to get things back to a "lean" setup it is necessary to make a full backup of the hard drive before the system becomes bloated. Plenty of third-party backup software is available, but the Windows XP Backup utility is just about adequate for most purposes. Combined with an additional hard disc drive, it provides a fast and cost-effective method of providing a full system backup.

The Windows Backup program can be used to backup selected files, or to provide a full backup of the hard disc. Regularly backing up the full contents of a hard disc is relatively time consuming, but restoring a full backup is the quickest way to get the computer into full working order again if a major problem occurs.

The Windows XP Backup program can be used without wizards, but for most purposes the wizards provide the easiest and most reliable means of handling backup and restore operations.

It is necessary to buy a backup program such as Drive Image in order to make a backup copy on CDR discs. This method has the advantage of placing the backup copy beyond the reach of viruses. Another advantage is that the cost is quite low provided your PC already has a CD writer (as most do). It is relatively slow though.

Reinstalling XP

Clean sweep

A fresh installation of Windows works quickly and efficiently, but things tend to slow down as more programs are installed, data files are added, and the hard disc begins to fill up with tens of thousands of files. The obvious solution to this problem is to periodically reinstall Windows from scratch so that you are taken back to a new "lean and mean" installation from time to time, rather than having one that just gains more and more "baggage". Just revert to a clutter-free installation as soon as Windows starts to suffer from general clutter.

This method does indeed work well at keeping Windows running smoothly, and it has been used successfully by many Windows users. However, there are a few ifs and buts to consider before opting for this method. For a start, reinstalling an operating system is not something to be undertaken lightly. These days it is not actually that difficult, but it remains a substantial undertaking. Bear in mind that reinstalling Windows from scratch will result in all the data on the hard disc being lost, so anything important must be reliably backed-up prior to reinstallation.

Windows can be installed over an existing installation, which should preserve all the data on the hard disc. Unfortunately, this method will usually be of little help in the current context. This type of reinstallation is mainly used in an attempt to fix Windows when it has been seriously damaged and will not boot properly. This type of reinstallation will not remove accumulated clutter from the hard disc drive, and is unlikely give any improvement in the boot-up time, etc.

It will only help if a serious problem is causing Windows to take an excessive time to boot-up, or a problem is causing Windows to run slowly. Both are possible, although a serious fault is more likely to bring Windows to a halt rather than slow it down. Note also that a major problem in the original installation might simply be copied into the new one. Reinstallation from scratch is the only "sure fire" method of eradicating a serious fault in Windows. Installing Windows over the existing installation is quicker than doing everything from scratch, so you might prefer to try this approach first. Both methods of reinstallation are described in this chapter.

Keep it simple

An important point to bear in mind is that the new "lean and mean" installation will not stay that way for very long if you immediately install dozens of application programs, utilities, and anything else you can lay your hands on. When reinstalling Windows, you will only reap the full benefit if you think carefully about which programs you really need and use. Only include those that are really necessary in the new installation.

These days the main problem in installing Windows from scratch is that it can be a very time-consuming business. Reinstalling Windows itself is likely to take less than an hour, but in order to get things working properly it will then be necessary to spend a little time installing device drivers for items of hardware such as the sound and video cards. With Windows fully operational it is then a matter of installing all the application programs and any utility software that you use. Next, any updates to the application programs must be installed. Remember that any updates installed over the Internet, automatic or otherwise, will be lost when Windows is reinstalled. Finally, any customisation of Windows and the application programs must be undertaken. Customisation can be very time-consuming if it has to be handled manually, which is usually the case.

Before deciding to reinstall Windows from scratch it is essential to make a realistic assessment of the situation. With a fairly simple Windows setup it is likely that redoing everything from scratch will not take too long, and that it will give a major improvement if things have become seriously "gummed up". With a complex installation it could take days rather than hours to get everything back in place and working well again. The general improvement in speed might not be very great, with the new installation necessarily carrying a lot of "baggage".

The reinstallation process is rather different depending on whether the PC runs under Windows XP or ME. We will start by considering the reinstallation of Windows XP.

The process is very similar whether the operating system is installed from scratch or on top of an existing Windows installation. If Windows XP is already on the hard disc it will be detected by the Setup program, which can then reinstall Windows XP on top of the existing installation.

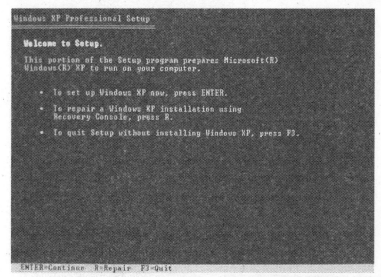

Fig.5.1 The opening screen of the Windows XP Setup program

Note that the versions of Windows XP supplied with some PCs do not have the standard installation disc. The methods described here are only applicable if you have the standard Windows XP installation disc. If your PC was not supplied with a standard installation disc it probably came complete with a recovery disc that makes it easy to return to a basic Windows installation. With a PC of this type you should consult the instruction manual, and this should give concise information about reinstalling Windows.

Booting from CD-ROM

Whether reinstalling on top of the current installation or reinstalling Windows XP from scratch, the first step is to boot from the installation CD-ROM. The BIOS must be set to boot from the CD-ROM drive before it tries to boot from the hard disc. It is unlikely that the computer will attempt to boot from the CD-ROM drive if the priorities are the other way around, and it will certainly not do so unless the CD-ROM is set as one of the boot devices. If all is well, a message will probably appear on the screen indicating that any key can be pressed in order to boot from the CD-ROM drive. This message appears quite briefly, so be ready to press one of the keys. The computer will try to boot from the hard disc if you

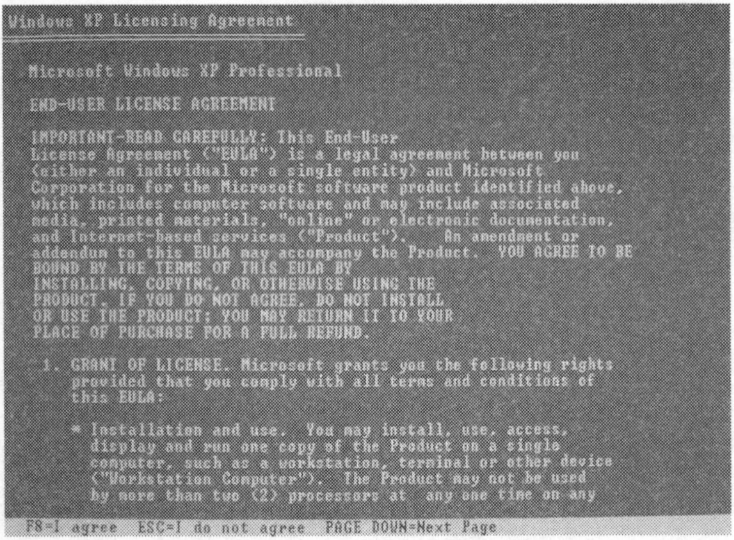

Fig.5.2 You must agree to the licensing conditions to proceed

"miss the boat". It will then be necessary to restart the computer and try again.

After various files have been loaded from the CD-ROM, things should come to a halt with the screen of Figure 5.1. The Setup program is needed to reinstall Windows XP, so press the Enter (Return) key. The Next screen (Figure 5.2) is the usual licence agreement, and the F8 key is pressed in order to agree to the licensing terms. Note that Windows XP can not be installed unless you do agree to the licensing conditions. The installations on the hard disc are listed on the next screen (Figure 5.3), and in most cases there will only be one. Where appropriate, select the installation that you wish to repair or replace.

Repair (rather than replacement) of the operating system will be considered first. In other words, reinstalling Windows on top of the existing installation rather than starting afresh. Press the R key to indicate that the selected installation must be repaired. The Setup program then examines the discs (Figure 5.4), and this process is usually quite brief. Next the Setup program copies files from the CD-ROM to the installation folders on the hard disc drive. This will take a few minutes, and the usual bargraph display shows how far the copying has progressed (Figure 5.5). Once the copying has finished, it is time for the computer to reboot for the first time. You can press the Enter key to start the reboot (Figure 5.6), but after 30 seconds it will automatically reboot anyway. Make sure that there is no floppy disc in drive A:, as this would prevent the PC from rebooting properly. Also, when the message appears on the screen, do

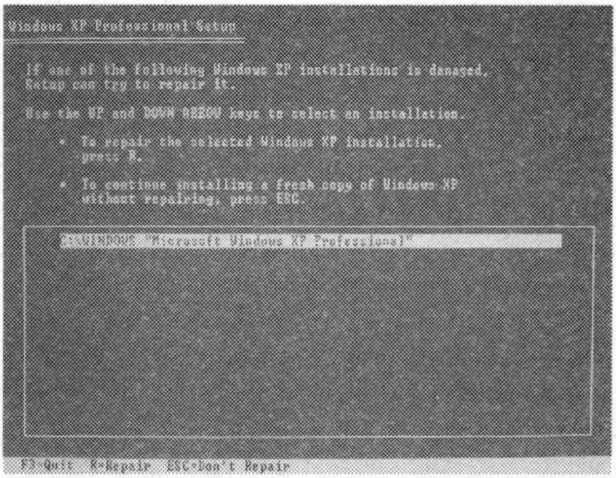

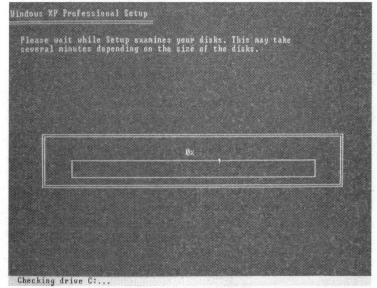

Fig.5.3 Select the correct installation

not press a key to cause the system to boot from the CD-ROM drive. At this stage it must boot from the hard disc drive.

A screen like the one in Figure 5.7 will appear once the reboot has completed, and this keeps you informed about the progress of the

Fig.5.4 Setup will briefly examine the disc drives

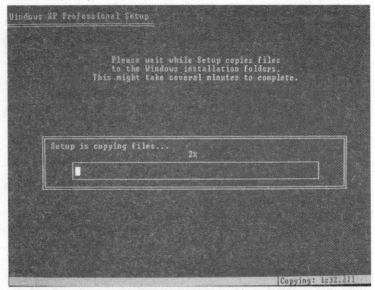

Fig.5.5 It will take some time for the files to be copied to the hard disc

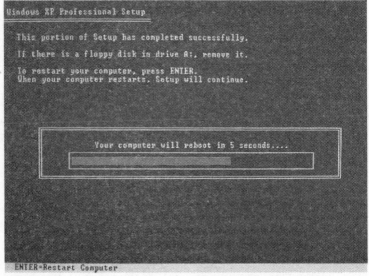

Fig.5.6 The computer will automatically reboot after 5 seconds

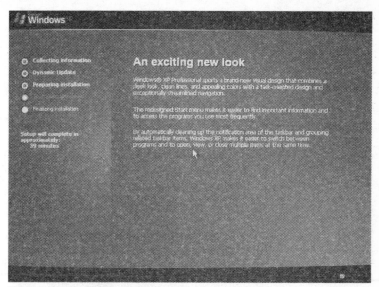

Fig.5.7 Setup indicates which stage of the process it is on, and gives an estimate of the time left until completion

reinstallation. A warning message like the one in Figure 5.8 might appear during the reinstallation. This points out that one of the device drivers in use on the computer is not one that has officially passed the Windows XP compatibility test. This does not necessarily mean that it is the cause of the problems with Windows XP, but it is obviously a possibility that has to be given serious consideration. In this case the audio driver in question had been in use for some weeks without any problems arising, so it was unlikely to cause any problems. If you operate the No button so that the driver is not loaded, the corresponding piece of hardware will be rendered inoperative until a suitable driver has been installed.

Language settings

Eventually a screen like the one in Figure 5.9 will appear. This permits the language settings to be customised, and it is advisable to operate the Customise button and check that the settings are suitable. This brings up an initial window like the one on Figure 5.10, but further windows and menus can be brought up by operating the Customise buttons and the tabs. Figures 5.11 and 5.12 show a couple of examples. Look through the various windows and menus, changing any settings that are incorrect. Mistakes here will not have dire consequences, but

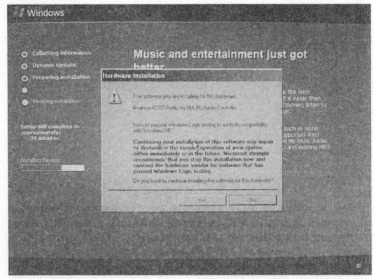

Fig.5.8 A warning message appears if a non-approved driver is found

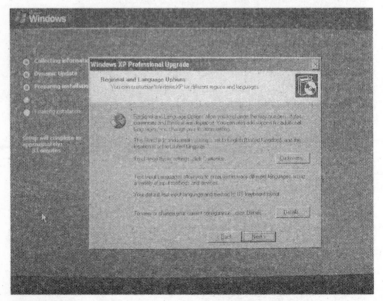

Fig.5.9 This window enables the language settings to be altered

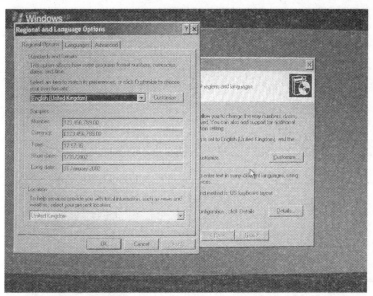

Fig.5.10 *These settings determine such things as how large numbers and the time will be displayed*

there could be a problem such as the keyboard producing some incorrect characters. It should be possible to correct any mistake of this type once Windows XP has been installed.

Even though Windows is being installed over an existing installation, it is still necessary to enter the product key when the screen of Figure 5.13 appears. The Windows XP installation disc is supplied in a cardboard folder rather than the usual jewel case. The 25-digit product key is on the rear of this folder. Keep the folder safe because it is not possible to reinstall Windows XP without it. With the correct product key typed into the textboxes, operating the Next button will produce a screen like the one in Figure 5.14, and the installation process will continue. The computer may then reboot, and the Welcome screen of Figure 5.15 will appear.

Operate the Next button to move on to the screen of Figure 5.16. Using the two radio buttons you can opt to activate the new Windows XP installation or leave this until later. It is probably best to defer the activation process until the PC is fully operational again. Activating Windows via the telephone method is a bit awkward, so in due course it is best to opt

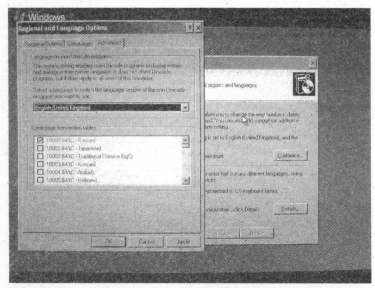

Fig.5.11 Various regional and language settings are available

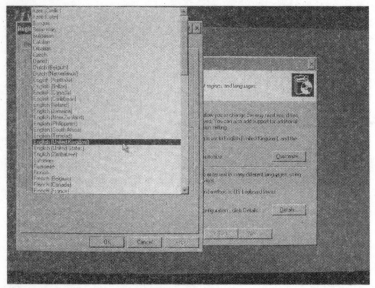

Fig.5.12 Setting the correct region

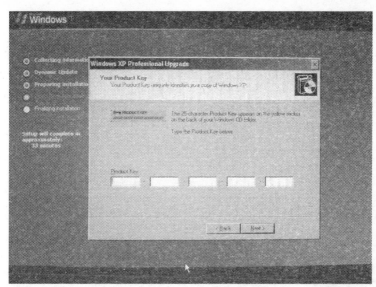

Fig.5.13 The product key is still needed when reinstalling Windows XP

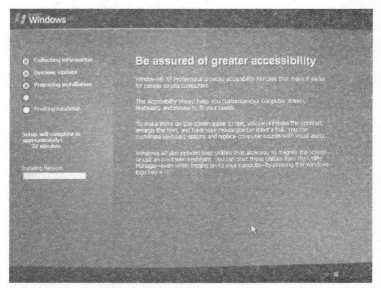

Fig.5.14 The reinstallation process resumes

Fig.5.15 With reinstallation complete, the Welcome screen is
displayed

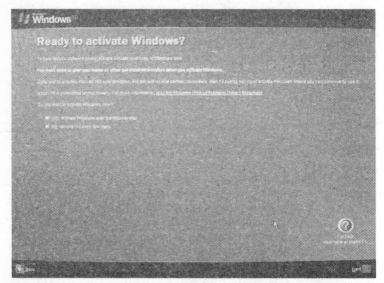

Fig.5.16 It is not essential to activate Windows XP at this stage

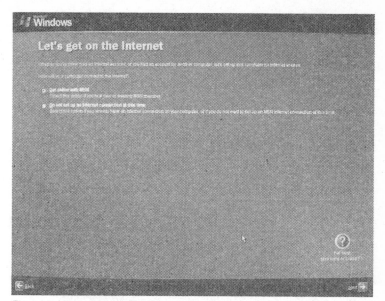

Fig.5.17 You are given the opportunity to get online with MSN.

for the web option if you have an Internet connection. At the next screen (Figure 5.17) you can sign on to MSN or continue with reinstallation. Assuming that the second option is taken, the Windows reinstallation is then finished, and the screen of Figure 5.18 will appear to confirm that the process has been completed.

To try out the new installation, operate the Finish button. The computer should then boot into the usual login screen (Figure 5.19). Login using your normal password (where appropriate), and the computer should go into the Windows XP desktop (Figure 5.20). After reinstalling Windows XP it is necessary to adjust some of the settings in order to provide normal operation. In particular, the reinstalled version of Windows uses very basic video settings, which have to be adjusted to your normal settings. As can be seen from Figure 5.20, Windows XP uses the previous video settings, and the new installation should be usable without any adjustments.

The application programs should remain installed and fully usable. Of course, any programs that were giving problems previously might not have been fixed by reinstalling Windows. This depends on whether the

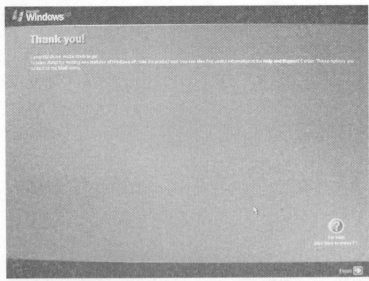

Fig.5.18 This screen confirms that reinstallation is complete

Fig.5.19 The next screen is the usual login type

Fig.5.20 The Windows desktop should look the same as it did before

root of the problem was Windows or the application program. Simply reinstalling a program over the original will usually fix any problems. Failing that, uninstalling the original, manually deleting any remaining files and folders, and then reinstalling the application should restore normality. If there are any major problems with reinstallation, as a last resort a program can be installed to a different folder.

From scratch

The initial stages of installation are much the same if it is necessary to install Windows XP from scratch. As before, the computer is booted from the installation CD-ROM and it is only at the screen of Figure 5.3 that things change. It is a fresh installation that is required and not a repair, so the Escape key is pressed. This moves things on to the screen of Figure 5.21 where there are three options. Two of these permit the disc partitioning to be changed, and you will presumably wish to retain the existing set-up.

On the face of it, the best course of action is to make sure that the correct partition for the installation is selected in the lower part of the

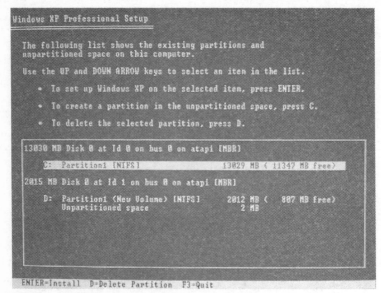

Fig.5.21 *Three options are available from this screen*

screen and then press the Enter key. However, this will produce the warning screen of Figure 5.22. Although you are not trying to install two operating systems on one partition, the existing Windows XP installation (if still to some extent intact) might give problems with the new one. After all, the idea is to completely do away with the old installation and start afresh with a new one. Therefore, the D key is pressed so that the partition used for Windows XP is deleted. This will delete everything in the partition, and a warning message to this effect appears when the D key is operated (Figure 5.23). Assuming that you have previously rescued any important data from the partition, press the L key to go ahead and delete the partition.

The previous screen then returns, but this time it indicates that disc C: has unpartitioned space (Figure 5.24). The next step is to create a partition for the new Windows XP installation, and to format that space. With the unpartitioned space selected in the lower section of the screen, operate the C key to create the partition. The next screen (Figure 5.25) enables the partition to be set to the required size. Presumably you will simply wish to reinstate the previous partition that used all the space

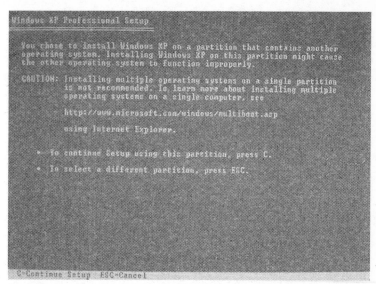

Fig.5.22 Remove the old Windows XP installation before proceeding

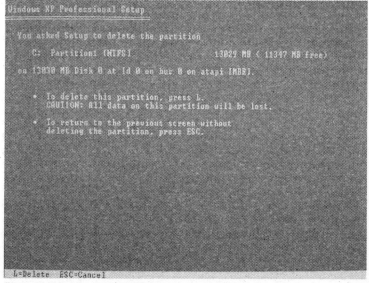

Fig.5.23 All data in the deleted partition will be lost

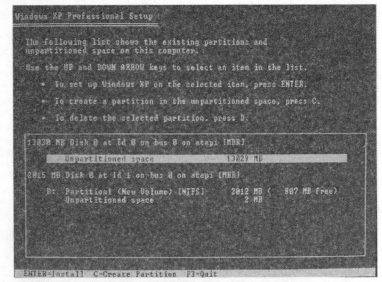

Fig.5.24 Disc C: now has unpartitioned space available

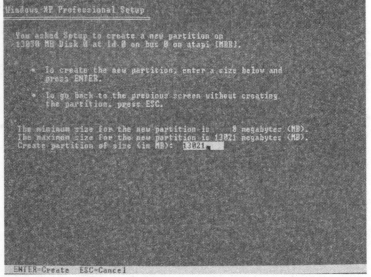

Fig.5.25 The partition will normally be set at the maximum size

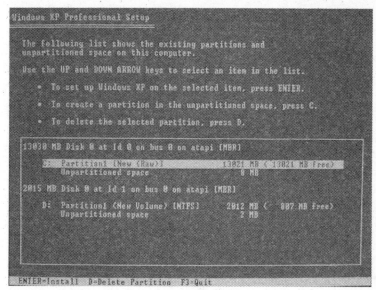

Fig.5.26 Drive C: now has an empty partition

just vacated. In that case, simply press Enter to accept the default partition
size. This returns things more or less to the way they were originally
(Figure 5.26), but the partition is now empty. It is not even formatted,
which is why it is described as "Raw" in the partition table.

Formatting

Next press the Enter key to go ahead and install Windows XP on the
partition. This produces the screen of Figure 5.27, where the desired
file system is selected. Unless there is a good reason to use the FAT or
FAT32 file systems, such as compatibility with another file system, choose
the NTFS option. This file system makes the best use of Windows XP's
capabilities. Having selected the required file system, press the Enter
key to go ahead and format the partition. This brings up the screen of
Figure 5.28, complete with the usual bargraph to show how far the
formatting has progressed.

Once the partition has been formatted, the Setup program will start
copying files to the hard disc, and thereafter the process is much the

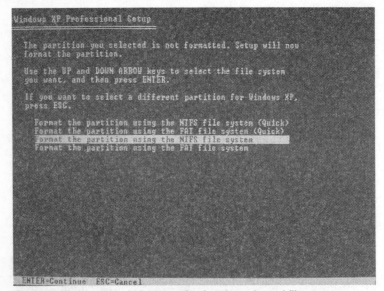

Fig.5.27 The partition is formatted using the selected file system

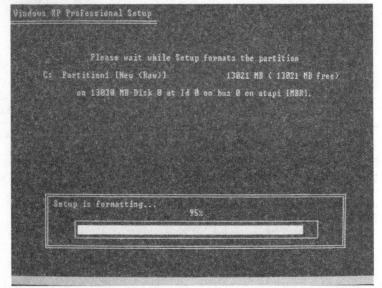

Fig.5.28 Formatting a large partition can take a long time

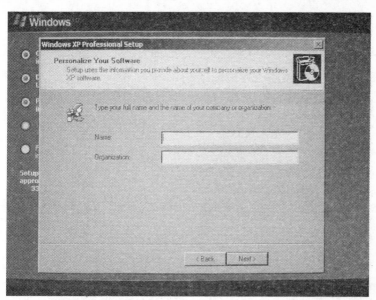

Fig.5.29 Add your name and (where appropriate) organisation in the textboxes

same as when reinstalling Windows XP on top of an existing installation. There are one or two differences though. As the original installation has been cleared from the hard disc, it is not possible for the new installation to read any information from it. You must re-enter your details when the screen of Figure 5.29 appears. The same is true of the passwords, and a new administrator password must be used when the screen of Figure 5.30 appears. Some general information has to be entered at the screens of Figures 5.31 and 5.32.

Near the end of the installation process there may be a small window that asks if Windows can automatically adjust the screen settings. Normally it is best to operate the OK button if this appears. Windows will then start in something better than the basic 640 by 480 pixel resolution. It will probably opt for only 800 by 600 pixel resolution, but this is still much more usable that the basic 640 by 480 pixel mode. After negotiating the usual login screen the computer should go into Windows XP (Figure 5.33). A window asking if you wish to activate Windows XP might appear, but it is probably best to leave activation until you are sure that everything is installed and working perfectly.

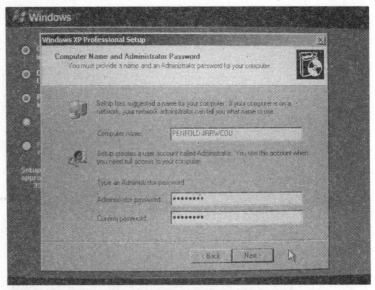

Fig.5.30 Type the administrator password into the textboxes

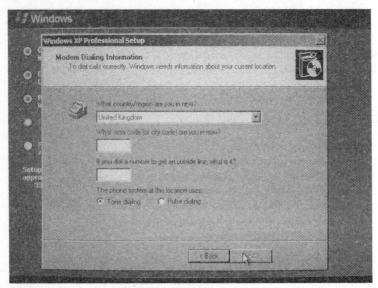

Fig.5.31 The modem dialling information is added here

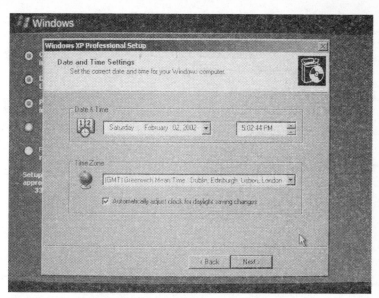

Fig.5.32 Use this window to set the time zone, etc.

Fig.5.33 Finally, you are into the newly installed Windows XP

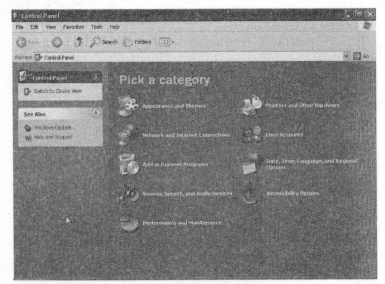

Fig.5.34 The default version of the Windows Control Panel

Hardware drivers

At this stage you have Windows XP reinstalled, but it is likely that some items of hardware will be either partially operational, or simply ignored by Windows. It is possible that Windows will detect all the hardware on the motherboard and install the necessary drivers. If the motherboard hardware is more recent than the version of Windows XP that you are using, then Windows is unlikely to have the correct drivers in its standard repertoire. It is virtually certain that proper video drivers will be needed. Even if the graphics card can be set to use high resolutions and colour depths, it is almost certainly using a generic driver rather than one designed specifically for the video card in use. Although high resolutions and colour depths can be used, the video system will probably be very slow in operation. There might be other items of hardware that Windows has missed completely, or has been unable to identify.

The first step is to go into Device Manager to look for any obvious problems with the hardware. First choose Control Panel from the Start menu, which will produce a window like the one in Figure 5.34. It is advisable to left-click on the Switch to Classic View link, which will change the window to the familiar Control Panel layout of Figure 5.35. This

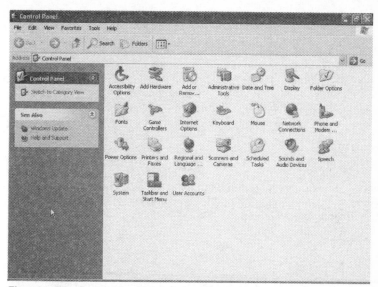

Fig.5.35 The Control Panel using the Classic View

provides easy access to the hardware settings and other useful facilities. Launch the System Properties window by double-clicking on the System icon and then operate the Hardware tab. Left-click the Device Manager button, and a window similar to the one in Figure 5.36 will appear.

The important thing to look for here is the yellow exclamation marks that indicate problems with the hardware. In this case the hardware appears to be trouble-free apart from the integrated audio system and the video card. It is worthwhile double-clicking some of the other entries to check that the hardware has been identified correctly. Internal modems can sometimes be troublesome, although the modem has been correctly identified and installed in this case.

If there are any problems with the main hardware on the motherboard, it is advisable to install the drivers for this hardware first. The main hardware means things like the IDE controllers and the PCI slots, and not integrated hardware such as audio systems and network adapters. Where appropriate, your PC should have been supplied with a CD-ROM containing the device drivers for the hardware on the motherboard. Next the video drivers should be installed, and then the device drivers for other hardware such as audio systems and modems.

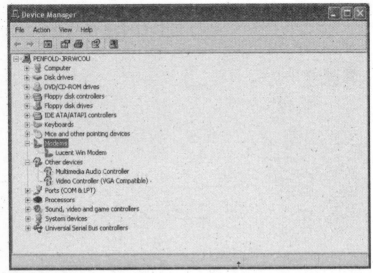

Fig.5.36 Check Device Manager for hardware problems

Driver installation

Windows has built-in facilities for adding device drivers, but few manufacturers seem to make use of these. Most hardware has its own installation program. This copies the device drivers onto the hard disc,

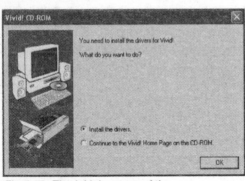

Fig.5.37 The initial screen of the installation program

and then the computer is restarted. The device drivers are installed automatically during the boot process. The instruction manuals for the hardware should give concise information about installing the device drivers, and the installation instructions should

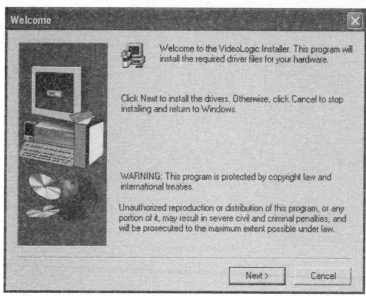

Fig.5.38 The Welcome window includes the usual copyright notice

be followed "to the letter". Note that the installation process is not always the same for each version of Windows, so make sure that you follow the right instructions and use the Windows XP device drivers. Fortunately, Windows XP will almost certainly display a warning message if you try to install inappropriate device drivers.

In this example there is no need to install any additional drivers for the motherboard's system hardware, so the first task is to install the proper video drivers. The installation CD-ROM will usually auto-run, as in this case, and

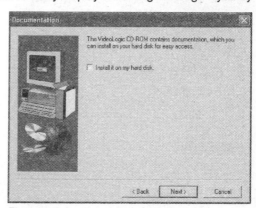

Fig.5.39 It is advisable to load the manual

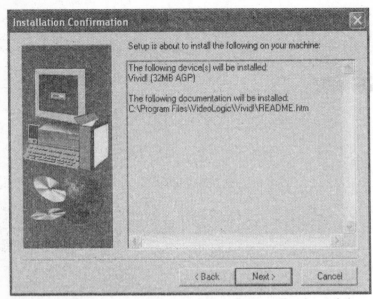

Fig.5.40 This window gives you an opportunity to review the options that have been selected

Figure 5.37 shows the initial window. This provides two options, and in this case it is clearly the default "Install the drivers" option that is required.

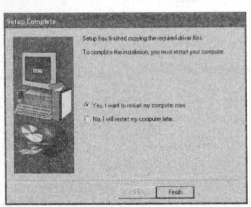

Fig.5.41 Restart the computer to complete the installation

The next window (Figure 5.38) has the usual copyright notice, and operating the Next button moves things on to the licence agreement. Left-clicking the Next button brings up a further window (Figure 5.39), and this one gives the option of loading the on-disc instruction manual onto the hard disc. Since the manual is unlikely to require much disc space, it is a good idea to install the documentation onto the hard disc when this option is available.

The next window (Figure 5.40) simply shows the options that have been selected, and assuming everything is in order it is just a matter of left-clicking the Next button to start installation. Once the files have been copied to the hard disc, the window of Figure 5.41 appears. It is definitely advisable to restart the computer immediately rather than waiting until later. This finalises the installation of the drivers and gives you an opportunity to check that they are functioning correctly. Installing several sets of device drivers and then restarting the computer might seem to be a more efficient way of doing things, because the computer only has to be restarted once. In practice it is not a good idea and is simply inviting problems.

Video settings

Windows will almost certainly detect that a new video card has been installed, and it will then produce the message window of Figure 5.42 when the reboot has been completed. Operate the OK button and then adjust the video settings using the Display Properties Window (Figure 5.43), which will be launched automatically. If the newly installed video card is not detected by Windows, the display settings window must be run manually. Launch the Control Panel, double-click the Display icon, and then operate the Settings tab in the window that appears.

Having set the required screen resolution and colour depth, operate the Apply button. It is likely that Windows is overestimating the abilities of the monitor if the screen goes blank or produces an unstable image. The screen should return to normal in a few seconds though. One way of tackling the problem is to operate the

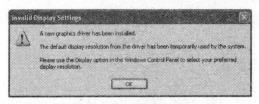

Fig.5.42 *Windows will probably detect the newly installed video card*

Troubleshoot button, which launches the Video Display Troubleshooter (Figure 5.44). By going through the questions and suggested cures it is likely that the problem would soon be solved. However, the most likely cause of the problem is Windows setting a scan rate that is too high for the monitor, and this is easily corrected.

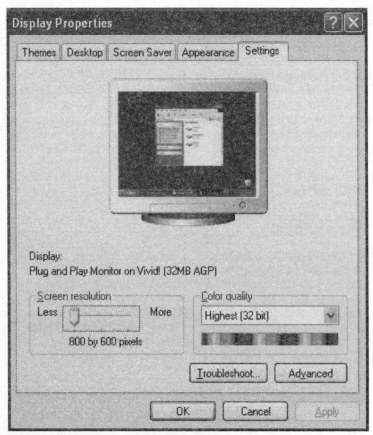

Fig.5.43 Set the required screen resolution and colour depth

First set the required screen resolution again, and then left-click the Advanced button to bring up a window like the one in Figure 5.45. Next, operate the Monitor tab to switch the window to one like Figure 5.46. Activate the Screen refresh rate menu, and choose a lower rate than the one currently in use. In this example the rate was reduced from 85 hertz to 75 hertz. Left-click the Apply button and observe the screen. With luck, this time a small window like the one shown in Figure 5.47 will be visible on the screen. If so, operate the Yes button to keep the new scan rate. If not, wait for a proper display to return and then repeat this process

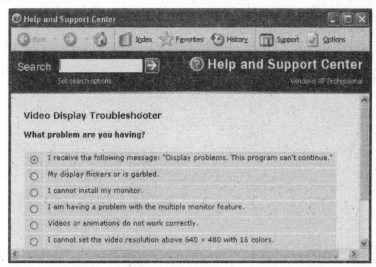

Fig.5.44 The Video Display Troubleshooter

using an even lower scan rate. Note that the maximum scan rate for a monitor generally reduces as the screen resolution is increased. Consequently, the higher the screen resolution used, the lower the scan rate that will have to be set.

Obviously the installation of the video card will vary slightly from one card to another, but most cards are installed using the general method

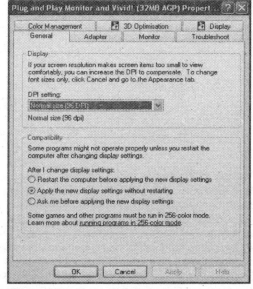

Fig.5.45 The Advanced Settings window

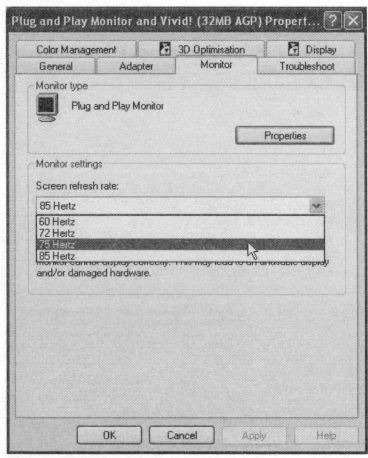

Fig.5.46 A lower scan rate should cure the problem

outlined here. With the video card installed and set up correctly, any further drivers that are needed can be installed. In this example it was only necessary to install the device drivers for the audio system. Device Manager then showed no problems with any of the hardware (Figure 5.48), indicating that the hardware was all installed successfully. With the hardware installed properly, it is then a matter of installing all the application software, undertaking any customisation of the software, and then reinstating your data files. The PC is then ready for use again.

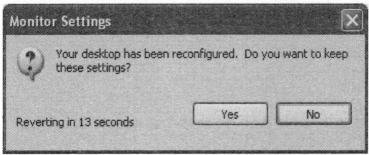

Fig.5.47 The settings return to normal unless the Yes button is operated

Correct channels

The installation CD-ROMs supplied with most hardware includes a Setup program. However, in some cases the disc contains device drivers but it does not include a program to install the drivers. If the instruction manual gives installation instructions, then follow them. With some low-cost hardware you are simply left to work it out yourself. One way of

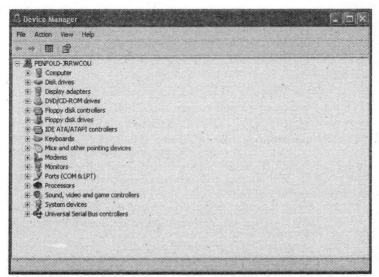

Fig.5.48 The problems with the hardware have been cleared

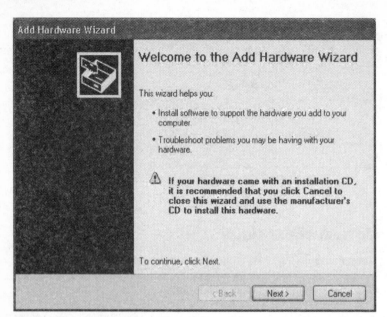

Fig.5.49 The Add Hardware Wizard

tackling the installation of hardware of this type is to launch the Add Hardware Wizard. Go to the Control Panel, double-click the System icon, and then operate the Hardware tab in the System Properties window. In the upper section of this window there is an Add Hardware Wizard button, and operating this launches the wizard (Figure 5.49).

Heed the warning notice about using the manufacturer's installation program wherever possible. Check the installation CD-ROM to ensure that it does not contain an Install or Setup program. If you are sure that it does not, operate the Next button to move the wizard on to the next stage (Figure 5.50). The Add Hardware Wizard uses the normal technique of suggestions and questions to (hopefully) find the right answers. The first screen simply determines whether the hardware is already connected to the PC. Unless the manufacturer specifically advises otherwise, the hardware must be physically installed before the device drivers are loaded.

Assuming that the hardware is already connected, the next window provides a list of the detected hardware. Obviously the entry for the

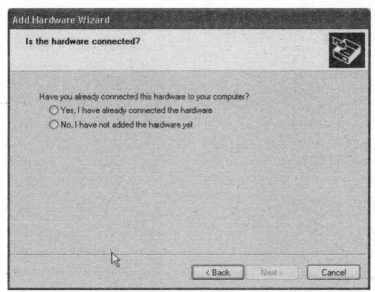

Fig.5.50 The first check looks for the hardware

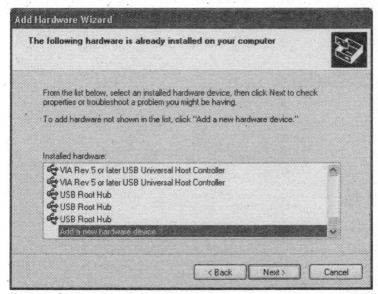

Fig.5.51 Select Add new hardware device

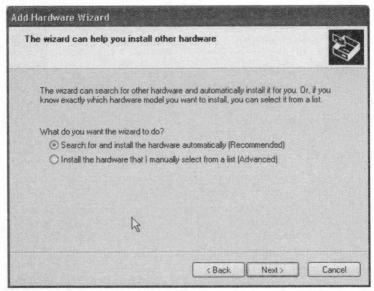

Fig.5.52 Manual installation is probably the best option here

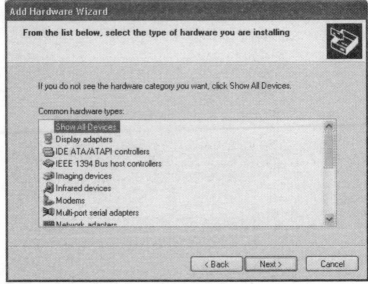

Fig.5.53 Select the correct category for the new hardware

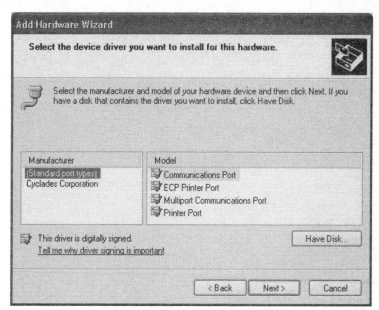

Fig.5.54 It is normally the Have Disk option that is needed here

hardware should be selected if it is found in the list. If it has not been detected and listed by Windows, select the Add a new device option (Figure 5.51). The next window (Figure 5.52) gives the option of installing the device manually or having Windows try to detect it. There is no harm in trying the detection method, but it is likely Windows is incapable of detecting the hardware if it has not done so already. Taking the manual route produces a window like the one of Figure 5.53. This gives a list of hardware types, and you must select the correct category for the device you are trying to install.

Moving on to the next window (Figure 5.54) gives a

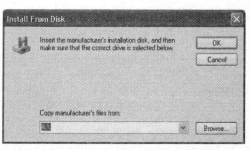

Fig.5.55 Give the location of the driver files

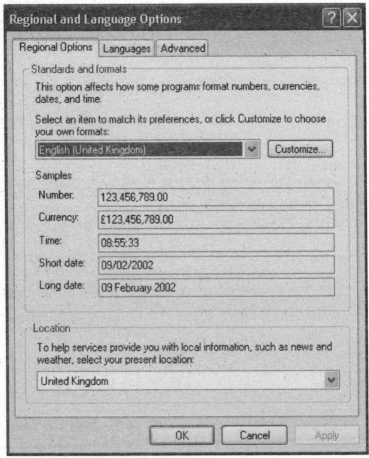

Fig.5.56 Check the the Regional and Language settings are correct

list of manufacturers in the left-hand section, and devices for the selected manufacturer in the right-hand section. Obviously you should select the appropriate entry for your device if it is listed, but this is unlikely. It is normally necessary to operate the Have Disk button, which brings up a window like the one of Figure 5.55. Either type the path to the disc and folder containing the device drivers, or use the Browse option to locate the drivers. Having pointed Windows to the drivers, the installation process then follows along normal lines.

Language problems

Back in the days of MS-DOS it was often quite tricky to persuade the operating system that you were using a keyboard having the English version of the English layout, rather than one having the US English characters and layout. The differences are quite minor, but they result in the double quotes and @ symbol being transposed. Also, the pound sign (£) tends to disappear or be replaced with the hash (#) symbol. Some of the little used symbols also disappear or become assigned to the wrong keys.

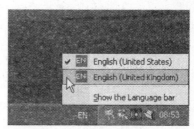

Fig.5.57 Choose the correct language version

Windows XP can suffer from a similar problem after it has been reinstalled from scratch. The obvious first step is to go to the Control Panel and double-click the keyboard icon. This is the first thing to try if the keyboard is not working at all, but with a language problem it is unlikely to be of any help. It is better to start by going to the Control Panel and double-clicking the Regional and Language icon. This produces a properties window like the one in Figure 5.56, which is essentially the same as the one that appears during the installation process. Check the various sections to make sure that the correct language is set.

If everything is correct, look at the bottom right-hand corner of the Windows desktop. Here there will be a button that indicates the language in use. This will usually be marked EN for English, but more than one version of the language will probably be available. Left-click the button to produce a small popup menu (Figure 5.57), and then select the English (United Kingdom) option. The keyboard should then function properly, producing the pound sign, etc. However, the wrong version of English

Fig.5.58 Choose the Settings option from the popup menu

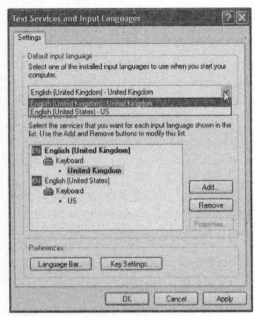

will be set as the default.

To correct this, activate the menu again and select the "Show the language bar" option. This removes the button and produces a small floating bar instead (Figure 5.58). Operate the tiny button in the bottom right-hand corner of the bar and select Settings from the popup menu. This launches the Text Services and Input Languages window (Figure 5.59). Use the drop-down menu near the top of the window to select the correct default language. Next operate the OK button, and then restart the computer to check that the default has switched to the right language.

Fig.5.59 Set the correct default language

User accounts

At least two user accounts would have been produced automatically if the original Windows XP installation was an upgrade from Windows 9x, the Administrator account and one for the name used during the upgrade process. Both accounts are assigned the same password. Some computer retailers supply their PCs completely set up and ready for use, sometimes complete with one or more user accounts installed. Only an Administrator account is produced when Windows XP is installed from scratch. Any other accounts you require have to be set up manually.

The Administrator account is usually reserved for making changes to the system or troubleshooting, since it gives full control over the system. As a minimum, you should install one additional account for normal

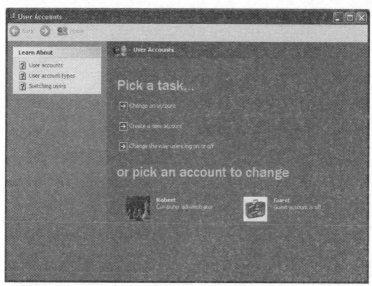

Fig.5.60 The initial version of the User Accounts window

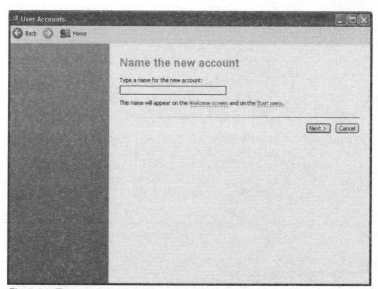

Fig.5.61 Type a name for the account into the textbox

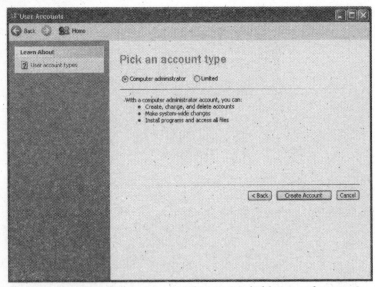

Fig.5.62 Use this window to select the most suitable type of account

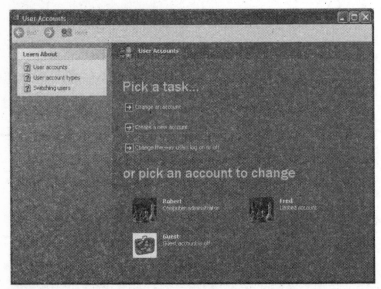

Fig.5.63 An icon has been added for the newly created account

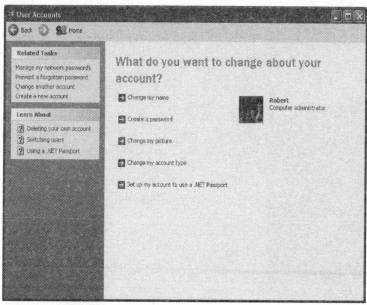

Fig.5.64 Operate the Create password link

use. The first step in adding a new account is to go to the Control Panel and double-click the User Accounts icon. This launches a window like the one in Figure 5.60. Left-click the link for Create a new account, which switches the window to the one shown in Figure 5.61. Type a name for the account into the textbox and then operate the Next button.

The type of account is selected at the next window (Figure 5.62). An administrator account provides freedom to make changes to the system, but these abilities are not needed for day to day use of the computer. A limited account is generally considered to be the better choice for normal use, since the restrictions reduce the risk of the system being accidentally damaged. Note that you might not be able to install programs when using a limited account. Also, some programs produced prior to Windows 2000 and XP might not be usable with a limited account. Consequently, there is no alternative to an administrator account if maximum flexibility is required.

Having selected the type of account using the radio buttons, operate the Create Account button. The original User Accounts window then

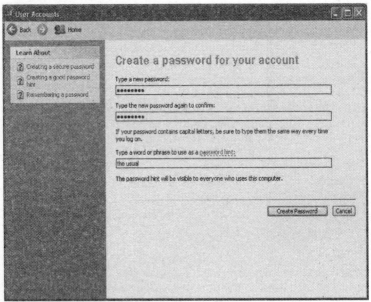

Fig.5.65 Type the password into the top two textboxes

returns, but it should now contain the newly created account (Figure 5.63). There are other facilities in the User Accounts window that enable the login and logout settings to be altered. By default, the Welcome screen is shown at start-up, and you simply have to left-click the entry for the new account in order to use it. Note that the new account will start with a largely blank desktop. Each account has its own desktop and other settings, so each account can be customised with the best settings for its particular user.

Accounts are not password protected by default. To add a password, go to the User Accounts window and left-click the entry for the account that you wish to password protect. This switches the window to look like Figure 5.64, and here the Create password link is activated. At the next window (Figure 5.65) the password is typed into the top two textboxes, and a hint is entered into the other textbox. The hint is something that will jog your memory if you should happen to forget the password. Next operate the Create Password button, which moves things on to the window of Figure 5.66. This window explains that password protection does not prevent other users from reading your files. Operate

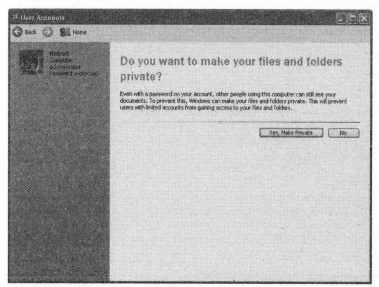

Fig.5.66 If desired, your files and folders can be kept private

the Yes Make Private button if you would like to prevent other users from accessing your files. This completes the process, and the password will be needed the next time you login to that account.

Points to remember

PCs that are supplied with Windows XP preinstalled are not necessarily supplied with a normal Windows installation disc. Windows then has to be installed in accordance with the computer manufacturer's instructions. The exact method of reinstallation varies somewhat from one manufacturer to another.

Installing Windows XP on top of an existing installation might speed up a PC that has started "crawling", but it is by no means guaranteed to do so.

Installing Windows XP "from scratch", with all the previous files removed from the hard disc should effect a cure to any Windows problems, including sluggish operation. Reinstalling dozens of programs as well could largely undo the benefits of reinstalling Windows.

When reinstalling Windows XP from scratch it is not necessary to reformat the hard disc prior to reinstallation. The appropriate disc partition can be deleted and then added again during installation. This clears away any trace of the original installation, but all data will also be removed from the partition.

Make sure that any important data is reliably backed up prior to installing Windows XP from scratch. Data should not be lost when reinstalling Windows XP on top of the existing version, but it is a good idea to backup any important data in case there are problems.

The process is largely automatic with either type of reinstallation. The user provides some basic information and then the Setup program installs the Windows files and sets up the essential hardware.

Once Windows XP has been reinstalled, some further work is required to get all the hardware properly installed, the screen resolution and colour depth set correctly, etc. Most hardware has its own installation routines and does not go through the normal Windows routes. Always install hardware in accordance with the manufacturer's instructions.

Install the device drivers for system hardware on the motherboard first, followed by the video drivers, and then any other drivers that are needed. Do not install application software until all the hardware is installed and working properly.

The "Text Services and Input Languages" window can be used to correct things if the computer defaults to using the US English keyboard layout.

Any user accounts and passwords are lost when Windows XP is installed from scratch. These can be rebuilt by going to the User Accounts window, which is accessed via the Control Panel.

Reinstalling ME

Clean sweep 2

The method used to reinstall Windows ME and its predecessors is rather different to the one used for Windows XP. It is perhaps a bit cruder, with no option of booting from the installation CD-ROM. Instead it is necessary to boot from a floppy disc that contains the MS/DOS operating system, or the Windows version of it. I would not recommend trying to reinstall Windows by booting into Windows. With Windows seriously damaged this will probably not be an option anyway. If you can boot into Windows but only in Safe Mode there will be no CD-ROM support, so it will not be possible to install Windows from the installation CD-ROM.

Where the PC can be booted into a largely working version of Windows, an installation started from within Windows will simply place the new version on top of the old one. As with Windows XP, this type of reinstallation will not necessarily repair any problems in the existing Windows set up, and it is unlikely to speed-up a bloated Windows installation. Of course, there is no harm in trying this method. If this fails to give an improvement then it is time to install Windows from scratch.

Whichever type of reinstallation you try, I would suggest booting from a Windows Startup disc in drive A: and selecting CD-ROM support when the menu appears. This method seems to be more reliable than starting reinstallation from within Windows. When installing Windows "from scratch" it is necessary to wipe the hard disc clean first. When installing Windows over an existing version, all the existing files on the hard disc are left in place. Simply run the Windows Setup program once the computer has booted into MS/DOS.

Although the description provided here is for an installation of Windows ME, the basic procedure is much the same for Windows 95 and 98 (first or second edition). Also, the process is much the same whether the operating system is installed from scratch or on top of an existing

Windows installation. If Windows is already on the hard disc it will be detected by the Setup program, which will then reinstall it on top of the existing Windows installation by default. Any Windows application programs on the disc should remain properly installed with the new Windows installation. Any data and configuration files should also be left unchanged.

Of course, if the hard disc is wiped of its contents and Windows is installed from scratch, all programs, data, customisation, etc., will be lost. Any important data must therefore be reliably backed up prior to clearing the contents of the disc, and you must be prepared to redo any customisation of Windows and the application programs. Do not proceed with this method unless you have backed up any important data.

Booting up

The first task is to boot the computer from a Windows Startup disc. If you do not have a Startup disc, one can be made by selecting Settings from the Start menu, then Control Panel and Add/Remove Programs. Left-click on the Startup Disk tab, operate the Create Disk button, and then follow the onscreen prompts. It will be necessary to make the disc on another computer if your PC can not even boot into Windows in Safe Mode.

With the Startup disc in drive A, restart the computer and with luck it will boot using the Startup disc. The BIOS settings are unsuitable if the computer ignores this disc and tries to boot from the hard disc instead. In this event you must go into the BIOS and choose a boot-up option that has A: as the initial boot disc and drive C: as the second boot disc. Any subsequent boot options are irrelevant, because the PC will boot before it gets to them.

Once the PC starts to boot-up using the Startup disc, you will be presented with a menu offering three or four choices. Select the one that boots the computer using CD-ROM support. This is important, because you can not run the Setup program on the Windows CD-ROM without the CD-ROM support. The CD-ROM support works with the vast majority of CD-ROM drives, including virtually all types that use an IDE interface. However, it does not work with all drives. If it does not work with the CD-ROM drive of your computer you must make your own boot disc with CD-ROM drivers. To make a boot disc, first boot the PC in MS/DOS mode. To do this you must operate function key F8 as the system starts to boot into Windows, and then select the appropriate option from the menu that appears. Once the computer has booted into MS/DOS, put a blank disc in drive A: and issue this command:

format A: /s

This will format the disc and add the system files needed to make it bootable. In Windows ME there is no option to boot in MS/DOS mode, but the computer can be booted using a Startup disc, and then this command can be used:

format B: /s

In the unlikely event that your PC has a drive B:, this will format the disc in drive B: and place the system files onto it. If there is no drive B:, the operating system will use drive A: as both drive A: and drive B:, and you will have to do some disc swapping when indicated by the onscreen instructions. The CD-ROM and mouse drivers should then be installed onto the floppy disc. The PC should have been supplied with this driver software, together with instructions for using the installation programs. Once this has been done the PC should be rebooted, and it should then be possible to access the CD-ROM drive.

As explained previously, it is necessary to wipe everything from the hard disc if Windows and the application programs are to be installed from scratch. The easiest way of achieving this is to reformat the hard disc. It will presumably be drive C: that will take the new installation, so this command would be used to format this disc:

format C:

It does not seem to be necessary to have the system files placed on the disc, and they are presumably added by the Windows Setup program during the installation process. The "/s" switch is therefore unnecessary, although adding it will not do any harm. Before formatting the disc the program will warn that all data on the disc will be lost. Heed this warning and only proceed if you are completely sure that all important data has been backed up properly.

Windows Setup

Once the mouse and CD-ROM drive have been installed, it should be possible to run the Setup program on the Windows 95/98/ME installation disc. If the PC was booted using a Startup disc, this command is all that is needed:

setup

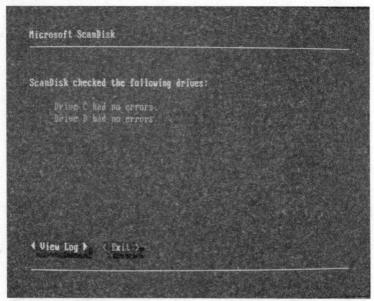

*Fig.6.1 The MS/DOS version of Scandisk is run automatically as the
initial stage of the Setup routine*

If the PC was booted using another boot-up disc, the CD-ROM's drive
letter must be specified in the command. For example, if the CD-ROM is
drive D:, this command would be used:

D:\setup

After a welcome message on the screen the Scandisk utility will be run,
and it will check for errors on the hard disc drives and any logical drives.
Assuming all is well, a screen like Figure 6.1 will appear. Press the "x"
key to exit Scandisk and (if necessary) operate the Enter key to remove
the onscreen message and go into the first screen of the Windows Setup
program (Figure 6.2). It is then a matter of following the on-screen
prompts to complete the Windows installation, providing the information
that is requested, as described in the next section.

Note that you can install the upgrade version of Windows 95, 98 or ME
onto a "clean" hard disc, and that it is not essential to load your old
version of Windows first so that you have something to upgrade.
However, during the installation process you will probably be asked to
prove that you have a qualifying upgrade product by putting the Setup
disc into the floppy drive or CD-ROM drive, as appropriate. Do not

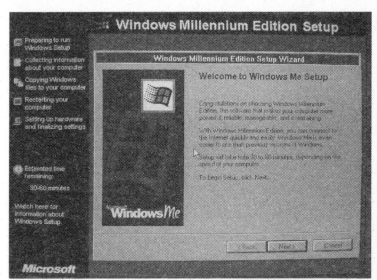

Fig.6.2 *The Welcome screen of the Windows Setup program*

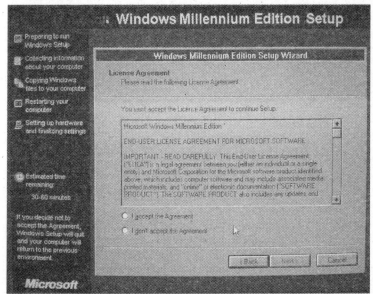

Fig.6.3 *You must agree to the conditions in order to proceed*

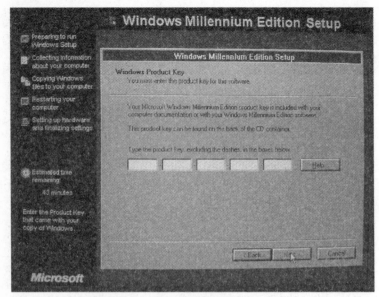

Fig.6.4 With an installation "from scratch" the product key is required

throw away or recycle your old Windows discs, as this could leave you unable to reinstall the Windows upgrade.

Installation

First you have to agree to the licensing conditions (Figure 6.3), and it is not possible to install Windows unless you do. At the next screen the Windows Product Key has to be entered (Figure 6.4). This code number will be found on the Windows certificate of authenticity and/or on the back of the CD's jewel case. Next you are asked to select the directory into which Windows will be installed (Figure 6.5), but unless there is good reason to do otherwise, simply accept the default (C:\Windows). After some checking of the hard disc you are offered several installation options (Figure 6.6), but for most users the default option of a Typical installation will suffice. Remember that you can add and delete Windows components once the operating system is installed, so you are not tied to the typical installation forever.

The Custom option enables the user to select precisely the required components, but this can be time consuming and you need to know

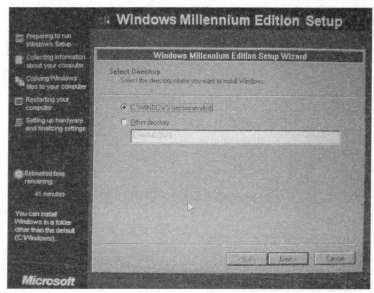

Fig.6.5 It is normally best to install Windows in the default folder

what you are doing. The Compact option is useful if hard disc space is limited, but with a new PC the hard disc will probably be large enough to make this option superfluous. The Portable option is optimised for portable PCs, and is the obvious choice if you are installing the system on a computer of this type.

At the next screen you type your name and company name into the textboxes (Figure 6.7). If an individual owns the PC, the box for the company name can be left blank. The purpose of the next screen (Figure 6.8) is to give you a chance to check the information entered so far, and to provide an opportunity to change your mind before moving on to the actual installation process. Operating the Next button may bring up a network identification screen (Figure 6.9). Where appropriate, make sure that this contains the correct information. In most cases the PC will not be used on a network, and the default settings can be used. Next the appropriate country has to be selected from a list (Figure 6.10), and then the required time zone is selected (Figure 6.11). This screen also provides the option of automatically implementing daylight saving changes. The next screen (Figure 6.12) enables a Windows Startup disc to be produced. If you already have one of these you may prefer to

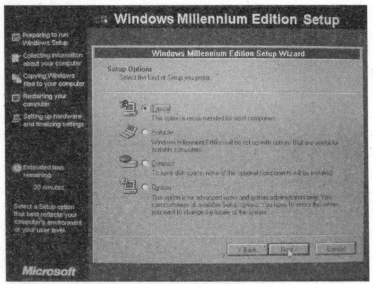

Fig.6.6 Four types of installation are available

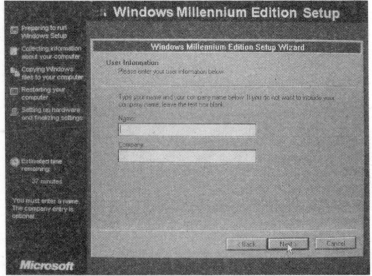

Fig.6.7 You must enter your name, but the company name is optional

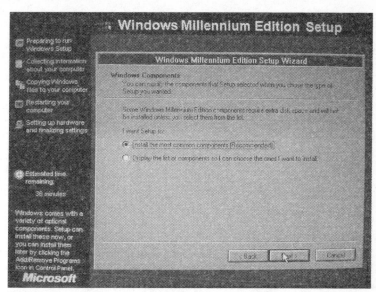

Fig.6.8 The "most common" components are normally sufficient

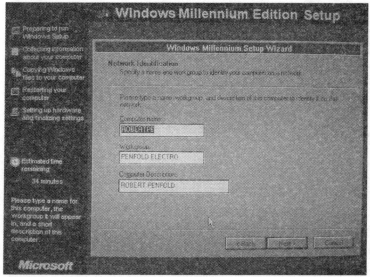

Fig.6.9 The network selection screen is not relevant to most users

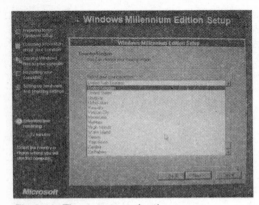

Fig.6.10 The country selection screen

skip this section by operating the Cancel button and then the OK button. Unfortunately, floppy discs are not the most reliable of storage mediums. If you only have one Startup disc already, I would suggest that you go ahead and make another one so that you have a standby copy.

If you are using an upgrade version of Windows, there will be an additional section in the setting up procedure where you have to prove that you have a qualifying product to upgrade from. The screen of Figure 6.13 will appear, so that you can point the Setup program towards the disc that contains the

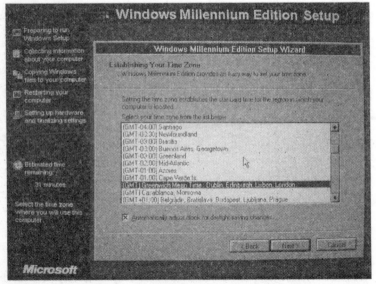

Fig.6.11 This screen is used to select the correct time zone

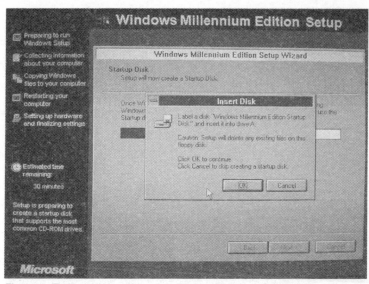

Fig.6.12 There is the option of making a Windows Startup disc

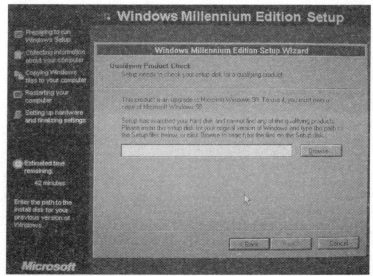

Fig.6.13 An upgrade product requires evidence of a previous version

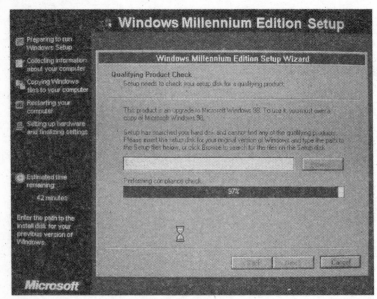

Fig.6.14 The bar shows how the (often slow) check is progressing

earlier version of Windows. To do this you will have to remove the upgrade disc from the CD-ROM drive and replace it with the disc for the previous version of Windows. Then either type the path to the CD-ROM drive in the text box (e.g. E:\) or operate the Browse button and point to the appropriate drive in standard Windows fashion. Note that this stage will be passed over if you are reinstalling an upgrade version on top of an existing Windows installation. Windows will find the existing installation and will deduce from this that you are a bona fide user.

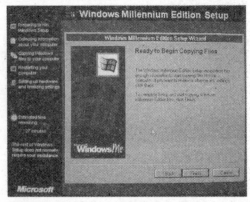

Fig.6.15 The main installation screen

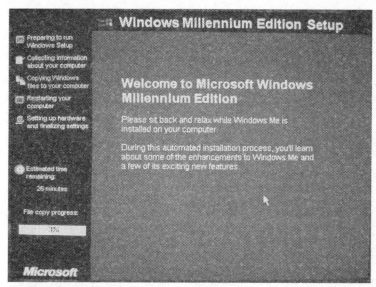

Fig.6.16 *Eventually the installation begins*

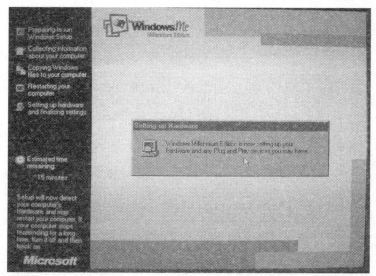

Fig.6.17 *The Setup program keeps you informed of what it is doing*

Fig.6.18 The password is optional

Having completed all this you will have finally progressed to the main installation screen (Figure 6.15), and from thereon installation is largely automatic. A screen showing how the installation is progressing will appear (Figure 6.16). The computer will reboot itself two or three times during the installation process, so if you opted to produce a Windows Startup disc during the initial set up procedure remember to remove it from the floppy drive. Otherwise the computer might reboot from the floppy rather than the hard disc, which would interfere with the installation process. In the later stages of the installation there will be further screens telling you what the computer is doing, and giving an indication of how far things have progressed (Figure 6.17). No input is required from the user during all this, so you can let the computer get on with the installation. The one exception is that near the end of the installation process you will be asked to supply a user name and password (Figure 6.18). Simply leave the password text box blank if you do not require password protection. Eventually you should end up with a basic Windows installation, and the familiar initial screen (Figure 6.19).

Fig.6.19 With installation complete, the familiar Windows screen appears

Sometimes the Windows Setup program comes to a halt. Either the computer shows no signs of any disc activity for some time, or there may be repeated disc activity with the installation failing to make any progress. The usual cure is to switch off the computer, wait a few seconds, and then switch on again. The Setup program will usually detect that there was a problem, and will avoid making the same mistake again. If the computer is switched on and off on several occasions, but the installation still fails to complete, it will be necessary to reboot using the Startup disc, wipe the hard disc clean, and try again. If Windows repeatedly refuses to install it is likely that the PC has a hardware fault.

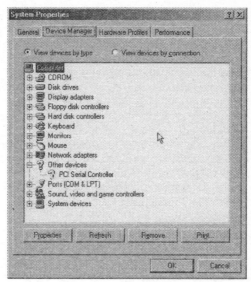

Fig.6.20 Use Device Manager to check for hardware problems

Hardware drivers

There will probably still be a certain amount of work to be done in order to get all the hardware fully installed, the required screen resolution set, and so on. Windows 95/98/ME might have built-in support for all the hardware in your PC such as the sound and video cards, but this is unlikely. In order to get everything installed correctly you will probably require the installation discs provided with the various items of hardware used in the PC. These discs may be required during the installation of Windows 95/98/ME, or they may have to be used after the basic installation has been completed. The instruction manuals provided with the hardware should explain the options available and provide precise installation instructions.

These days even the motherboards seem to come complete with driver software for things such as special chipset features and the hard disc interface. It is once again a matter of reading the instruction manual to determine which drivers have to be installed, and how to go about it. Get all the hardware properly installed before you install the application software. It is best to start with the drivers for hardware on the motherboard. Next the video drivers are installed and then any additional drivers for a soundcard, ports, or whatever.

Once everything is supposedly installed correctly it is a good idea to go into the Control Panel program and double-click the System icon. Then select the Device Manager tab to bring up a window of the type shown in Figure 6.20. Look down the various entries to check for any problems. These are indicated by yellow exclamation marks, or possibly by yellow question marks. Certain items of hardware will not be picked up properly by Windows, and often some types of modem fall into this category. The question mark in Figure 6.20 is caused by a Windows modem that the system is unable to sort out on its own. A Windows modem uses relatively simple hardware plus software in the computer to provide the encoding and decoding. Unlike a conventional modem, a Windows modem does not interface to the computer via a true serial port. It is interfaced via a sort of pseudo serial port, and it is this factor that makes it difficult to correctly identify the hardware.

If a problem is indicated, or an item of hardware is missing from the list, it will be necessary to load the drivers for the hardware concerned in order to get things working properly. This would be a good time to search the relevant web sites for updated driver software for the hardware in your PC. You may well find some newer and better drivers for the hardware in your PC. The hardware can be integrated into Windows using the Add New Hardware facility in the Control Panel. However, many items of PC hardware do not take the standard Windows route and have special installation programs instead. Read the installation manuals carefully and use the exact methods described therein.

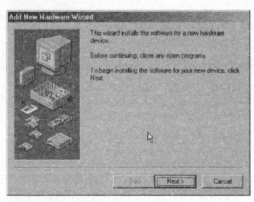

Fig.6.21 The initial Add New Hardware screen

Awkward hardware

Any awkward hardware will have to be added via the Add New Hardware facility without utilizing Windows's hardware detection facility. First Windows tries to detect Plug and Play devices, and then it can try to find non-

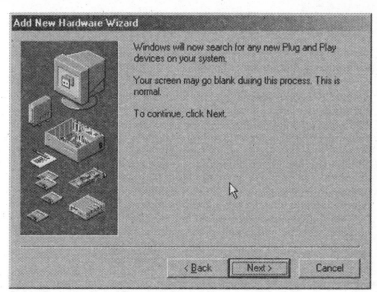

Fig.6.22 A search for Plug and Play devices is made first

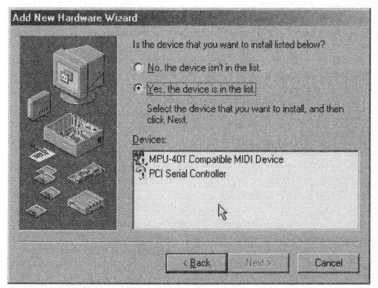

Fig.6.23 Any Plug and Play devices that are found are listed

Plug and Play hardware. Failing that, the new hardware has to be installed manually using the driver disc or discs provided with the item of hardware. The process is slightly different depending on the version of Windows you are using, but the basic process is the same with all three versions.

Here we will consider the Windows ME version.

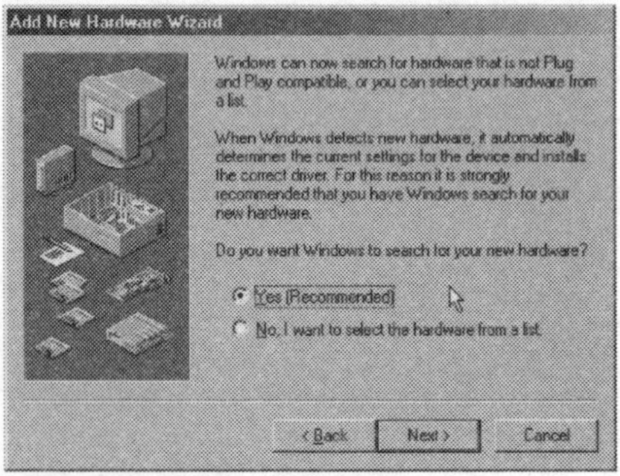

The opening screen of Figure 6.21 appears when the Add New Hardware program is run. Heed the warning and close any programs that are running before proceeding further. To continue, left-click on the Next button, which will bring up a screen like the one in Figure 6.22. This informs you that the program will look for Plug and Play devices connected to the system, and not to panic if the screen goes blank for a time. Press the Next button to proceed with the search. Eventually you

Fig.6.24 A search can be made for more Plug and Play devices

will get a screen something like the one in Figure 6.23, complete with a list of any Plug and Play devices that have been found. If the device you wish to install is in the list, leave the Yes radio button selected, left-click on the device you wish to install, and then operate the Next button to proceed with the installation.

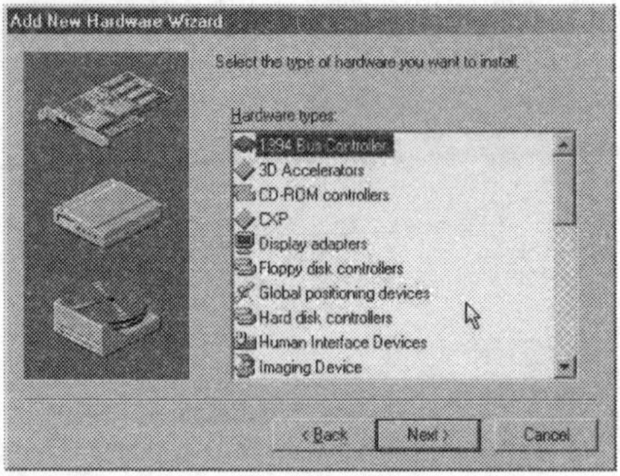

Fig.6.25 This screen enables the type of device to be selected manually

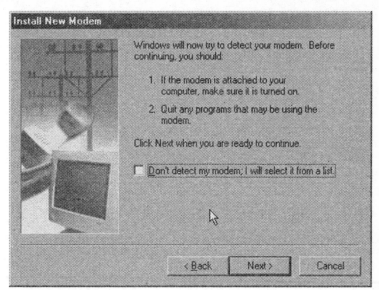

Fig.6.26 Even at this stage, automatic detection is still possible

Any non-Plug and Play devices will not be in the list, and it is then a matter of selecting the No radio button and operating the Next button. This brings up the window of Figure 6.24, which provides the option of having the program search for the hardware you wish to install. There is no harm in letting the program search for the hardware, although this can be quite time consuming. It is likely that a standard item of hardware such as an additional serial or parallel port will be detected, but it is by no means certain that anything exotic will be located.

If you decide not to opt for automatic detection, check the No radio button and operate the Next button. This produces the window of Figure 6.25 from where you can select the appropriate category for the hardware you are installing. A wide variety of devices are covered, with more available under the "Other" category. In this example the modem category was selected, and operating the Next button moved things on to the window of Figure 6.26. Here you are once again offered the option of automatic detection, but this does not work properly with most "soft" modems, so the checkbox was ticked and the Next button was operated.

If you opt for manual selection you will eventually be shown a window containing a list of devices, as in Figure 6.27. The correct device might

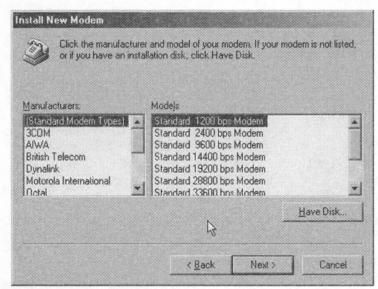

Fig.6.27 The Have Disk option is used if you have a driver disc

appear in the list, but with recent hardware or generic devices you will probably be out of luck. It is then a matter of selecting the Have Disk option, which brings up a file browser so that you can direct the program to the correct disc drive, and where appropriate, the correct folder of the disc in that drive. With the drivers installed, the computer will probably have to be rebooted before the hardware will operate properly.

Screen settings

Once the video card has been installed properly, the required screen parameters can be set. To alter the screen resolution and colour depth, go to the Windows Control Panel and double-click on the Display icon. Then left-click on the Settings tab to bring up a screen of the type shown in Figure 6.28. It is then just a matter of using the onscreen controls to set the required screen resolution and colour depth. To use the new settings left-click the Apply button. It may be necessary to let the computer reboot in order to use the new settings, but in most cases they can be applied without doing this. Instead Windows will apply the new settings for a few seconds so that you can see that all is well. Simply left-click on the Yes button to start using the new screen settings.

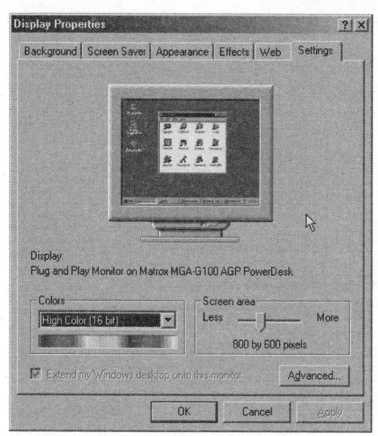

Fig.6.28 The Display Properties screen is used to set screen resolution, colour depth, etc.

If there is a problem with the picture stability then do nothing, and things should return to the original settings after a few seconds. This should not really happen if the monitor is installed correctly, because Windows will not try to use scan rates that are beyond the capabilities of the installed monitor. If a problem of this type should occur, check that the monitor is installed properly. In the Display window of Control Panel select Settings, Advanced, and then Monitor. This will bring up a screen like Figure 6.29, which shows the type of monitor that is installed. If the installed monitor is not the correct one, or is just one of the generic monitor types, left-click the Change button and select the correct one. If the picture is stable with the new settings but the size and position are completely

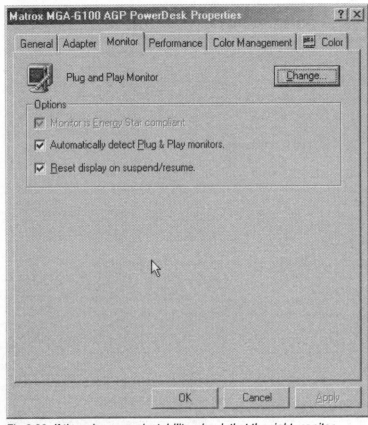

Fig.6.29 If there is screen instability, check that the right monitor is installed

wrong, there is probably no problem. It should be possible to position and size the picture correctly using the monitor's controls. Many graphics cards are supplied with utility software that helps to get the best possible display from the system, and it is worth trying any software of this type to see if it gives better results.

Disc-free ME

It has been assumed in this chapter that you have a Windows installation CD-ROM. Some computers are supplied with Windows ME pre-installed, and they do not come complete with a Windows installation CD-ROM. Instead, the hard disc has two partitions, with drive C: acting as the main disc and a much smaller drive D: containing the Windows files. There is usually a CD-ROM that can be used to recover the situation in the event of a hard disc failure, but this is not an ordinary Windows installation disc. With a computer of this type it is necessary to resort to the instruction manual for details of reinstalling Windows.

Manufacturers are able to customise the installation software to suit their PCs and any software bundled with them. Consequently there are differences in the installation procedures, but there should be a quick and easy way of getting back to a basic Windows installation. In fact some manufacturers provide a quick means of getting back to the factory settings. In other words, the computer will have Windows installed and set up correctly for the hardware installed at the factory. Of course, if you have changed the hardware configuration of the PC, it will be necessary to install the drivers for the new items of hardware.

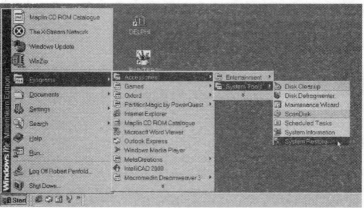

Fig.6.30 The System Restore program is deep in the menu structure

System Restore

Windows XP and Windows ME have a useful facility called System Restore. Unfortunately, this feature is not present in earlier versions of Windows. System Restore effectively winds the operating system back to the system settings of an earlier date where the PC functioned properly.

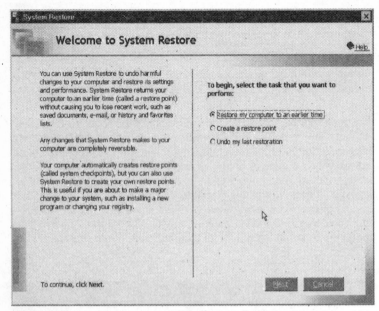

Fig.6.31 The welcome screen of the System Restore program

Hopefully, reverting to an earlier setup will return a faulty system to normal operation. Using System Restore will leave the data and configuration files intact. However, any programs installed after the restoration point will have to be reinstalled, and any changes made to the system have to be reinstated.

It can be useful to try going back a day or two using the System Restore facility if the PC suddenly seems to slow down for no apparent reason. This will sometimes remove adware, spyware, or other pests that are causing problems. It can also repair damage to the system that is causing it to run inefficiently. There is little point in trying this method with a PC that is suffering from a bad case of "Windows bloat".

Here we will consider the Windows ME version of System Restore, but it is essentially the same as the Windows XP equivalent, with a few minor differences in points of detail. The System Restore program is buried deep in the menu structure (Figure 6.30); it can be started by going to the Start menu and then selecting Programs, Accessories, System Tools, and System Restore. The program is controlled via a Wizard, so when it is run you get the screen of Figure 6.31 and not a conventional Windows

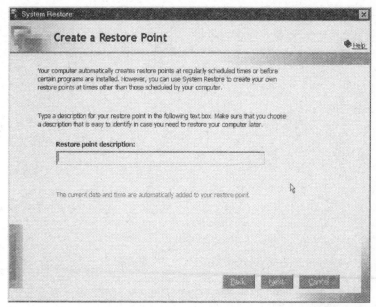

Fig.6.32 The system creates restore points, but you can add your own

style interface. The radio buttons give three options, which are to go back to a restoration point, create a new one, or undo the last restoration. When the program is run for the first time there is no restoration to undo, so this option will not be present.

As pointed out previously, the system will automatically create restoration points from time to time, but you will probably wish to create your own before doing anything that will make large changes to the system. Start by selecting the "Create a restore point" option and then operate the Next button. The next screen (Figure 6.32) asks the user to provide a name for the restore point, and it is helpful if the name is something meaningful. There is no need to bother about including a date, as the program automatically records the date and time for you. There will be a delay of at least several seconds when the Next button is pressed, and then a screen like the one shown in Figure 6.33 will appear. This gives you a chance to check that everything is correct before the restoration point is created. If everything is all right, operate the OK button to create the restoration point and terminate the program.

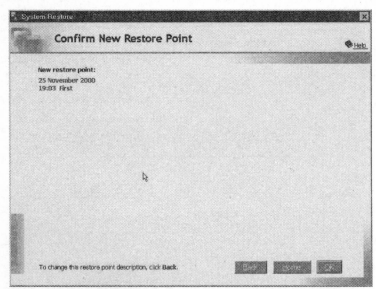

Fig.6.33 This screen gives you a chance to check your selections

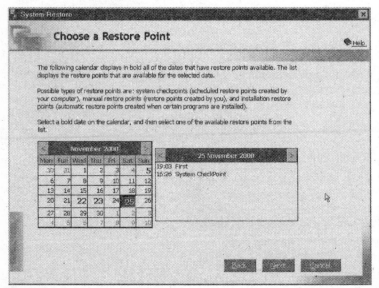

Fig.6.34 Choosing a restore point

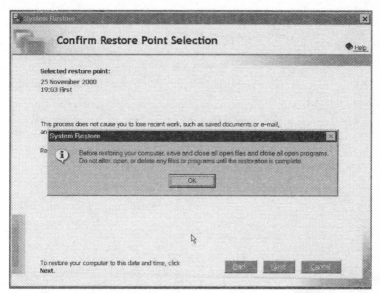

Fig.6.35 A warning message gives you a chance to change your mind

To go back to a restoration point, run the program as before, and select the "Return my computer to an earlier time" option. Operate the Next button, and after a short delay a screen like the one of Figure 6.34 will appear. If there are a number of restore points available you can use the arrow heads in the calendar to find the one you require. The dates on the calendar in larger text are the ones that have restore points. Left-clicking on one of these will show the available points in the screen area just to the right of the calendar. Left-click on the required restoration point and then operate the Next button. This brings up a screen and warning message, like Figure 6.35. Left-click the OK button to remove the warning message, and close any programs that are running. If you are satisfied that the correct restore point has been selected, operate the Next button and the program will begin the restoration process. A screen showing how things are progressing will appear (Figure 6.36). Heed the warning on this screen, and do not do anything that will alter, open or delete any files while the program is running. Just sit back and do not touch the computer until the program has finished its task. Once the restoration has been completed the computer will reboot, and a message will appear on the screen (Figure 6.37). This confirms the

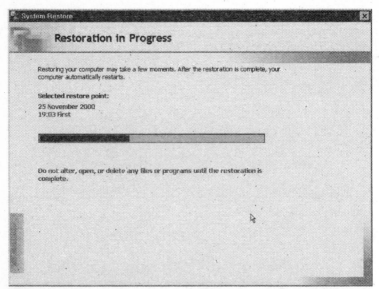

Fig.6.36 You can see how the restoration process is proceeding

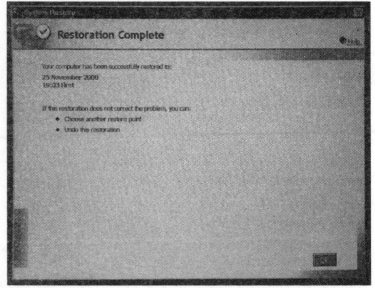

Fig.6.37 This message appears after the computer has rebooted

point to which the computer has been returned, and indicates the options if the PC fails to operate properly using this restoration point. Left-click the OK button to finish the boot process, and the computer should then have shifted back in time to the appropriate restoration point.

Points to remember

Whether reinstalling Windows over an existing installation or "from scratch" it is advisable to boot from a Windows Startup disc, opting for CD-ROM support.

The basic installation process is largely automatic. The user provides some basic information and then the Setup program installs the Windows files and sets up the essential hardware. Some further installation is then required to get all the hardware properly installed, the screen resolution and colour depth set correctly, etc.

Not all hardware can be installed with the aid of the automatic detection facilities. Manual installation of hardware drivers is not difficult, but where appropriate, make sure that items of hardware are supplied complete with a disc or discs containing the driver software. Some hardware has its own installation routines and does not go through the normal Windows routes. Always install hardware in accordance with the manufacturer's instructions.

PCs that are supplied with Windows ME preinstalled are not necessarily supplied with a normal Windows installation disc. Windows then has to be installed in accordance with the computer manufacturer's instructions. The exact method of reinstallation varies somewhat from one manufacturer to another.

Windows ME has the System Restore facility, but it is not a feature of Windows 98 or 95. Windows XP also has the System Restore feature.

Hardware
upgrades

Problems, problems

When getting your PC fully tuned and operating as quickly as possible does not provide sufficient speed there are two main options available. Either buy a faster PC or upgrade the hardware of your current base unit. Before deciding to do either, it is a good idea to question whether a faster PC is really necessary. Provided it is operating efficiently, a modern PC, even if it is not the latest "wonder machine", will take most computing tasks in its stride.

If you really have applications that would benefit from increased speed, will new or additional hardware make that much difference? I am producing this book using a far from new PC that has a 2.4GHz Pentium 4 processor with masses of memory. Software that "crawls" using this PC will certainly run faster on the latest hardware, but all this means is that it will "crawl" less slowly! You might need the PC to operate as fast as possible in order to obtain the most realistic results from the latest games, but with most applications a moderate increase in speed is either unnoticeable or of little practical value.

On the face of it, upgrading the microprocessor is the ideal way of giving a PC a new lease of life. A new, faster processor would give the computer increased speed, enabling it to cope with the increasing demands of modern software. The cost of the upgrade would be quite low compared to the cost of a new PC, and the speed increase would certainly justify the expense. Upgrading a processor is usually difficult though, if it is possible at all. Unfortunately, the older the PC the more it would benefit from a processor upgrade, but the lower the chances of it being feasible.

The problem with a processor upgrade is that as newer and better processors are developed, new and improved motherboards are also required. The most obvious problem is that of the processor requiring a faster clock speed than the motherboard can provide. Newly designed motherboards are often capable of going faster than the quickest of the processors available at the time. Although a motherboard is fitted with (say) a one gigahertz chip, it could be that it will actually work perfectly well with a 1.6 gigahertz type, even if that chip did not exist when the motherboard was made. On the other hand, the motherboard may have been struggling to accommodate the one gigahertz chip fitted when the PC was made, and there might be no upgrade path.

Even where an upgrade is possible, it will usually be necessary to upgrade the BIOS first, so that the motherboard recognises the new chip and can set the correct operating parameters for it. This process is covered later in this chapter. It is usually necessary to do some investigating at the web site of the relevant motherboard manufacturer in order to discover if there is an upgrade path available. Where there is, the updated BIOS is usually available as a free download from the manufacturer's web site.

In some cases there is no possibility of an upgrade because later processors used a different type of socket. A further complication is that AMD and Intel have gone their separate ways in recent years, and this means that different motherboards are required for each make of processor. If the existing processor in your PC is an Intel type, then there is no possibility of upgrading to anything other than another Intel chip. Similarly, if your PC currently uses an AMD chip, it is only possible to upgrade to another AMD chip, if an upgrade is actually possible. The only exception is where the mother board uses Socket 7 processors. However, PCs based on these motherboards now have to be regarded as obsolete and undertaking an upgrade is unlikely to be possible.

Options

The first task with a processor upgrade is to determine what processor is fitted at present. You will probably know this already if you are dealing with your own PC. When helping others with upgrades I have found that they usually have little knowledge of their PC's specification. The type of processor and its clock frequency are often displayed by the BIOS during the initial start-up period. The PC might be helpfully labelled something like "Pentium III 800MHz". Labels are not totally reliable because the PC could have already been upgraded, so if there is any doubt it is advisable to use some system analysis software to check. This type of software can provide masses of useful facts for a "mystery" computer.

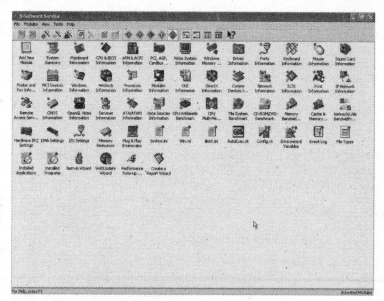

Fig.7.1 The initial screen of the Sandra system analyser

There are numerous analysis programs available, but this example will be based on the very popular Sisoft Sandra Standard, which is available as a free download on the Internet. The Sisoft Sandra web site is at:

www.sisoftware.co.uk/sandra

This program is available from several of the large shareware download sites such as www.download.com. Having downloaded, installed and run this program, a window like the one in Figure 7.1 is obtained. A number of program modules are available, with each one giving detailed information on a different part of the PC. In this case it is information on the processor that is required, which is obtained by double-clicking the "CPU and BIOS Information" icon. Incidentally, CPU stands for central processing unit, and it is simply an alternative name for the processor.

The CPU and BIOS Information program produces a screen like the one in Figure 7.2, and the processor information is at the top. In this example an AMD Athlon processor has been correctly identified. The processor is a 1.2 gigahertz type, but the program has correctly pointed out that it is actually running at 1.260 gigahertz. This is because the motherboard's clock frequency has been set slightly too high, which has resulted in slight over-clocking of the entire system.

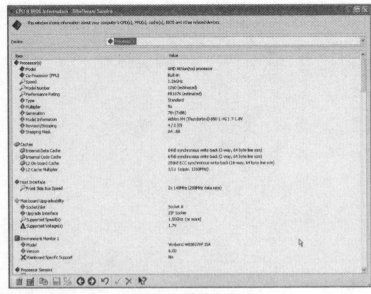

Fig.7.2 The program correctly identifies the processor

It is possible to get some basic information on a PC using the built-in facilities of Windows. From the Program menu select Accessories, System Tools, and then System Information. This produces a screen like the one of Figure 7.3. A great deal of useful information is available here, but it is usually too vague on the subjects that are of interest in the current context. The clock frequency of the processor and its manufacturer have been identified correctly, but there is no mention of it being an Athlon. The system manufacturer is given as VIA, which is the maker of the support chips. The motherboard is made by Jetway. For the present purposes it is better to use a program such as Sisoft Sandra, which will give the more detailed information that is required in this case.

To obtain information on the motherboard using Sisoft Sandra, close the CPU information window and then double-click the Mainboard Information icon in the main window. This launches a window like the one of Figure 7.4, and this shows a large amount of technical information about the motherboard; in particular, it provides the manufacturer and model number.

It has to be pointed out that the model number provided by the program can be different to the one used by the manufacturer when marketing

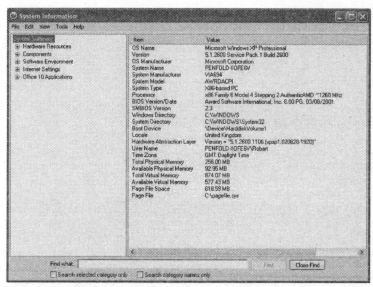

Fig.7.3 The Windows System Information Screen

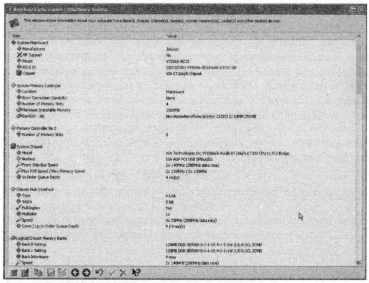

Fig.7.4 The Sandra Mainboard Information screen

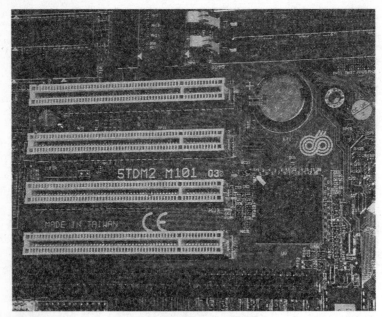

Fig.7.5 This motherboard is a Chaintech 5TDM2

the board. This complicates the next step, which is to go to the manufacturer's web site to look for information about the board and the availability of an updated BIOS. Where more than one type number is in use it is likely that the web site will give details for the board under both numbers. An Email to the manufacturer should soon get things sorted out if there is any doubt about the identity of a board. Do not try to update a BIOS unless you are certain that the new BIOS is suitable for your motherboard. Loading the wrong BIOS would almost certainly render the board unusable.

The type number of the motherboard plus the BIOS version and date are often shown near the top left-hand corner of the screen during the initial start-up process. It can be difficult to make sense of all the material displayed during start-up, but it is worth noting it all down and looking for a correlation between the type numbers on the manufacturer's web site and the numbers you have noted.

If all else fails you can try looking on the motherboard itself for the board's name or type number. This might seem to be the obvious approach, but

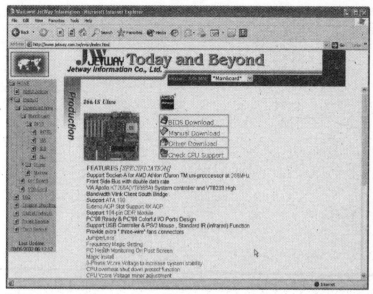

Fig.7.6 The page for the Jetway 866AS has useful links

not all motherboards are actually marked with this information. Where it is present, the situation will probably be confused by other markings. In the example of Figure 7.5 there is no manufacturer's name on the board, but the logo for Chaintech is present. The board is a 5TDM2, not an M101 or an O30.

A visual inspection of the board will probably reveal the name of the manufacturer and the model number for the board, but it might require a certain amount of sleuthing. It is worth looking through the documentation supplied with the PC. This might include a detailed specification including details of the motherboard. There could even be a copy of the instruction manual for the motherboard, which should tell you everything you need to know.

CPU compatibility

An Internet search engine should soon find the web site for the motherboard's manufacturer. Having found the site it is then a matter of looking for information about the CPU compatibility of the motherboard you are using. Most sites have charts that give information about the

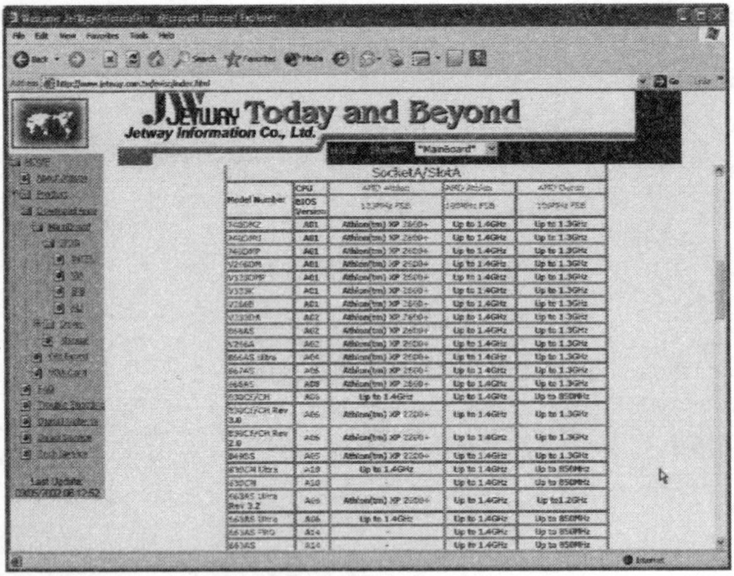

Fig.7.7 The CPU compatibility chart of Jetway motherboards

processor compatibility of each motherboard, and the various BIOS updates that are available. In this Jetway example I selected the Mainboards section of the site, followed by the VIA section, and then finally the page for the particular board fitted to the PC (a Jetway 866AS). This page of the site is shown in Figure 7.6, and it helpfully has links to a CPU compatibility page and a page for BIOS updates.

Checking the CPU compatibility page is the next step. There is no point in upgrading the BIOS unless it is possible to fit a faster processor. Upgrading the BIOS is something that should not be done unless it is really necessary. Left-clicking the appropriate link produces the compatibility chart shown in Figure 7.7. With the original BIOS it is not possible to fit anything beyond a 1.4 gigahertz Athlon processor, which is not a great deal faster than the 1.2 gigahertz chip already fitted.

The aim is to fit an Athlon XP2000+ processor, which actually runs at about 1.633 gigahertz. The higher clock rate and improved circuitry of this processor means that it provides something like a 50 percent increase in performance over the existing processor. Surprisingly perhaps, the chart shows that this motherboard can accommodate Athlon processors

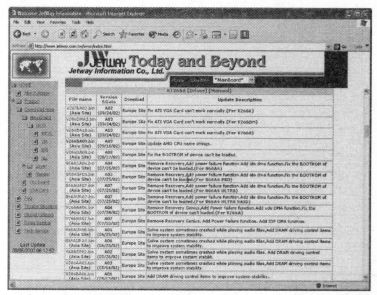

Fig.7.8 The list of BIOS updates. Make sure you download one intended for your motherboard

up to the XP2600+ if it is equipped with the latest BIOS. Although a substantial upgrade, a Athlon XP2000+ is by no means stretching the motherboard to its limits.

The BIOS page (Figure 7.8) lists the available BIOS updates, and it is simply a matter of downloading it in the usual way. The BIOS file is usually just the data to be blown into the EEPROM chip on the motherboard. A program is needed in order to write this data to the chip. Your PC might have been supplied complete with this program, but if not it should be available from the manufacturer's web site.

Some modern PCs can do a BIOS update from within Windows, but this is not the normal way of doing things. Most motherboards require the PC to be booted into MS/DOS in order to update the BIOS. There should be some documentation available from the web site and/or supplied with the PC that gives precise instructions for updating the BIOS. Read through this documentation a couple of times and follow the instructions "to the letter". Do not proceed until you are sure that you know exactly what you are doing.

Flash upgrade?

If you look through the specifications for motherboards you will often encounter something like "Flash upgradeable BIOS" or just "Flash BIOS". In days gone by, the only way of upgrading the BIOS was to buy a new chip, or pair of chips as it was in those days. Some of the ROMs that were used to store the BIOS were actually re-programmable, but only by removing them from the PC and putting them into a programmer unit. This was not a practical proposition for most users. New BIOS chips were very difficult to obtain and you were usually stuck with the BIOS supplied with the motherboard.

The rate at which modern computing changes makes it beneficial to upgrade the BIOS from time to time in order to keep PCs up to date, and not just to accommodate a processor upgrade. The BIOS sometimes has to be updated to cure compatibility problems with certain items of hardware. There could even be one or two minor bugs in the original BIOS.

With a modern BIOS there is no need to replace the BIOS ROM chip or to remove it from the motherboard for reprogramming. The ROM for a modern BIOS can be electronically erased and reprogrammed while it is still on the motherboard. This is why it is possible to download a new BIOS and a "blower" program and upgrade the BIOS. Of course, an upgrade of this type is dependent on the motherboard having the BIOS in Flash memory. Unless you are using a very old PC there is little likelihood of it lacking support for the Flash method of upgrading the BIOS. If you are using an old PC and the manufacturer's web site does not give details of BIOS upgrades, it is reasonable to assume that the BIOS can not be upgraded.

Write protection

If you get an error message such as "Flash type unrecognised" during the upgrade, this does not mean that the BIOS is a non-reprogrammable type. It usually just means that the Flash memory is write-protected, making it impossible for the upgrade program to alter its contents. Write protection is used as a means of preventing viruses and other malicious programs from corrupting the BIOS and rendering the PC unusable. It would be prudent to check for write-protection before trying to upgrade the BIOS.

The manual for your PC or its motherboard should give instructions for disabling this facility. In some cases the write protection is provided via

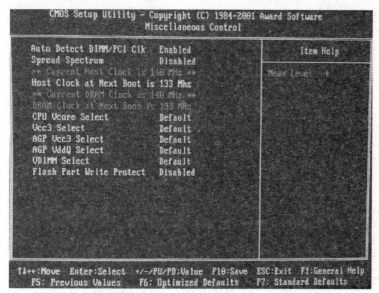

Fig.7.9 The BIOS can not be updated if it is write-protected

a switch or jumper on the motherboard. These days it is more usual for this facility to be controlled via a setting in the BIOS itself (Figure 7.9). There should be no difficulty in upgrading the BIOS once the write-protection has been switched off. Having completed the upgrade, it is a good idea to enable this facility again, so that the BIOS is protected from attack.

Risk factor

It is only fair to point out that a BIOS upgrade is a bit risky. As explained previously, you need to be absolutely certain that the data file you are using is the correct one for your motherboard. Using the wrong BIOS data file could easily render the computer unusable, and if it will not boot-up correctly it is impossible to restore the original BIOS. Another slight worry is that a power failure during the upgrade could leave the PC with a BI (half a BIOS)! With an incomplete or corrupted BIOS it is unlikely that the PC could be rebooted to restore the original or complete the upgrade. It only takes a few seconds to carry out the upgrade, so you would be very unlucky indeed if a power failure interrupted the

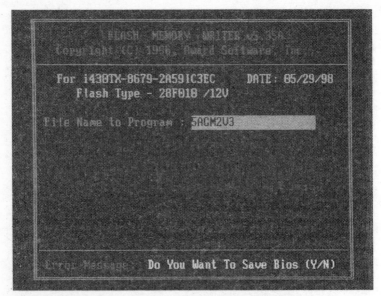

Fig.7.10 The BIOS upgrade program running from a floppy disc

process, but it is a slight risk. A serious error when upgrading the BIOS could necessitate the fitting of a complete new motherboard.

The upgrade program usually has to be run from MS/DOS, and is very simple to operate (Figure 7.10). After you have supplied the name of the data file for the new BIOS (including any extension to the filename) the program should give the option of saving the existing BIOS onto disc. It is as well to do this so that you can revert to the original BIOS if the new version proves to be troublesome. After you have confirmed that you wish to continue with the upgrade, the new data will be written to the BIOS ROM chip. Do not touch the computer during the flash upgrade, just stand back and let the upgrade program get on with it. The computer is then ready for rebooting and checking to see if the new BIOS has the desired effect.

Boot disc

The boot disc used when upgrading has to be a very basic type that does not run some form of memory management software such as

EMM386. Making a suitable boot disc from a system running Windows XP is very straightforward. Place a blank disc in the floppy drive, launch Windows Explorer, and then locate drive A in Windows Explorer. Right-click on the entry for drive A and select the Format option from the popup menu. This produces the window for the Format program, which looks like the one in Figure 7.11. Tick the Create an MS-DOS Startup Disc checkbox and then operate the Start button. A warning message will probably appear, pointing out that any data on the disc will be lost. Operate the Yes button to continue and create the boot disc.

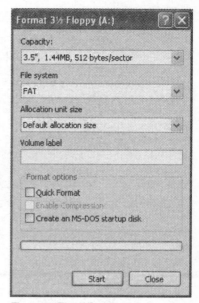

When the formatting has been completed, copy the BIOS data file and the upgrade program to

Fig.7.11 The Windows XP Format program

the floppy disc. Leave the disc in the floppy drive and restart the computer. With luck the floppy drive will be used as the boot drive, and you will be ready to proceed with the upgrade once the boot process has been completed. It is possible that the computer will simply boot into Windows. This occurs because the floppy drive is not set as the first boot disc in the BIOS. The BIOS therefore looks for the hard drive first, finds it, and then boots into Windows as normal. Restart the PC, go into the BIOS and set the floppy as the first boot disc, then save the changes and exit the BIOS Setup program. The computer should then boot into MS/DOS using the floppy disc in drive A.

Unfortunately, the Windows ME Format program does not provide a boot disc option. It is possible to make a Startup disc via the Control Panel and the Add/Remove Programs facility. However, this option results in various utilities being placed on the disc, and some of these could interfere with the upgrade process. Make sure that the Minimal Boot option is selected from the boot options menu during the initial boot process, and the memory management programs, etc., will not be run. It should then be safe to go ahead with the BIOS upgrade.

Switches

Most BIOS upgrade programs allow certain switches to be added after the command name. For example, it is possible to specify the file containing the data for the new version of the BIOS. Another common option clears the CMOS memory of all the BIOS settings. It is generally considered advisable to use this switch, since some of the original settings might be inappropriate to the new BIOS. Using this switch means that the BIOS will have no settings when the PC is restarted, and you must enter the Setup program so that the Load Setup Defaults option can be selected. If necessary, the defaults can then be "fine tuned" to suit your requirements. The date and time will have to be reset, but this can be done from the Windows Control Panel.

If the BIOS has been updated correctly, a new BIOS version number and date should be displayed on the initial screen at start-up. It is also likely that Windows will detect that there has been a change and respond with various messages to the effect that new hardware has been detected. Actually, it is just detecting the same old hardware and reinstalling the drivers for it. Once this reinstallation has been completed the computer should perform much the same as it did before.

Out with the old

With the BIOS successfully updated it is time to move on to the hardware side of things. Switch off the PC and remove the plug from the wall socket, or ensure the socket is switched off if you wish to maintain an earth connection. Then remove the outer casing so that you have access to the motherboard. There is likely to be a problem with access to the processor, which is often hidden away underneath the power supply. This is certainly a problem with the example PC, where part of the processor's heatsink can just about be seen underneath the power supply (Figure 7.12). It is impossible to change a processor without good access to the relevant section of the motherboard, so the power supply must be dismounted from the case. It should not be necessary to disconnect the supply from the motherboard or any of the drives. There should be good access to the processor if the power supply unit is placed on the drive cage. In this example, removing the power supply gave good all-round access to the processor (Figure 7.13).

Removing the old processor usually presents no problems, but the same is rarely true of its heatsink and fan. The heatsink normally clips onto the socket using the arrangement shown in Figure 7.14. The heatsink must be firmly clipped into place in order to ensure that it operates efficiently.

Fig.7.12 This processor is largely obscured by the power supply

Fig.7.13 Access is greatly improved by removing the power supply

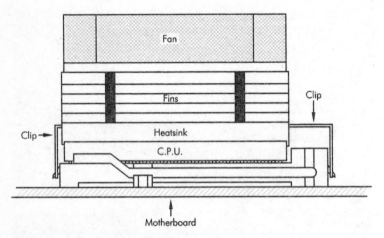

Fig.7.14 The heatsink and fan are clipped onto the processor's socket

The spring clip that holds it in place is therefore fairly strong. One side of the clip can be pressed down a relatively long way, but there is little movement on the other side. If you are lucky, pushing down on the side that has the greatest movement will result in it unhooking from the socket and the heatsink can then be pulled free.

In most cases it will not be quite as simple as this. Often it is necessary to use a screwdriver to gently lever the clip outwards as it is pushed downwards. This ensures that having been pushed down far enough it then moves out and free of the socket. Some heatsink clips can be very difficult to manoeuvre out of position because the clip is designed to press inwards quite firmly. Presumably it is done this way to make the heatsink easy to fit, with the clip tending to lock into place if it is pressed down far enough. Unfortunately, it makes things much more difficult when trying to remove the heatsink.

With some of them there is a notch in the clip that will take the blade of a medium size screwdriver. With the blade firmly fitted in place it is then quite easy to push downwards and then outwards to get the clip free of the socket. Take due care though. Slipping and gouging the motherboard with the blade of the screwdriver could seriously damage it. It is advisable to use a screwdriver with an earthed blade, as this will prevent anything from being zapped if it should come into electrical contact with the blade.

Do not get a case of "computer rage" if the heatsink is very reluctant to unclip. Trying to use brute force is a good way of damaging the

Fig.7.15 The Athlon processor can be seen once the heatsink and fan have been removed

motherboard and possibly injuring yourself in the process. In cases where the heatsink refuses to unclip there is little option other than removing the motherboard from the case so that you have totally unrestricted access to the heatsink. Try to get a good side-on view so that you can see what is preventing the clip from pulling free. What was previously an unsuccessful struggle can usually be solved in a few seconds once there is better access to the heatsink.

Some people advocate removing the motherboard from the case whenever undertaking memory or processor upgrades. The reason for this is that both types of upgrade usually involve pressing down on the motherboard, causing it to flex slightly. This puts the motherboard at slight risk, but it is unlikely to be damaged unless you adopt a "hammer and tongs" approach. Some motherboards now have provision for extra stand-offs around the processor, which greatly reduces the risk of damage occurring. Removing the motherboard and reinstalling it is a time-consuming business, and it is not entirely risk-free. It is an approach that I only use where there is no other way of getting adequate access to the motherboard.

*Fig.7.16 Older processors do not have the
metal heat pad*

With the heatsink removed you should be able to see the processor in the socket (Figure 7.15). The metal pad in the middle is the bit that conducts heat from the processor and into the heatsink. This is a feature of virtually all modern processors, but it is lacking on some older types (Figure 7.16). The four rubber pads are included on many processors, and they help to keep the underside of the heatsink parallel to the top of the processor. The heatsink would operate very inefficiently if it was allowed to keel over slightly. It is unlikely that any damage would occur, because most motherboards have protection circuits that shut down the system if the processor gets too hot. It is best not to put this type of thing to the "acid test" though.

*Fig.7.17 A "missing" hole ensures that the
processor can be fitted only correctly*

There should be a dot, arrow, or other marking near one corner of the processor. In the example of Figure 7.15 the top left-hand corner of the chip's case is missing. On the underside of the processor there is one pin "missing" in this corner, which matches a missing hole in one corner of the socket. In Figure 7.17 the absent hole is in the top right-

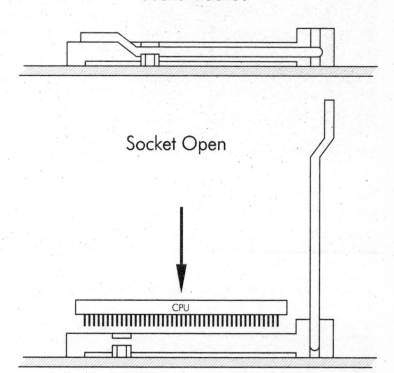

Fig.7.18 The lever is raised to open the socket and lowered to lock it

hand corner of the socket. The point of this is to ensure that processor can only be inserted into the socket the right way around. Make a note of the processor's orientation so that it is quick and easy to fit the replacement.

The processors in modern PCs are fitted on the board via a form of ZIF (zero insertion force) socket. This simply means that the chip can be dropped into place without having to push it down into the socket. Similarly, the chip can be easily lifted from the socket with no need to prise it free or to use any special tools. The socket has a locking mechanism that keeps the processor in place and electrically connected to the motherboard during use. In order to remove the processor it is merely necessary to raise the lever situated at one side of the socket to

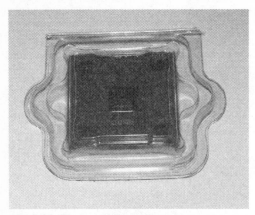

Fig.7.19 The new Athlon XP processor in its anti-static packing

unlock it, and then lift it free. Figure 7.18 shows how this system of locking operates.

Next, the new processor (Figure 7.19) is removed from its anti-static packaging and placed in the socket, being careful to get the orientation correct. Make sure that the standard anti-static handling precautions are rigidly observed when dealing with the processors (see page 301). Put the old processor in the anti-static packing so that it can be stored safely.

Fig.7.20 The Athlon XP processor installed on the motherboard

The new processor should simply fall into place but it might take a certain amount of manoeuvring to get it into just the right position. Lower the locking lever back to its original position once the processor is in position. If the processor will not fall into place, check that its orientation is correct.

If it still fails to drop into place it is likely that one of the pins has become bent out of position. Look closely at all the pins and if necessary use the blade of a small screwdriver to carefully straighten any that are seriously bent out of place. Proceed very careful and gently, because the processor will be a write-off if one of the pins is broken off. Fortunately, the pins on modern processors are quite short and strong, so there should be no problems with bent pins unless the device has been seriously mistreated. Figure 7.20 shows the new AMD XP2000+ processor in place in the example PC.

New heatsink?

Next, the heatsink and fan are fitted to the processor's socket. In general, heatsinks have become bigger over the years as more complex processors consume higher power levels and generate more heat. The latest processors actually consume less power than some of their predecessors even though they are more complex and operate at higher clock frequencies. This is apparently due to the use of smaller transistors that give greater speed with reduced power consumption. Even so, it is a good idea not to simply fit the old heatsink and fan onto the new processor.

The safe option is to buy a new heatsink and fan assembly that is properly matched

Fig.7.21 A fan fitted with a three-way lead and connector

to the new chip. Most processors are offered in retail boxed and OEM (original equipment manufacturer) versions. The retail boxed version costs more, but it is usually complete with a heatsink and fan that are guaranteed to be up to the task. The heatsink and fan are not included with the OEM version. The retail boxed processor is the safer option, and it is unlikely to cost much more than an OEM chip plus a heatsink and fan bought separately.

There is a potential problem with supplying power to the new fan since there is more than one way of powering PC cooling fans. The two most common methods are to power the fan from the motherboard via a three-way lead and connector (Figure 7.21), or to tap off power from the power lead for a drive (Figure 7.22). Most of the current fans have the three-way lead and connector for the motherboard, the third wire incidentally, enables the motherboard to monitor the speed of the fan and give a warning if it is too slow or stops. If the original fan is a type that taps off power from a drive, and there are no fan power connectors on the motherboard, you

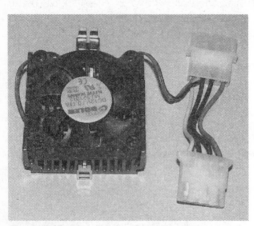

Fig.7.22 This fan taps off power from a
5.25-inch drive power lead

must be careful to order a new fan that has drive power connectors. Alternatively, it will probably be possible to fit the fan from the old heatsink in place of the fan supplied with the new heatsink.

Heatsink compound

As supplied, the underside of the heatsink will probably look something like the one in Figure 7.23. The paper tear-off strip should be removed prior to fitting the heatsink. Removing it reveals a square of heatsink compound (Figure 7.24) which helps to produce a good thermal contact between the processor and the heatsink. This pad is not needed for older processors that lack the metal heat conductor on the top, and it will not be present on heatsinks intended for use with such processors.

If the heatsink from the original processor is being used for the new one, any existing pad of heatsink compound will be largely obliterated. The old pad must be carefully cleaned away and then some new heatsink compound must be added in its place. Most of the larger computer component retailers supply at least one grade of heatsink compound.

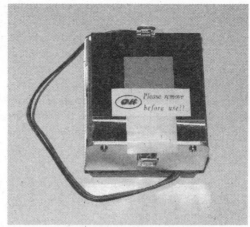

Fig.7.23 The heatsink compound has a protective covering

One of the cheaper grades will suffice. The expensive types are intended for use in over-clocking and not for general use. Very little heatsink compound is needed, so one of the small sachets will be more than sufficient.

The heatsink is fitted in place by first clipping the less springy side of the clip under the lug on the socket. With the heatsink accurately in position on the socket it should then be reasonably easy to press the other side of the clip down and into place. Heatsinks are usually much easier to install than they are to remove. It is advisable to pull firmly on the heatsink to make sure that it is reliably secured to the socket. There could be dire consequences for the processor if the heatsink should come

Fig.7.24 Here the heatsink compound has been revealed

Fig.7.25 The heatsink and fan in position on the processor

adrift. Figure 7.25 shows the heatsink securely fitted in place on the example PC.

Pentium 4

The method of mounting the heatsink described previously is the one used for most processors, including those that fit Socket 7, Socket 370, and Socket A boards. There are some processors that use a different type of heatsink. The Slot processors fall into this category, but it is unlikely that a suitable processor to upgrade one of these boards will be obtainable. Pentium 4 processors are another exception, and these are much more likely upgrade candidates.

The socket for a Pentium 4 processor looks quite conventional (Figure 7.26), and there is the usual lever that is used to lock or release the processor. Figure 7.27 shows the processor fitted into its socket. The processor itself also looks fairly conventional, but it is smaller than previous Pentiums, Athlons, etc. Around the processor there is a black

Fig.7.26 A Pentium 4 requires a different heatsink and fan

Fig.7.27 The Pentium 4 processor installed in its socket

Fig.7.28 The heatsink and fan for the 2.4 gigahertz Pentium 4

plastic mounting bracket that is used to clip the heatsink in place. This can be seen in Figures 7.26 and 7.27. The heatsink itself (Figure 7.28) is relatively large, and it has two locking levers, one at each end.

Fitting the heatsink onto the motherboard is very easy, and it simply presses down into place on the black plastic mounting bracket. If it is reluctant to fit into place you probably have one or both of the levers in the locked position, and correcting this should enable it to be pressed down into place. The levers are set to the locked position once the heatsink has properly clipped into place. The levers operate a cam mechanism that forces the heatsink down onto the processor. Figure 7.29 shows the heatsink locked in position, and one of the cams can be seen in the side-on view of Figure 7.30.

Fig.7.29 The heatsink and fan locked in position

Fig.7.30 One of the locking cams can be seen in front of the fan

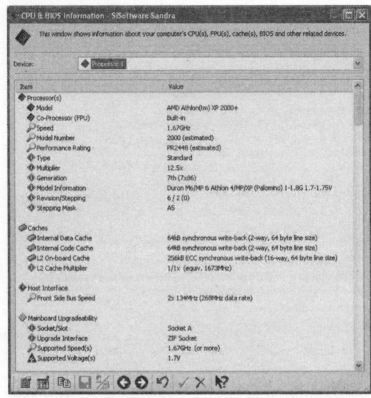

Fig.7.31 The Sandra analyser program shows that the new processor is present and correct

Jumperless motherboard

With the heatsink and fan in place it is time to do any reassembly such as refitting the power supply, check that no cables have come adrift, and then try out the new processor. It is assumed here that the motherboard is a so-called "jumperless" type that does not require things such as voltages and clock frequencies to be set via jumpers or switches on the motherboard. With an older motherboard it might be necessary to adjust some settings to produce the right operating conditions for the new processor. Some modern motherboards have a few settings set via switches or jumpers, and the front side bus frequency is often set in this way. The motherboard manufacturer's web site should have details of

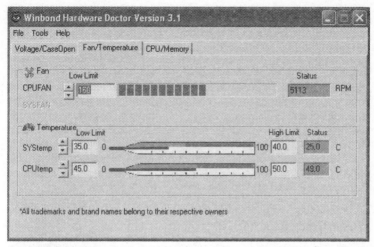

Fig.7.32 The motherboard's monitor program in action

the correct settings for each processor that the board will accept. Motherboard settings are covered in the next chapter, so refer to this if necessary.

With the example PC, the new processor was detected and the BIOS automatically configured itself to suit. The onscreen messages during the start-up procedure suggested that the new chip was installed and functioning well. This was confirmed using the CPU reporting section of Sisoftware Sandra. As can be seen from the results (Figure 7.31) the processor is operating at the correct speed of 1.67 megahertz and it has been correctly identified an AMD Athlon XP2000+. The system proved to be very stable with the new settings.

If the motherboard has a built-in temperature monitor for the processor, it is advisable to use this after the PC has been running for a few minutes. The BIOS often displays the CPU temperature during the initial start-up sequence, or POST (power on self test) as it is often called. This enables the temperature to be checked by restarting Windows and watching the screen carefully during the POST sequence. The CPU temperature can usually be checked by going to the relevant section of the BIOS Setup program.

Many PCs are supplied with a monitoring utility for the motherboard, and this provides the most convenient means of checking the processor's temperature, fans speeds, etc. Figure 7.32 shows the monitor program for the example PC, and with the processor at only 49 degrees Celsius it is operating quite coolly by current standards, and the upgrade has been completely successful.

It is only fair to point out that each processor upgrade tends to be a bit different to any other processor upgrade. With so many different processors and motherboards being manufactured in the last few years there are numerous permutations, with each one being slightly different in points of detail. Consequently, it is often necessary to use some common sense in order to get everything sorted out correctly. If your PC was not supplied with a manual for the motherboard, it is definitely worthwhile searching the manufacturer's web site for a downloadable version. Even the skimpier manuals should tell you any important facts that you need to know when dealing with the processor.

Overclocking

Overclocking is sometimes referred to as the "free upgrade", and it is the practice of using electronic components beyond their maximum speed rating. In practice it usually means running the processor beyond its rated maximum frequency, and with modern PCs it usually means running most of the computer beyond its normal operating frequency. Many motherboards have the ability to overclock the processor, but the manufacturers do not encourage this practice.

The motherboard's instruction manual will usually contain one or two disclaimers, saying something along the lines that the board has the ability to use overclocking, but the manufacturer does not condone this practice. This may seem rather two-faced, but the manufacturer is basically saying that the board has the overclocking facility, but you use it at your own risk. Overclocking the motherboard's chipset is unlikely to damage anything, but good reliability can not be guaranteed.

The processor's clock frequency is set at some multiple of the system's clock frequency. Most motherboards have the processor's multiplier set automatically. The BIOS detects which version of the processor is installed and sets the appropriate multiplier. The user has no control over the multiplier, and can not overclock the processor by setting a higher multiplier. Some boards use DIP-switches or jumpers to control the multiplier, or have this as an option. With these boards it should be possible to operate the processor at a higher multiplier, but there is obviously no guarantee that it will work.

The other approach to overclocking is to boost the bus frequency of the motherboard. A big advantage of this system is that it boosts the speed

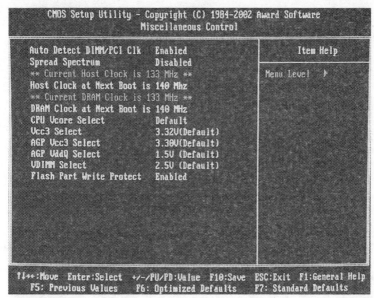

```
        CMOS Setup Utility - Copyright (C) 1984-2002 Award Software
                          Miscellaneous Control

    Auto Detect DIMM/PCI Clk    Enabled                      Item Help
    Spread Spectrum             Disabled
    ** Current Host Clock is 133 MHz **               Menu Level   ▶
    Host Clock at Next Boot is 140 Mhz
    ** Current DRAM Clock is 133 MHz **
    DRAM Clock at Next Boot is 140 MHz
    CPU Vcore Select            Default
    Vcc3 Select                 3.32V(Default)
    AGP Vcc3 Select             3.30V(Default)
    AGP VddQ Select             1.5V (Default)
    VDIMM Select                2.5V (Default)
    Flash Part Write Protect    Enabled




    ↑↓←→:Move  Enter:Select  +/-/PU/PD:Value  F10:Save  ESC:Exit  F1:General Help
       F5: Previous Values    F6: Optimized Defaults   F7: Standard Defaults
```

*Fig.7.33 With this BIOS the system frequency can be incremented in
          1MHz steps*

of virtually the whole system, not just the processor. The memory, video
card, and just about everything else will be speeded up by boosting the
bus frequency. Increasing the clock frequency of the whole system gives
a greater boost to performance than boosting the frequency of just the
processor by the same amount.

The main drawback of this system of overclocking is that by boosting
the speed of virtually the entire system it increases the chances of
something going wrong. While this method has a big advantage if it
works, it is less likely to work than simply boosting the processor's clock
rate. The overclocking will fail to work if any part of the system is unable
to handle the higher operating frequency. It is quite likely that even a
modest amount of overclocking will result in one of the components
failing to work properly.

This type of overclocking is usually achieved via the BIOS Setup program.
The PC used for the Athlon XP2000+ processor upgrade has the ability
to alter the motherboard bus frequency in one megahertz increments.
Before the upgrade it was overclocked by about five percent by having
the system bus frequency raised from 133 megahertz to 140 megahertz.

With the new processor installed I tried the same thing (Figure 7.33) and this did not seem to compromise stability. The processor still ran quite coolly at about 50 degrees Celsius or so.

Whether such a small increase in speed made any noticeable difference in use is another matter. Even with the more demanding application programs it is unlikely that a change of less than about 10 to 20 percent will be of significance. With the less demanding application programs it is unlikely that a huge boost in speed would be noticeable. Where things already happen almost instantly there is no real room for improvement.

When trying any overclocking technique you need to bear in mind that the increased clock frequency will produce increased power consumption and heat generation. It is unlikely that any chips will overheat if their clock frequency is increased slightly, and this certainly did not happen when the example system was moderately overclocked.

It is very unlikely that the processor or system as a whole will function properly if their clock rates are increased by a large amount. Therefore, overheating is not a major worry, but if a fault should occur when you are using a component beyond its normal maximum operating frequency it will not be covered by the guarantee. If you experiment with overclocking, you do so entirely at your own risk. You will have to pay to replace any components that fail, whether or not the overclocking had anything to do with the failure.

Memory

On the face of it, fitting additional memory will not make a PC run any faster. The processor will still run at the same speed, so surely the PC will run no faster than it did prior to the memory upgrade? When running simple application software this is probably true, and any increase in speed is unlikely. However, with the more demanding applications or when running several programs at once, increasing the amount of memory can give a significant increase in speed. When a PC has large amounts of memory, this memory is used as temporary storage space for data. If a PC has only a small amount of memory, it is soon used up and the hard disc is then used for storing temporary data. The disc is far slower than memory, and this is reflected in the speed at which heavyweight programs run on a PC with limited memory capacity.

Fitting additional memory to a PC is fairly straightforward, but determining the type of memory required can be problematic. Several types of

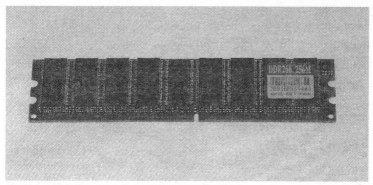

Fig.7.34 This is a 184-pin PC2100 DDR DIMM

memory module have been used in PCs over the years, and there are numerous variations on each type. A few older PCs actually have sockets for two different types of memory, but they can usually take only one type or the other, not a mixture of the two. Computers of this vintage have probably reached the stage where it is not worth spending money on an upgrade. Also, the older types of memory are generally hard to track down and expensive when you do manage to find the right type.

Modern PCs mainly use 184-pin DIMMs (dual in-line memory modules), but some Pentium 4 based PCs use so-called RIMMs from Rambus Inc. These two types of memory are shown in Figures 7.34 and 7.35 respectively. Older PCs use 168-pin DIMMs (Figure 7.36), which are slightly smaller versions of the modern 184-pin variety. A few of the larger PC manufacturers have been known to "do their own thing" with memory modules,

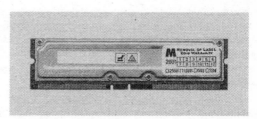

Fig.7.35 A Rambus memory module (RIMM)

and in these cases it is usually necessary to buy the special modules from the PC manufacturer, or have them upgrade the memory for you.

It is important to realise that not all memory modules of the same general type are the same. In addition to different capacities, various memory

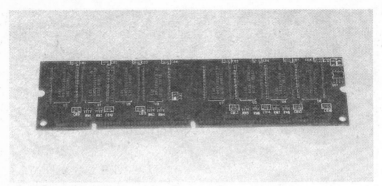

Fig.7.36 A 168-pin DIMM (dual in-line memory module)

modules have been produced using different memory technologies. Thankfully, this kind of thing is less common these days. Most types of memory module can be obtained in more than one speed. Modern DIMMs contain DDR (double data rate) memory chips, which have a speed rating that reflects the bandwidth in megabits per second. These are the memory modules called PC1600, PC2100, PC2700, etc., in the catalogues. In general, fitting a faster module than the PC requires will give satisfactory results, but it is preferable to be cautious and use the right type. With a few exceptions, prices tend to be higher for the faster modules, so there is no point in using a faster module unless there are supply problems with the correct type.

Before buying extra memory it is clearly essential to determine the type of memory used in the PC and its speed. There are programs that will produce a list of a PC's hardware, but one of these will probably not give a sufficiently detailed description of the memory fitted in the PC. The paperwork supplied with the PC is likely to prove more helpful. This should give precise details about the amount and type of memory fitted.

Next you must ascertain the maximum amount of memory that the motherboard can accommodate. Modern PCs can mostly accommodate a few gigabytes of memory, but with older units there could be a limit of 512 megabytes or even less. Do not make the common mistake of assuming that the computer can accommodate any variety of memory modules of the correct type and speed. Particularly with older base units, modern high capacity modules could be unsuitable. For example, a PC that can have up to 512 megabytes of memory and that has three memory holders might require two 256 megabyte modules or two 128

Fig.7.37 A DIMM has a polarising key than matches a bar in the socket

megabyte and one 256 megabyte type. Using one 512 megabyte module might not be an option.

It will sometimes be necessary to remove one or more of the existing memory modules in order to increase the memory capacity of the computer. With only a few memory sockets on the motherboard, you can not go on increasing the amount of memory fitted by simply adding more and more memory modules. It therefore pays to think ahead and fit large memory modules, rather than working your way up to high capacity modules, wasting a lot of smaller ones along the way. You really need to look at all the possible upgrade options, and cost them. Where possible, avoid scrapping any of the existing memory modules, but be prepared to do so if there is no practical alternative.

Fitting memory

Fitting numerous RAM chips into their sockets is a tedious task, and it is easy to accidentally buckle one of the pins or to fit a chip around the wrong way. Memory modules were produced in an attempt to make fitting and removing memory much easier, and something that practically

Fig.7.38 There are actually two polarising keys in each DIMM

anyone could undertake. Fitting DIMMs is certainly very easy, and it is impossible to fit them the wrong way round because the circuit board has a polarising "key". This is just an off-centre notch cut in the circuit board that matches a bar in the DIMM socket (see Figure 7.37). In fact there are two of these keys (Figure 7.38), and they are apparently in

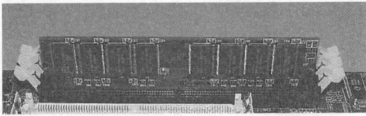

Fig.7.39 A DIMM fitted into its socket but not yet locked into place

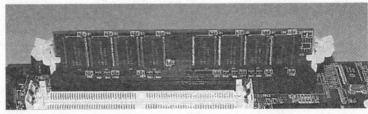

Fig.7.40 Here the DIMM has been fully pushed down into position

slightly different positions depending on the supply voltage of the module and the type of RAM fitted. This should make it impossible to fit a DIMM of the wrong type.

When fitting a DIMM, always look for the notch that is well off centre. This, plus the bar in the socket, makes it clear which way round the module must be fitted. The module simply drops into place vertically and as it is pressed down into position the plastic lever at each end of the socket should start to close up. Pressing both levers into the vertical position should securely lock the module in place. Of course, the two levers must be set fully downwards and outwards before you start to insert the module.

Do not try to fit these modules by simply pressing hard until they click into place. They will probably fit into place correctly using this method, but it risks damaging the motherboard. Operating the levers enables modules to be fully inserted into their sockets without having to exert much force on the modules and motherboard. Figures 7.39 and 7.40 respectively show a DIMM before and after it has been locked into place. To remove a DIMM, simply press the two levers outwards as far as they will go. This should unlock the memory module so that it can be lifted free of the socket. Always observe the standard static handling precautions when dealing with memory modules (see page 301)

Video card

A "bog standard" video system is more than adequate for many applications, but for games and certain specialist uses it is necessary to have a top quality video card. Indeed, no matter how fast the rest of the PC happens to be, without a video system of adequate quality it will be impossible to run some applications in a satisfactory manner. In most cases a video upgrade is just a matter of swapping the existing video card for a newer and better type, but there are a few points that have to be considered before purchasing a new card.

Does the PC actually have a slot for a video card? Many budget PCs have an integrated video system, which means that the video circuits are included on the main board and there is no video card as such. The fact that the existing video circuits are part of the motherboard does not necessarily mean that there is no AGP (Accelerated Graphics Port) slot for a video card. Many boards that have integrated video circuits also have an AGP expansion slot. However, in order to use the AGP slot it is normally necessary to manually switch off the built-in video circuits.

Fig.7.41 The cut-out for the locking lever at the front of an AGP card

This is sometimes achieved via a jumper or switch on the main board, but these days it is more likely to be accomplished via the BIOS Setup program. Either way, the documentation supplied with the PC should provide information about disabling the built-in video adaptor. Failing that, the PC manufacturer's customer support service should be able to supply the information you require.

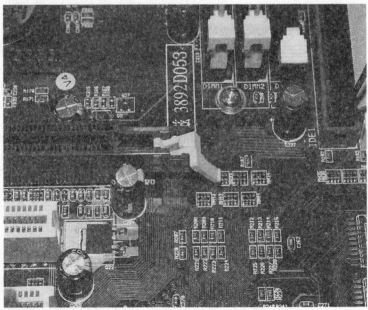

Fig.7.42 The locking lever of an AGP expansion slot

Fig.7.43 Here the video card has been locked into the AGP slot

You have to bear in mind that AGP slots and cards have various speed ratings (1x, 2x, etc.), and that some slots are incompatible with cards of certain speeds. Also, if you run the latest high performance video card in an older PC it is quite likely that the card will be running below its maximum speed rating. There should be no problem provided it is designed to run at the lower speed, but the card will obviously provide reduced performance if used in this way.

With the PC's outer casing removed it should not be difficult to spot the video card. This is the only type of expansion card that uses an AGP slot. It is usually the slot nearest the port cluster on the rear of the PC, and it is set further forward than the other expansion slots. The metal bracket at the rear of the card is bolted to the rear of the case, so this bolt must be removed before the old video card can be pulled free.

Modern AGP slots have a locking lever at the front of the slot, which avoids the common problem of the card skewing slightly when the mounting bracket is bolted to the case. There are a lot of terminals crammed into a small space on an AGP connector, so even a slight skewing of the card could cause problems. The locking mechanism in

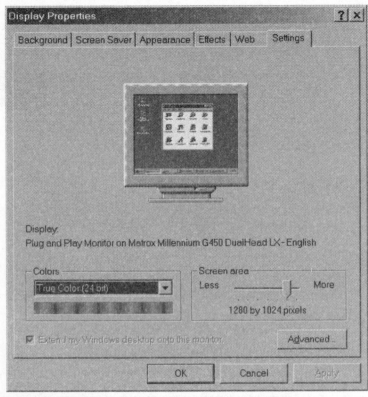

Fig.7.44 Adjusting the colour depth and screen resolution

the AGP slot latches into a cut-out in the front of the video card's connector (Figure 7.41). This is rather like the locking mechanism used at each end of a DIMM, and the locking lever on the slot certainly looks very similar (Figure 7.42). However, only one locking mechanism is used for an AGP card. Make sure that the lever is in the open (down) position before attempting to remove or fit the video card. The lever will probably move into the locking position automatically when the video card is inserted into the AGP slot, but if necessary it can be given a little help. Figure 7.43 shows an AGP card locked into its expansion slot, with the lever in the locked (up) position.

At one time it was necessary to uninstall the old card from Windows before installing the new card, but this should not be necessary with a modern version of Windows. In theory there should be the usual Plug N

Play installation process the first time the PC is booted with the new card fitted. However, in practice it is quite common for the card manufacturer to recommend a different approach, so it is important to read the installation information supplied with the card and follow it "to the letter".

It will almost certainly be necessary to manually return the screen resolution and colour depth settings to their original values. From the Windows Control Panel select Display and then operate the Settings tab on the new window that appears. This gives a window like the one in Figure 7.44. Here the required screen resolution is selected using the slider control and the colour depth is chosen via the Colors menu.

Shocking truth

When dealing with a PC's hardware it is essential to bear in mind that many modern semiconductors are vulnerable to damage by static electricity, as is any equipment that incorporates these devices. I think it is worth making the point that it does not take a large static charge complete with sparks and "cracking" sounds to damage sensitive electronic components. Large static discharges of that type are sufficient to damage most modern semiconductor components, and not just the more sensitive ones.

Many of the components used in computing are so sensitive to static charges that they can be damaged by relatively small voltages. In this context "small" still means a potential of perhaps a hundred volts or so, but by static standards this is not particularly large. Charges of this order will not generate noticeable sparks or make your hair stand on end, but they are nevertheless harmful to many electronic components. Hence you can "zap" these components simply by touching them, and in most cases you would not be aware that anything had happened.

I think it is also worth making the point that it is not just the processor and memory modules that are vulnerable. Complete circuit boards such as video and soundcards are often vulnerable to static damage, as is the motherboard itself. Even components such as the hard disc drive and CD-ROM drive can be damaged by static charges. Anything that contains a static-sensitive component has to be regarded as vulnerable. The case and power supply assembly plus any heatsinks and cooling fans represent the only major components that you can assume to be zap-proof. Everything else should be regarded as potentially at risk and handled accordingly.

When handling any vulnerable computer components you should always keep well away from any known or likely sources of static electricity.

These includes such things as computer monitors, television sets, any carpets or furnishings that are known to be prone to static generation, and even any pets that are known to get charged-up fur coats. Also avoid wearing any clothes that are known to give problems with static charges. This seems to be less of a problem than it once was, because few clothes these days are made from a cloth that consists entirely of man-made fibres. There is normally a significant content of natural fibres, and this seems to be sufficient to prevent any significant build-up of static charges. However, if you should have any garments that might give problems, make sure that you do not wear them when handling any computer equipment or components.

Anti-static equipment

Electronics and computing professionals often use quite expensive equipment to ensure that static charges are kept at bay. Most of these are not practical propositions for amateur computer enthusiasts or those who only deal with computers professionally on a very part-time basis. If you will only be working on computers from time to time, some very simple anti-static equipment is all that you need to ensure that there are no expensive accidents.

If you wish to make quite sure that your body remains static-free, you can earth yourself to the computer by way of a proper earthing wristband. This is basically just a wristband made from electrically conductive material that connects to the earth via a lead and a high-value resistor. The lead is terminated in a clip that permits easy connection to the chassis of the computer. The resistor does not prevent any static build-up in your body from leaking away to earth, but it will protect you from a significant shock if a fault should result in the earthing point becoming "live". A variation on this system has a special mains plug that enables the wristband to be safely earthed to the mains supply. Earthing wristbands are available from some of the larger computer component suppliers, and from electronics component retailers.

A typical wristband, complete with lead and special earthing plug, is shown in Figure 7.45. Note that these are sometimes sold together as a kit, but they are also sold as separate items. Make sure you know what you are buying before you part with your money. The wristband on its own is about as much good as a monitor without the rest of the PC. It is possible to buy disposable wristband kits, but if you are likely to do a fair amount of PC upgrading from time to time it is probably worthwhile

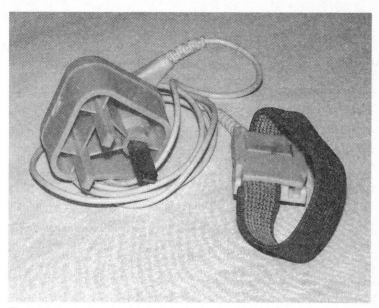

Fig.7.45 An anti-static wristband with lead and earthing plug

obtaining one of the cheaper non-disposable types. With intermittent use one of these should last many years.

If you do not want to go to the expense of buying a wristband, a simple but effective alternative is to touch the conductive worktop or the metal chassis of the computer from time to time. This will leak away any gradual build-up of static electricity before it has time to reach dangerous proportions. Again, the computer must be connected to the mains supply, but it should be switched off and the mains supply should be switched off at the mains outlet. The more frequently you touch the computer or other earthed object the lower the likelihood of static build-up in your body. Before removing any component from its anti-static packing, touch the earthed chassis while holding the component and its packing.

That is really all there is to it. Simply having a large chunk of earthed metal (in the form of the computer case) near the work area helps to discourage the build-up of any static charges in the first place. The few simple precautions outlined previously are then sufficient to ensure that there is no significant risk to the components. Do not be tempted to simply ignore the dangers of static electricity when handling computer components. To do so could be a costly mistake.

Points to remember

The processor upgrade options available, if any, are determined by the motherboard fitted to your PC. Each motherboard only takes a limited range of processors, and modern boards are only designed to handle processors from one manufacturer (either AMD or Intel).

It is often possible to extend the range of processors that a board can accommodate by upgrading the BIOS. Most modern boards have the BIOS in Flash memory, and it can be upgraded using the appropriate program and a new BIOS downloaded from the Internet.

Check the available options before deciding on an upgrade. Find the model name or number of the motherboard and its maker. Some delving on the Internet should then produce a choice of available upgrade options. If the motherboard was "a bit long in the tooth" when the PC was built it is possible that there will be no upgrade options.

If a BIOS upgrade is needed, follow the manufacturer's upgrade instructions "to the letter". Make absolutely certain that you are using the correct BIOS data file. A mistake when upgrading the BIOS could leave the motherboard unusable, so only upgrade when it is really necessary.

Some motherboards are supplied with utilities that permit the BIOS to be upgraded from within Windows. In most cases though, it is necessary to make a boot disc and boot from drive A. The disc should provide a very basic MS/DOS system with no memory management software or anything else that could cause the BIOS upgrade program to malfunction.

Do not use the "armstrong" method if the old heatsink is difficult to remove. Using brute force is more likely to damage the motherboard than to release the heatsink. If necessary, remove the motherboard from the case in order to gain better access to the heatsink.

The heatsink for the old processor is unlikely to be suitable for the new one. The safest option is to buy a retail boxed version of the replacement processor that includes a matching heatsink and fan.

If the motherboard does not have a three-terminal power connector for the fan, you must use a fan that takes its power from one of the drive power connectors via a simple adapter. This will presumably be the same system that is used to supply power to the existing fan.

With many motherboards it is unnecessary to change any settings in order to get the it to function correctly with the new processor. The BIOS will detect the new processor and make any adjustments that are required. In some cases it will be necessary to make one or two changes, such as increasing the bus speed of the motherboard. Sometimes this is done via switches or jumpers on the motherboard, but in most cases it is just a matter of changing one or two BIOS settings.

Many motherboards have the ability to use overclocking. In most cases only a small amount of overclocking can be used, if it works at all. If you use overclocking and "cook" the processor it will not be covered by the manufacturer's or retailer's guarantees.

The hardest part of a memory upgrade is determining the correct type of memory to use. Start by ascertaining the amount and type of memory already fitted to the PC and the number of free memory sockets. Then check the maximum amount of memory that can be used and the maximum size per module. You are then in a position to work out the upgrade possibilities.

Not all PCs use standard memory modules. There will be relatively few sources of supply if your PC uses proprietary memory modules. In the case of an old PC, it might not be possible to obtain suitable modules at all.

Although the risk of damaging computer components with static charges is perhaps not as great as the manufacturer's warnings would suggest, it is a very real risk. It is certainly not worth taking risks when dealing with even the cheaper computer components.

Static-sensitive components are supplied in some form of packing to protect them against static charges. Leave them in this packing until it is time to fit them into the computer. Avoid the temptation to remove the components from the packing just to have a good look at them.

Index